"A witty and insightful read, Boys Who Like Boys *is a rallying cry for all queer men to date, love and care for one another better."*
— **Vaneet Mehta, Author of *Bisexual Men Exist***

"This is a much-needed, highly relevant and thought-provoking book, ideal for queer men looking to develop deeper connections and relationships. Without a doubt I would recommend this book to any queer man."
— **Thomas Smithson, LGBTQ+ Therapist (@newhcounselling)**

BOYS WHO LIKE BOYS

Boys Who Like Boys

*How we date, love, and find fulfillment
in the age of the internet*

MAX THOMAS

earth sign books

ISBN 978-1-7393679-0-9 (paperback)

ISBN 978-1-7393679-1-6 (eBook)

contact@earthsignbooks.com

To all the boys who like boys who made my heart a little bigger. I'm grateful for you.

Contents

PART II: SEX

PART III: REALITIES

PART IV: MAKING CONNECTIONS

I Hate to Say It... But Men Kind of *Are* Trash

"Like, wow, Claire. I'm astounded. ASTOUNDED!"

I'd been coming to see Claire for over a year at this point.[1]

"A thirty-seven-year-old GROWN-ASS MAN. With a good job. And his own home!"

I'd sat on the couch opposite her and spilled all kinds of personal, shameful, heart-wrenchingly painful things before.

"And — APPARENTLY — the emotional maturity of a fourteen-year-old!"

But this one felt different.

"This feels like a big thing to say..."

Claire nodded invitingly, as therapists do.

"But I think it's true. Men are trash, aren't they? Men. Are. Trash."

We sat in silence for a moment. It felt appropriate to let that thought reverberate around the room, perhaps the universe.

"Like, I'm at the point in dating where, for my own self-protection, I think I have to start each new connection assuming that he *is* trash, then wait to be proven wrong instead of the other way around."

I took a deep breath.

"That feels devastating. That's not usually how I navigate the world AT ALL. But I don't think I have any choice."

Let's rewind six weeks earlier.

---

[1] I've changed most of the names in this book, obviously.

It was the typical twenty-first-century queer love story. We'd matched on one of the more relationship-friendly apps, and a few messages in, it felt — to me, at least — like we were clicking. I was out of town with work for a month just after that, but we stayed in touch over message while I was away.

The conversations felt pretty substantial. We'd shared photos of our families. We'd both thirsted over Mena Massoud in the new *Aladdin* movie. We talked about his passion for horse riding and, at his request, swapped cute voice notes. It didn't feel too much too soon. It didn't feel clingy. It was just a few conversations each week, all leading to — I thought — meeting in person later, once I'd made it back to London.

When later rolled around, we were still checking in a couple of times a week, which felt vaguely, faintly promising. And whether we were going to be a hit or a flop in person, I was excited to find out.

"Heyy so I just booked my ticket. I'll be back on Thursday. So clear your calendar :)"

"Oh that's nice," he shot back. "Are you excited to be back?"

That felt weird. We'd had that conversation literally a couple of days before.

"Haha yeah, it'll be nice to be home." Maybe he'd just forgotten. "So are we hanging out sometime? What's your schedule like?"

Then... there it was. Or more accurately, wasn't.

Message delivered, not read.

Twenty-four hours later, the same. This was not how it had played out the past six weeks. He'd replied within a few hours, without fail.

On the train back to London, I figured I'd try one more time. Messages get lost. People get distracted.

"Hey Mike, hope you're doing OK. Just wanted to check in. If you're down to catch up sometime, I'm still game. Or if you're not feeling it, it's 100% cool, just let me know."

The train pulled into Euston. Nothing. I got off the tube and through my front door. Still nothing. I woke up the next morning. Still nothing.

Nothing. Nada. Not one thing.

It wasn't a chain of events I especially enjoyed. But back in Claire's office, I was grateful to have someone who was literally paid to hear me sound off about it.

"I know, Claire! Call *The New York Fucking Times*!! 'Gay man in big city fails to communicate openly with other gay man!' It's the scoop of the decade!

"Because honestly," I went on, "now I feel like an idiot for daring to get excited about this. I'm mad at myself for assuming this was going somewhere it wasn't, and assuming if he wasn't interested, he'd just say that. Like, I literally set him up for the easiest rejection ever. I literally threw that ball in the air, ready for him to knock it out of the park with the TINIEST bit of effort, but then... nothing."

"Right," Claire said.

"I get that we've normalized this shit. I get this isn't even CLOSE to the worst thing some gay man will have done to some other gay man this week. And I can deal with rejection. I can cope with being told no — even if I really like someone. So why does this sting so much?"

To me, that was a rhetorical question. But Claire had an answer.

"Well, if I can chime in..." she said.

Now I nodded. For extra flair I raised my eyebrows as if to say, "Please, chime away!!"

"It sounds like, whether it was reciprocated or not, you felt like you'd formed a connection with this person. And when that happens, once you assume you've reached a point of mutual trust and respect with someone, but they violate that, it does hurt. It's bound to hurt."

"Right," I said. "So it's not really about the rejection. It's about trust and expectations."

"Yes," Claire said, "exactly."

"And in your case," she went on, "you care a lot about making meaningful connections. Your expectation is that you should be able to trust and form connections with other queer men. But from what you've told me, it sounds like it's been a struggle to do that recently."

I resisted the homosexual urge to say, "Gurl, you think!?" and just thought quietly about that a moment.

"You know what, that's it," I said. "It's not just that I got excited because this connection lasted more than three messages on a dating app. It's that I dared to feel optimistic about something that turned out to be another massive fucking letdown."

I slunk into the couch a little (dejectedly).

"So here I am, at the point where every time I connect with someone new, I'm actively wondering what kind of new emotionally devastating experience is going to end it this time.

"Yep, that's it. I'm not even mad at myself for being optimistic. I'm wondering whether queer men even *get* to be optimistic. I'm wondering whether I'm even allowed to think I'll couple up with someone I actually like someday. I'm wondering whether 'men are trash' — maybe myself included — is the mantra I need to keep my expectations in check. Because that's what it feels like right now."

* * *

In theory, we've never had it better.

Queer people across the globe are more accepted than ever. Queer people are more visible than ever. Yes, there are equality battles still to win, but in lots of places we can legally marry, adopt, share bank accounts and share lives. We can meet, flirt and stroke each other's butts in public. We're not watching each other die of a devastating viral illness. Queer life is much more than hanky codes and underground bars now. The internet has given us easy access to more friends, dates and sex than ever. It's easier to connect with other queer people now than at literally any other time in human history.

In theory, we've never had it better. But it doesn't always feel like it.

Not just to me. A lot of us are bouncing through life facing more than our fair share of disconnection, disappointment and — as if that wasn't enough — loneliness and isolation.

Because the truth is, a lot of us do struggle with dating and relationships. A lot of us aren't finding much success in building meaningful, supportive connections with each other.

Because, in a phrase, men often *are* trash when it comes to dating and relationships. Collectively, we really can be trash to each other.

I'm not proud to say it. And as I'll explain, it's not entirely our fault we ended up here. But somehow we did, and I for one think we should talk about it.

I could talk about how men learn that being sensitive and emotionally open is a sign of weakness.[2] I could talk about how men learn to dominate, compete and control.[3] I could talk about how men encourage each other with weirdly violent phrases like "smash it," "knock 'em dead" and "kill it, bro." I could talk about the devastating truth that our fear of showing any signs of struggle or weakness is actually killing *us* — that up to *four* times as many men die by suicide as women.[4]

I could talk about all of that. But I might not need to.

If you're anything like the myriad of gay, bi and other queer men I spoke to while I was writing this book, there's a good chance you've already had your own "are men... trash?" moment.

Without even thinking about it, you might be able to rattle off a list of your own bad dating or relationship experiences that left you feeling not just hurt and let down, but wounded. And if you've been

---

[2] Seriously though fellas, is it gay to have feelings?

[3] See Selin Kesebir, "Research: How Women and Men View Competition Differently," *Harvard Business Review* ◆ (November 6, 2019). Dr. Kesebir really uses her full doctorate to say men are competitive trash: "On the negative side, competition potentially (1) encourages unethical behaviors, (2) damages people's self-confidence, and (3) hurts relationships."

(By the way, the lil' diamond symbol above means the source is available freely online. If you want to look any of them up, I've put the applicable URLs in the "Internet Reference Links" section at the end of the book.)

[4] See Helene Schumacher, "Why more men than women die by suicide," *BBC News* ◆ (March 18, 2019). If you or someone you know is at risk, visit befrienders.org for help and support worldwide.

trying to date men for more than a few months, there's also a good chance you've taken at least one "Urgh, men are trash!" time-out — or just given up altogether — because it felt too stressful, disappointing or just like a massive waste of time.

And sure, maybe as queer men we are a bit ahead of straight men. Maybe you're more likely to say "you go, gurl!" than "smash it, dude!" Maybe you once tried to exorcise every trace of toxic masculinity from your soul at a self-actualization retreat in Peru.

But for all we've done as queer men to evolve our own culture, a lot of us still wrestle with the baggage we pick up from being raised culturally as men.

A lot of us are surprisingly competitive. We feel pressure to have the biggest pecs, the hottest partner or the fanciest job. A lot of us feel like we have to constantly assert our manliness. We put on deeper voices, look down on more "feminine" queer men — whatever we decide that means[5] — and can be super guarded with our emotions. And then, lots of us struggle to be kind and empathetic. We're not always very nice to each other.

And OK, it's not all men, all of the time. But it's enough of us, enough of the time, that a lot of us do struggle to connect with each other — or at least connect through anything more emotionally meaningful than no-strings sex, shirtless mirror selfies and/or sweaty dancing.

As queer men, we often define ourselves mostly by the queer part. (Maybe because that's the part that gets us called "faggot" for holding another guy's hand in public.) But part of why we're the way we are is also because we're men. We grew up in the "man box" about as much as straight men do, and many of us haven't grown out of it.

Being a man is not a stigmatized identity (though personally, I would sometimes like to make it one), so most of us assume it's an easy identity to live with. And in some ways, it is. But when it comes

---

5 Fellas, is it gay to be gay?

to emotions and connection, let me go out on a limb and say that being raised as men *does* put us at a disadvantage.

Put it this way: research shows that overall, gay men suffer from significantly more mental health issues than lesbian women do.[6] So while being attracted to people of the same gender in a world that's still deciding whether it's cool with that or not isn't great for anyone's mental health, the fact that we're men seems to make things worse.

And that, of course, brings us to the rainbow-colored elephant in the room. (Let's call her Justine.) Being queer *is* hard.

Despite all the reasons our lives are much better than they were or would have been forty years ago, it doesn't always feel like it. We still have to think twice about public displays of affection with other men. We can't take for granted that a bakery or hotel or wedding venue won't tell us "Umm, no fags." If we raise kids, we still have to go through a whole process of not just explaining to them that it's completely normal to have two dads, but also preparing them for the fact that other kids and their parents might not see it that way.

Even worse, as queer men who were raised to fit our society's very limited definition of what a man should be, liking other men makes us failures there, too. We have sucked dick and brought shame to our society *and* our gender.

And unfortunately — as we'll come to again and again in this book — that shame creates all kinds of psychological obstacles for us. It makes it harder for us to connect more deeply with each other, treat each other kindly, and communicate openly with each other. It cuts at our self-esteem and our ability to give and receive love.

So if the question is "Why does queer dating suck so much?" part of the answer is "because queer men can be kind of shitty to each other" and part of the answer is "because society is still shitty to queer

---

6 See Wendy B. Bostick, Carol J. Boyd, Tonda L. Hughes and Sean Esteban McCabe, "Dimensions of sexual orientation and the prevalence of mood and anxiety disorders in the United States," *American Journal of Public Health* 100/3 ◆ (March 2010), 468–75.

people." But don't get comfortable just yet, because that's actually not the whole picture either.

There's a digital elephant in the room too. (Her name is Antoinette.) See, the internet was supposed to make things — dating included — better. But, you might not be surprised to hear, in a lot of ways it hasn't. In fact, there are plenty of ways it's made dating worse.

Forty years ago — or even just fifteen — you might have found yourself meeting guys in a bar. And if one of them wasn't interested, he'd probably say so, but you might make a friend or get a nice conversation out of it.

Today, you're probably meeting people online, which means you're more likely to get rejected by being ghosted, blocked or — if you're lucky — told you're too fat or ugly or old or feminine to think you ever stood a chance.[7] The internet has connected us in all kinds of ways, sure, but it often leaves us feeling less connected, and less *human*, than we should.

So to recap, if the question is "Why does queer dating suck so much?" there are actually three broad categories of answers. One: men are trash. Two: society treats queer people like trash. And three: the internet encourages us to be trash.

And that's the hot, flaming trash heap that we, as queer men in the age of the internet, get to sit on. That is the universe we get to live in and where we have to try to find connection, love and fulfillment.

And then, we get basically zero help in learning to navigate said fiery trash heap. Sex and relationships education for straight people is usually pretty bad, but for queer people, it's often nonexistent. Maybe your high school taught you how to put condoms on a carrot, and that's definitely a start. But it probably didn't teach you how to have conversations about consent with a carrot, how to cope with being rejected by a carrot, how to figure out whether you should be in an open relationship with your carrot, or how the stress of being not-

---

[7] Fellas, is it gay to be nice to gay people?

straight in a straight-centric world takes a serious emotional toll that can harm your otherwise promising relationship with your carrot.

At the same time, your straight parents probably were — and still are — clueless about most of that too. There's no Faggot University. (Though there should be, if only because we'd call it "FU" for short.) Dating apps don't come with instructions. And nobody so far has written the handbook *Men: Embracing Your Inner Trashiness*.

And so, that's partly why we're here.

Sure, I wrote this book in part because I got my feelings hurt, and telling y'all about it in print feels intensely validating.[8] And sure, I wrote this book in part to understand more about why same-sex dating is so hard. I wanted to understand why so many of us find it hard to connect more deeply with each other, why so many of us are way more single than we'd like to be, and why a lot of queer men feel lonely and isolated from each other in general. (We'll talk more about that later, but spoiler alert: stigma, spoiler alert: trauma.)

But mostly, I wrote this book because I'm crazy enough to think we deserve better. And I think we *can* do better. It's not completely — or even really — our fault that we ended up here, but we did, and I'm crazy enough to think it would be great if we treated each other a little better. I'm crazy enough to think we should be able to connect more deeply with each other if we want to. And I'm crazy enough to think that if we worked just a bit harder at processing the emotional and cultural baggage that put us here, we'd all feel a bit more optimistic about finding the fulfilling relationships that so many of us crave.

Because truthfully, there *are* reasons to be optimistic. Within the forty-foot trash heap, there *is* a glowing orb of hope. (If you dig around a little.) Plenty of queer men do form happy and fulfilling relationships, and there's absolutely no reason any of us can't.

First, nothing about this is inevitable. Being a man is not some kind of curse. (Even if I'm making it sound like one.) Men learn to be

---

[8] I mean, Taylor Swift basically built a career out of sharing her bad dating experiences, so maybe you can extend a smaller version of that courtesy to me.

like we are mostly because of culture, not biology. As strong as the pull of "Man up, bro!* (*according to my very specific definition of masculinity)" might be, it's not fixed.

Second, the emotional maturity and self-assurance it takes to become much, much better at dating and relationships are absolutely things you can pick up. Learning to love and connect with other queer men more authentically and finding partners who are ready to do the same can be challenging, yes, but with time and patience it's something any of us can do. But we genuinely do have to learn how. It's not something we can just rely on our instincts for.[9]

The biggest problem is, again, that nobody really tells us this stuff. As queer men, we're regularly exposed to all kinds of things — stigma, gonorrhea, *RuPaul's Drag Race* — but we're only rarely exposed to positive and well-grounded attitudes toward dating and relationships. And that seems like a shame.

And so, here we are, a few pages into a book not just for boys who like boys, but for boys who like boys who like meaningful connections, who value emotional maturity, and who care about getting fulfilled and not just filled.

We'll start by looking at some key concepts about dating and connection — old favorites like authenticity, vulnerability, romantic compatibility, and what love even is, anyway. Then we'll talk a bit about sex. (I know, kind of weird not to start with that, huh?) Then we'll dive more deeply into how we can build the fulfilling queer relationships that are right for us, and the specific baggage that often holds us back. And in the last few chapters we'll look at some practical ways we can all date better, and try to figure out where in the holy titties of Jesus F. Christ we might go from there.

We're going to get serious and heartfelt sometimes. We're going to get mopey and introspective sometimes. We're going to be chaotic

---

[9] Yes, your three-time divorcée aunt Linda may disagree. But yes, she is wrong. See Maria Popova, "A 'Dynamic Interaction': How We Learn (and Unlearn) the Language of Love," *The Marginalian* ◆ (June 30, 2014).

and a bit unhinged sometimes. We're going to make points backed by serious psychological research sometimes. Basically, if it's part of the authentic experience of being a gay, bi and/or queer man, you bet we're going to be it somewhere.

At the same time, I'm going to encourage you to live your best life, in your way, on your terms. I'm going to encourage you to date, fuck and thirst after the various orifices of whoever you want. But yes, I'm also going to argue that, as a community, we can treat each other better. I'm going to suggest that, as a community, we can absolutely go after the things we want and build the relationships we want while minimizing the collateral damage we cause other people along the way. (Yes, we really can have it all.)

And yes, while we're talking about our wider community, I want you to know I am semi-embarrassed to be yet another cis, white gay man who's clearly privileged enough to afford regular therapy who wound up writing a book about queer culture. But I also want you to know I've tried do it in a way that resonates as widely with as many different types of men who are attracted to men as I know how. And I hope that will be enough.

Still, a lot of what we'll cover is nuanced and won't apply to every single person in every conceivable situation. Nobody else's lived experiences invalidate yours. So please take whatever you find helpful and feel free to ignore the rest.

Also while we're here, we should talk a bit about terminology.

You've probably spotted that I'm mostly using the word "queer" as an umbrella term for "not straight and/or cisgender," and "queer men" to mean "men who are attracted to men."

Yes, "queer" is a word that some gay and bi men don't love, for all kinds of reasons I'm not going to get into now. But since this is a book about all boys who like boys, whether they identify as gay or bisexual or queer or questioning or pansexual or polysexual or anything else, I wanted to use a word that's as inclusive as possible to refer to us all.

"Queer" is the word that does that, however we might all identify individually. ("LGBTQ+ men" felt weird because most of us don't identify with the "L," and, at least for now, "GBTQ+ men" isn't a widely used phrase.) So even if it's not a perfectly neutral term, "queer men" is how I'll usually refer to us as a group.[10]

Equally, I'm mostly going to refer to queer men with the pronouns "he," "him" and "his," though you or the people you like might use other pronouns, or even not identify as men. I'm also mostly going to use the word "partner," though what I have to say might apply more to someone you think of as your "boyfriend," "husband," "spouse," "fuckbuddy" or, sure, your "emotional support bottom." Using the word "partner" in the singular is also not me trying to ignore polyamory or invalidate the orgy you went to last weekend, I promise. I'm just trying to be as inclusive as possible without having to account for every possibility and permutation on every page.

In short, whether I use the exact language you use or not, if what I'm saying resonates with you and how you see yourself, please rest assured that you are invited to the table. Always.

So, yes, thanks for joining me on this strange journey to try to turn something as chaotic and bewildering as "being a man who is attracted to men" into some kind of meaningful discussion.

Because as queer people find more acceptance and become more visible, we probably shouldn't be surprised that more of us want more substantial connections, or at least something other than a string of casual relationships that just fizzle out or go nowhere. And a lot of us do expect more depth and respect from the people we date. We want to build relationships in our own ways, yes, but for more and more of us that includes longer-term, more meaningful connections. And if we want to build those longer-term connections, we absolutely can.

---

[10] And to trans readers: first and foremost, yes, I hope you'll also feel very welcome here. As a cis man, I don't feel qualified to write about the specific challenges of dating as a trans man, so I'll let other people's books cover that. Still, most of what I say about queer dating and connection should apply to all of us, and if this book mostly speaks to you, I hope you won't feel put off anytime I say something that doesn't fully represent you or just applies differently. (Including the occasional jokes about the bodies of cis men.)

It's not always the easiest path. It's easier to ignore or laugh about our emotional baggage and our learned trashiness than to fight it. It's easier to say, "Oh, that's just queer culture," and settle for less than many of us want. But we don't have to.

We can overcome our trashiness. We can understand ourselves and our motivations better. We can learn to identify behaviors that might feel good and natural in the moment but might be harming our odds of finding happiness and fulfillment longer-term.

We can learn to connect more deeply with each other.

And if we want to, we will.

* * *

"Yes, Max, I hear you," Claire said. "And I'm sorry you had to go through all of that. So where do you go from here?"

"Huh?" I replied.

I'd assumed I could just wallow in self-pity and blame everyone but myself until things got magically better.

"What are you going to do about it?" she said. "For what it's worth, I don't completely disagree with you that men can be trash. But what, you're giving up on dating now?"

"Well, no. I don't want that. I guess I need to be... better?" I said abstractly, still hoping things would improve without me changing myself or really doing anything at all.

"Because yes," Claire continued, "we aren't responsible for anyone else's behavior. But it's often in low moments like this that we can reflect on our choices and behaviors, readjust them based on what we've learned, and come back much better."

"A breakdown is just the prelude to a breakthrough, right!?" I said.

"Yes, Max, that's one way to put it."

It felt a bit like Claire said that just to be supportive. But whatever.

"Well, actually," I said, "I did have this idea a while back to write something about queer dating and relationships. A self-help book, I guess. Because Jesus Christ a lot of us need help, 'self' or otherwise."

"That's interesting," Claire said. "I know you're an experienced writer, but what happens if you start writing about this even just for you, to help get your head straight?"

It was a poor choice of phrase, but not a bad idea.

"What happens," she went on, "if you try to figure out some ways you — and your community, your dating pool, whatever you want to call it — might show up in relationships differently? What could you do to be better to yourselves *and* each other?"

"Right, like how would I fix queer dating forever!?" I said, a bit too eagerly.

"Maybe," Claire said. "Or just what could be different in the short term? If queer people rarely get the emotional help and support they need while they're growing up, what do you wish they knew?"

Oh, that was a topic I had plenty of thoughts about.

"Think about it," Claire said. "Speak to some other queer men. Read up on it, if you like. It could be really interesting to see what you discover."

PART I:
FUNDAMENTALS

Authenticity

OK, I know. What kind of basic-ass dating book starts with the advice "just be yourself"?

Because sure, "be yourself" might be just about the most clichéd dating advice there is. And yet, points were definitely made. Learning to present ourselves more authentically to the world is not only fundamental to dating well, it's also an essential part of how we fight back against the homophobia and stigma that keep us from finding more fulfilling relationships.

And what's more, "be yourself" isn't just damn good advice, it's an idea that underpins nearly everything else in this book. That's why it's the perfect place to start.

What authenticity is — and why it's so hot

If you ask a queer man to imagine his ideal partner, there's a nonzero chance he'll start to describe what that guy looks like. But let's go a bit deeper than just looks, and think about who that guy *is*.

Outside of physical characteristics, let's say our hypothetical queer man decides he'd like someone who is confident, kind, interesting and independent. Because let's face it, someone like that sounds pretty great. Who wouldn't want to have a partner who radiates confidence, who's completely assured in their right to be here and build great relationships, who lives their life in a way that makes them happy and fulfilled?

And sure, there are different ways to become a great partner who is a lot of those things. But they all have one essential ingredient in common: personal authenticity.

In a few words, **authenticity is the art of being yourself.**

In a few more, authenticity is the art of connecting with what you want, think and feel, then being comfortable presenting that to the world. And when someone does that well, it's usually really attractive. It tends to give off a vibe that says, "I'm a great person to be around!!"

But the reason achieving that level of authenticity, confidence and self-assurance is a challenge is that most of us — queer and otherwise — learn to care too much about other people's opinions. We worry about getting other people's approval so much we're willing to adapt the things we do, say and even think to fit in. We present ourselves as what we think the world wants to see, not what we are, because we think that's what will make us feel seen and, if we're lucky, even loved.

And on the surface, it sounds like a fucking great strategy. Only, in practice, it isn't.

Whether we're conscious of it or not, most of us are pretty great authenticity sleuths. (Yes, "sleuths" meaning "detectives," not a fancy French spelling of "sluts." Though "hoes for authenticity" is also a phrase I could have used.) Most of us are pretty good at sensing when someone is behaving in a certain way just to get our approval. And most of us are not hoes for that. Even if someone's inauthentic behavior technically gets us what we want, the inauthenticity often puts us off.

That's because inauthenticity tends to come across as neediness. Inauthentic behavior doesn't exactly say, "I value myself highly, boys, girls and people of all other genders!" More likely, it says something like "I base my opinion of myself on other people's!" or just "Someone — *anyone* — love me please??" And needless to say, that's generally not that attractive.

To be clear, it's not that highly authentic people don't care about other people's opinions at all. (You might be thinking of psychopaths.) We'll talk about this properly toward the end of the book, but unless you want to spend your entire life alone, we do need some approval and validation from others. And we do live a fuller life when we're open to other people's influence and ideas.

But the key is that highly authentic people are comfortable putting their opinions, their desires and their way of seeing things first. Even when they get input from other people, their own values and perspectives ultimately determine the decisions they make.

They spend time with the people they want to. They fill their lives with the things that are meaningful to them. They write a book that's like 80% well-intended dating advice and 20% random asides and dick jokes. And they do it knowing their exact brand of authenticity won't and can't be for everyone. But they do it anyway knowing it'll help them find the people their exact brand of authenticity *is* for — the people who will love and accept them *as they are*.

And that's hot, right? (In general, I mean. You can make up your own mind about the book thing.)

And sure, I know it's early in the book to be wheeling out the Insta-worthy comparison tables, but whatever. On the next page I've listed some specific ways people tend to reveal their authenticity — or how much they struggle with it — to the world.

In short, authentic people are comfortable being themselves and expressing themselves, even when that might make other people feel uncomfortable or let down, or even make other people reject them. And that's really important because while acting authentically can feel terrifying and even reckless in the moment, being inauthentic tends to have even bigger negative consequences in the long run.

Again, that's because inauthenticity tends to put people off. When someone really struggles to share their authentic opinion, it's harder to trust them. It's harder to believe them when they say "hell yes" if you suspect that they're afraid of saying "hell no" in case anyone gets mad or disappointed. It's draining when someone constantly needs reassurance to make even very small decisions — or when someone tries to change your mind about a deeply-held opinion instead of accepting that maybe you just see things differently to them.

Common in people who have a high level of authenticity	Common in people who struggle with authenticity
Pursues the things they like and value without worrying about what is popular	Usually follows the crowd and sticks with what is safely popular right now
Is comfortable saying no when necessary	Defaults to people pleasing — saying yes when they want to say no
Their words and behavior consistently align	What they say and how they act often don't align
Asks for input from people they trust, but ultimately makes their own decisions	Needs constant reassurance or validation from others before making decisions
Accepts other people authentically, without trying to change their mind or influence them excessively	Often encourages others to sacrifice their authenticity by trying to make them change their deeply held opinions
Expresses themselves confidently and clearly, even when their message might not be welcomed or understood	Often tells half-truths, lies by omission, or even outright lies
Acknowledges and accepts their imperfections and limitations, knowing they're part of being human	Struggles to accept their imperfections and limitations, afraid others will see them as weaknesses

In fact, another reason inauthenticity is unattractive is because it's a subtle kind of manipulation. It's a way of someone subtly altering who they really are to get other people's approval. And that's exactly why inauthenticity damages relationships. We don't like the feeling that we're being manipulated, that someone is *lying* about who they are in order to influence what we think or feel about them.

To be able to like and respect someone we have to know who they really are. (Not just in dating.) It's hard to build a trusting and genuine connection with someone who, on a personal level, is a moving target.

Yes, highly authentic people will be comfortable disappointing us sometimes, and yes, it sucks to feel disappointed. But we tend to admire people like that more in the long run, and trust them more deeply, precisely because we know they're not constantly hiding who they are. Ultimately, it's much more reassuring to be in a relationship with someone whose attitude is "Love me or hate me, THIS IS WHO I AM, bitch!" than "I change my thoughts and opinions more often than some twinks change their hair color!!!"

That's why high authenticity isn't just attractive but essential when it comes to forming secure and fulfilling relationships. It lets people see us as we authentically are so they can decide whether they're authentically into us, or not — which is always the best way to build more genuine relationships.

Because that's the thing: being more authentically yourself won't make you more attractive to everyone. In fact, it will usually put some people off. (Their loss, I'm sure.)

But importantly, being authentically yourself will always make you more attractive to the *right* people. It'll draw in the people who are ready to love and accept you as you are. It'll help you connect with, and keep, the people who are best suited to being in a fulfilling and genuine relationship with you specifically.

And, by the way, that's why relationships that begin with a lot of inauthenticity tend to become rocky or difficult over time. Sure, you can lie about your age or interests to get someone to talk to you. You can play games, like intentionally waiting to text someone back, to keep someone keen. You can even craft a whole fake profile online with fake photos, and it might even get you a whole lot of attention you wouldn't have gotten otherwise.

But those tactics tend to fail eventually because they're all about hiding who you authentically are or how you genuinely feel. They turn dating into a game, not an opportunity to build an authentic connection with someone. They help you attract people who aren't right for you, or just other people who think you have to play games to keep someone's interest. (Good luck with that.) Games also damage relationships because they usually involve actively deceiving or manipulating someone. And in my experience, at least, most people don't think it's hot to be openly lied to.

But the main reason that "just be yourself" is great advice is because it sends a strong message, to other people and yourself, that who you are is worth presenting to the world, as you are. It sends a message that you like yourself, and that always helps if you want other people to like you, too.

Why queer people struggle especially with authenticity

As simple as living more authentically might sound, in practice it's often hard work. It takes courage. And being your best most authentic self always comes with consequences.[1]

Before we talk about how to live more authentically, we should talk about what living authentically means when you're queer. Because as much as authenticity is something all kinds of people wrestle with, as queer people we face our own cornucopia of challenges when it comes to living more authentically.

The reason for that is depressingly simple: living in a homophobic, homo-uncomfortable, or even homo-just-about-tolerating society

---

[1] Perhaps you know the plot of the musical *Wicked*. (Yes, this might be a niche joke but no, I will not retract it.)

constantly forces us to compromise on being authentically ourselves in order to be basically accepted and even safe.

Yes, being queer is completely natural and queer people have existed throughout recorded history.[2] But obviously, plenty of people still don't see it that way. Instead of realizing that getting mad at queer people for naturally existing is exactly the same as getting mad at trees or clouds for naturally existing, some people still do that. And at best, those people make us feel uncomfortable and unwelcome. At worst, they physically harm us.

And as long as living authentically as queer people opens us up to stigma and rejection, not to mention actual harm, living authentically will be harder for us than it needs to be. All of that homophobia gives us a major incentive to hide who we are. And for our own safety and survival, most of us learn to adjust our behavior to avoid being too authentic when it might make our day-to-day lives harder.

And so, that means pretty much all of the behaviors that I told you are common in people who struggle with authenticity are things most of us have wrestled with at some point — and to some extent, probably still do — as we've come to terms with being queer.

Following the crowd? Sounds a lot like pretending to be like the straight majority to me.

Uncomfortable saying no? Sounds a lot like struggling to say "No bitch, I don't fit your exact image of how a man is supposed to look and love!!" to me.

Accustomed to half-truths, lying by omission and even outright lies? That sounds a lot like being closeted, or on the DL, to me.

Struggles to accept their imperfections and afraid others will see them as weaknesses? When you create a society that acts like being

---

[2] Same-sex attraction absolutely isn't just a thing in humans, either. See Juanita Bawagan, "Overturning 'Darwin's paradox': Imperial researchers are using a new approach to understand why same-sex behaviour is so common across the animal kingdom," *imperial.ac.uk* ♦ (2019).

anything but straight and cisgender is an imperfection or weakness, well, go figure.

And so, as queer people, we get very good at hiding behind inauthentic behaviors and defenses because that's what we learn to do to protect ourselves from prejudice and homophobia. We learn to become a version of ourselves that sacrifices authenticity in order to save ourselves from harm and humiliation. We get used to being loved and accepted as something false, something we're not. And as a result, we spend a lot of our adult lives trying to figure out which parts of us are truly us, and which parts of us we created to protect ourselves.

This fight to uncover our authentic selves is not trivial, by the way. That's because, without fighting that fight, without achieving a decent level of personal authenticity, we're unlikely to be able to build authentic and meaningful relationships with others. We might not even feel like we're worthy of the love and belonging all people — queer people included — are worthy of by birth.

Or, as Black queer writer James Baldwin once wrote: "It took many years of vomiting up all the filth I'd been taught about myself, and half-believed, before I was able to walk on the earth as though I had a right to be here."[3]

Without a strong sense of personal authenticity — a sense of what is true for us and within us — we don't have a yardstick to measure ourselves against. It's hard to feel proud of yourself and to see yourself as valid and lovable if you're not even sure who "yourself" really is.

As a result, a lot of queer men turn to external validation to fill the void where, ideally, a strong sense of internal validation should be. In the words of psychologist and author Alan Downs in his landmark book *The Velvet Rage*, a lot of queer men become "validation junkies" who organize their lives around seeking external reasons to prove to themselves they're valid and lovable.[4]

---

[3] James Baldwin, *Collected Essays* (Library of America, 1998), 636.

[4] See Alan Downs, *The Velvet Rage: Overcoming the Pain of Growing Up Gay in a Straight Man's World* (Hachette, 2012), especially chapters 1–3.

That can mean having lots of sex to feel wanted. It can mean bragging about the sex we're having to prove to other queer men that we're wanted. It can mean building perfectly sculpted bodies because we think it'll make us attractive to more and more people. Or it can mean chasing money, status and extravagant material things to prove to others that we're worthy of love and attention.

But of course, there's a catch. Because the validation is external — because it comes from outside, not within — it's never enough. Only true internal validation — genuine acceptance of ourselves, as we are — can build genuine and lasting self-esteem.

In short, because the society we live in teaches us to be ashamed of who we are, we tend to compensate for that shame by seeking out the quick highs of instant validation. But without attending to the source of that shame, without replacing that shame with authentic pride for who we are, that instant validation won't ever be enough. Because it's temporary, it passes and we're stuck looking for the next hit: the next hookup, the next shirtless selfie posted for attention, the next high-profile party or event we want to be seen at, and in many cases, the drugs or alcohol that can help numb the emptiness we feel.

And this, frankly, is a major part of why we behave so trashily to each other *and* are more likely to perceive each other's behavior as trashy and hurtful. To avoid shame, we have a habit of chasing the next hit of instant validation we need without caring or even thinking about who we affect in the process. And since a lot of us depend on this instant validation, when someone won't give it to us, say, through rejection or just indifference, we often feel not just disappointed but actively invalidated. We often end up feeling especially wounded by being turned down and — as if that wasn't fun enough — can even perceive rejection and invalidation where it doesn't exist. (We'll talk much more about that in a later chapter.)

And sure, by now you might be thinking "But surely homophobia isn't that bad anymore? Even my ninety-year-old grandpa adored my ex-boyfriend!"

And yes, you have a point. (And an exemplary grandpa.)

Queer people, at least in most of the Western world, are lucky to enjoy more freedom and more acceptance than we ever have before. But that doesn't mean all of us are surrounded by tons of acceptance. And the reality is, even small sacrifices of authenticity — like avoiding a public display of affection with your boyfriend, or ignoring a homophobic joke to keep the peace — still take a psychological toll.

Yes, what a privilege it is that lots of us get to worry more about hand-holding and homophobic jokes than about being beaten by the police, sent to conversion therapy, or stoned to death for being queer. But even these small compromises can have an outsized effect on us when we have to make them *constantly*.

The simple truth is, unless you were lucky enough to be raised by a pair of lesbian mountain goats in Nepal, you grew up in a society where homophobia existed. You'll have sensed, even unconsciously, that being queer is bad, or at least something you should, um, probably not be. And what's really fun is that you don't need to have been actively called a "fag" or a "queer" for that to be true — just understanding that "homo = bad" is enough.

When most of us grow up, we're confronted with more and more evidence of our queerness. Maybe we don't dress like other boys, or maybe we're more into art than sport, or we just start to notice we find other guys cute. So then, we start to confront this sinking feeling that there's something fundamentally unacceptable — and, importantly, unchangeable — about us. And before we've developed anything like the insight and maturity we'd need to understand what's going on, never mind deal with it, we respond in the only way we know how: we start adapting our behavior to try to become more acceptable.

We realize we can't get rid of homophobia, but we learn we can sacrifice our authenticity to save us from the worst of it. So we do. And when you spend years doing that over and over again, it's traumatic. It creates lasting and even lifelong trauma.[5]

---

[5] "'The trauma for gay men is the prolonged nature of it,' says William Elder, a sexual trauma researcher and psychologist. 'If you experience one

As a result, most queer people end up with a complicated relationship with authenticity. Most of us are still, one way or another, traumatized from the closet, from years of not being able to present ourselves as authentically as we'd like.

So yes, in theory authenticity is attractive — perhaps the most attractive trait there is. But in practice, a lot of queer men can't or just don't see it that way.

Even as adults we often fall into the trap of hiding who we are or how we feel, including from ourselves. Since we know what it feels like to be validated inauthentically — for being someone we're not — we can be good at dismissing even genuine support and admiration from other people. And maybe worst of all, we can end up feeling intimidated or repulsed by other queer people's authenticity. It can force us to confront how much of our own authenticity, or just our own queerness, we fearfully keep hidden.

We find ourselves preaching about how important self-love and self-acceptance are in long Facebook posts, then including phrases like "please be masc" or "muscular guys only" on our dating profiles. We compensate for feeling excluded from society in general by excluding and being cliquey with each other. We end up feeling disgusted and even invalidated by queer people whose queerness does not look exactly like ours. And knowing how much it hurts to be invalidated for being our authentic selves, a lot of us become masters at intentionally saying and doing things we know will hurt and invalidate the queer people *we* feel hurt or threatened by, like we're some kind of bitchy fallen Jedi.

These are the day-to-day struggles we face — and the less-than-ideal ways we behave — because of the internal battles we fight with

---

traumatic event, you have the kind of PTSD that can be resolved in four to six months of therapy. But if you experience years and years of small stressors — little things where you think, was that because of my sexuality? — that can be even worse.'" Michael Hobbes, "Together Alone: The Epidemic of Gay Loneliness," *The Huffington Post* ♦ (March 2, 2017).

authenticity. And again, it's why cultivating more authenticity as a queer person isn't just a fun thing to do because self-improvement is, like, so in right now. It's required of us if we want to find a healthy level of self-love and self-esteem, and build the meaningful relationships so many of us yearn for.

For queer people especially, our struggles with authenticity affect the foundation of how we see ourselves, how we value ourselves, how we interact with each other, and how we give and receive love in our relationships.

That's because the only real antidote to the disproportionate and uncalled-for invalidation we experience as queer people is authentic self-validation. Inauthentic validation — being validated for being someone we're not — doesn't work. It feels hollow, because it is. And relying on external validation — constantly looking for other people's approval to feel basically valid — puts our self-esteem in other people's hands, so it isn't a reliable strategy.

We fight the shame most of us struggle with for being queer by learning to be more authentic. By accepting and not hiding all the different parts of who we are. By presenting more of our authentic selves to the world. By learning to detach ourselves from other people's opinions, and relying more on our opinions of ourselves.

In turn, that's what helps us show up in relationships more authentically. It's what helps us build more genuine and meaningful connections. It's what can truly protect us from the worst effects of shame, stigma and rejection.

Yes, as queer people we might have to fight harder to cultivate a high level of authenticity. But equally, as queer people, doing that could not be more essential.

How to live more authentically

Again, learning to unlock more authenticity is not easy. So in the better, fairer world I often fantasize about, we wouldn't have to do this alone. We'd be able to call someone up called the Authenticity Fairy, who'd sit on our shoulders and help us make everyday decisions. She'd be just like Jiminy Cricket, if Jiminy Cricket cared less about gender norms and was banned in a handful of conservative states.

And just like that one friend who takes absolutely no shit and tells it like it is, the Authenticity Fairy would keep us on track anytime we're tempted to make a questionable decision or say something we don't mean. She'd know what's best for us — and that, deep down, we usually know it too.

And so, she'd always be on hand to whisper quiet encouragement like "Be yourself, king!" and "BISHHH, spit it out!" when we needed it. She'd also know when we don't say what we really mean or act in line with our true values. So she wouldn't hesitate to jump in with a "Bitch, you don't mean that!" or "GURL, that's not really what you want!!" She wouldn't even hold back with a "WHAT!? Stop lying just to fit in, hoe!!" or "Bitch, whyyyyy?!?" when we make choices that could really undermine our authenticity in the long run.

Her blunt honesty and peroxide-blonde hair would help us navigate the enormous daily challenge of living more authentically. Her strong female presence would help us overcome the fact that a lot of queer men don't respond well to earnestness or strong words from male figures, including ourselves.

But unfortunately, like Faggot University, the Authenticity Fairy is just a fantasy. Unfortunately, we're left to navigate the relentless challenges of living more authentically by ourselves. Unfortunately, only we can take responsibility for finding ways to bring more authenticity into our lives.

But if that's the bad news, there's also good news.

For starters, one reassuring thing about maintaining a high level of authenticity is that it rarely comes down to any single big decision. Living more authentically is about a *series* of choices, where we either decide to act in line with our values and desires, or do something that would make the Authenticity Fairy say, "Bitch, what the fuckkk!?"

That means that no single bad decision is catastrophic, and no matter what you've chosen to do in the past, you can always make more authentic decisions in the future. It also means there's plenty of room to screw up, change course, or make corrections if you need to — or just decide to do better next time.

And though living authentically can be hard, we tend to get better at it with practice. The more we build a habit of living authentically, the easier it gets to default to authentic decisions over inauthentic ones. So living more authentically is not about turning your entire life around overnight — as if that's even possible. It just means increasing your overall level of authenticity by choosing to replace inauthentic actions and decisions with more authentic ones.

Here are some specific ways you can do that.

Avoid saying things you don't mean

Yes, white lies and small fibs are often part of maintaining relationships with people. But if you start to bring significant untruths into your relationships, that comes at a cost — to the relationship and to you.

So stop saying things you really don't mean to fit in. Stop saying "Hey, let's hang out" to people if you have literally zero intention of hanging out with them. Avoid stringing people along by telling them you're looking for a relationship if all you want is a good fuck. Don't tell potential dates you're single if you're actually in an open relationship with a guy in the next town. Don't tell potential dates you're single if you're in a closed relationship with a guy you live with.

Stop yourself. Go back and correct yourself if you need to. But bring yourself, as you are, to your relationships and watch them deepen. And that starts by saying what you mean, as you mean it.

Stop saying yes to things you hate

Being more authentic means learning that "no" — or at least "No, I don't want to" — is a complete response. You don't have to do things you don't enjoy. You are not obligated to give your time to people you don't vibe with. If you know you'll resent saying yes to a project or commitment later, it's always better to face the discomfort of saying no now than letting someone down at the last minute or hating yourself for doing it.

Sure, carve out time for family get-togethers even if you decide to spend as little time as possible with your casually homophobic uncle. And sure, go to your best friend's comedy show because you really want to support them even if stand-up isn't your thing. But stop saying yes to things that drain you, depress you, or just offer no clear benefit to you. Being authentic means prioritizing the things, people, and relationships that bring you joy and fulfillment — and not just whatever's on offer.

Learn to tolerate being disliked

One of the biggest hurdles to living more authentically is that making more authentic choices for yourself often means someone else ends up feeling uncomfortable, disappointed or let down by your choices. That can be hard to accept — especially from people you're close to — but that's how it works.

Humans evolved to care about social acceptance because for most of our history we needed to be part of a large community to be safe and have enough food to eat. But that's not true anymore. We have supermarkets now. We can feel at home in smaller, less defined tribes. And actually, today it's often hard to thrive on a personal level *without* being misunderstood or disliked by some people.

Learning to live more authentically means accepting that you won't vibe with or be understood by everybody. It means accepting that it's usually more fulfilling to be accepted authentically by a small group of people than to sacrifice lots of personal authenticity to be accepted and understood by a lot of people.

Some queer men rely a lot on the approval and validation of others, and it's often a psychological defense mechanism we use to soften the feeling of being "othered" by a straight-centric —

"heteroppressive," if you will — society. But that's a major barrier to living and connecting more authentically.[6]

So surround yourself with people who accept you as you are, and learn to be comfortable with the fact that some people won't. Accept that being disliked or misunderstood by a few people is a small price to pay for the greater joy of living authentically. And remember that trying to be liked by everyone is a dumb game — you don't even like everyone, so it's nuts to expect the same in return.

Connect with what's important to you

Sometimes the challenge with authenticity isn't just acting on what you want, think and feel, but *knowing* what you want, think and feel in the first place.

That might sound like a crazy concept, but if you can remember a whole era when you assumed you were 100% straight, you might know what I'm talking about.

Unlocking more authenticity doesn't happen in one big lightbulb moment when you suddenly see the life you've always dreamed of. It's usually uncovering layers of wants and needs and feelings, like cutting into an (especially emotional) onion.

Plus, in a world where we're constantly bombarded with advertising trying to influence us, and social feeds drowning us in hundreds or thousands of other lives we could be living instead, it can be hard to drown out the noise and connect with exactly what is and isn't authentically you.

So take some time to do that. Go spend some time in nature. Decide to spend a weekend alone. Read something. Try journaling. Unplug, disconnect and put all the little queer people inside your phone you chat with on silent for a while. Make some time to get to know yourself, without anyone else to influence or distract you.

---

[6] Or as the Authenticity Fairy might paraphrase the Chinese philosopher Lao Tzu: "Care about what other people think and you will always be their prisoner, bitchhh!!"

Surround yourself with other authentic people

It takes courage to be authentic. That's part of why we admire it in others. But better yet, authenticity is often contagious: being around people who have the courage to live more authentically also tends to encourage us to be more authentic — and vice versa.

That's one reason queer men can struggle with authenticity as a group. If we watch our friends and the people we date do and say things we sense aren't authentic, there's a good chance we just think, "Fuck it, it doesn't matter," and watch our own authenticity slip away.

But we can break that cycle. As well as consciously choosing authenticity ourselves, we can prioritize spending time with people who also have a high level of authenticity, therefore turning a vicious circle into whatever the opposite of a vicious circle is. (A benevolent rhombus, I looked it up.)

In the real world, it's OK — and often necessary — to compromise on authenticity

It's true that consistently acting inauthentically tends to have negative long-term consequences. But when you're a queer person existing in an often-homophobic society, acting authentically can have negative consequences too. So strategic compromise is often a smart and necessary game plan.

This is often called "code-switching" — intentionally changing the way you talk or behave to be perceived differently around different groups of people. It's something most queer people still have to do sometimes, and yes, it can be exhausting.[7]

But if acting more authentically in a particular environment would actively put you in danger, then it's obviously not a good idea. If acting more authentically would explode a relationship that's important and otherwise fulfilling to you, such as a family relationship, you always have the option, within reason, to compromise.

---

[7] See Madeleine Holden, "The Exhausting Work of LGBTQ Code-Switching," *Vice* ◆ (August 12, 2019).

So if you find yourself putting on a deeper, more "masculine" voice around other men at work, that's OK. And no, you haven't failed as a queer man if you decide not to wear your sluttiest swim bikini to a family pool party. Even the Authenticity Fairy would say, "Don't make life any more difficult for yourself than you can handle, boo."

Because yes, it can also be authentic to value having a strong and stable relationship with your family. (Provided they're not stubbornly homophobic or abusive to you.) It can also be authentic to want to avoid dealing with awkwardness or weirdness from customers at work. It can also be authentic to accept that while you can be your queerest, most authentic self in some spaces, surviving in other spaces can require making small real-world compromises. And while that's often not right, it can — as Whitney taught us — be OK.

If authenticity is the sum (or really, the average) of the decisions you make, that doesn't mean it's game over if you make one compromise or inauthentic decision. Yes, for us, doing that can feel especially frustrating and insulting because of all the unjust sacrifices and adjustments queer people have to make, day in day out, to live peacefully. But again, authenticity isn't just about doing whatever you like and yelling "Fuck it!!" to the consequences. Unfortunately, being more authentic doesn't mean you'll get everything you want or even deserve all of the time.

When it comes to maintaining a high level of personal authenticity in difficult situations, what makes all the difference is that the adjustments are purposeful and strategic. When you're *choosing* to compromise on authenticity, any decision you make is less likely to feel like a personal betrayal that might have a lasting effect on your self-esteem.

Navigating this can feel like walking a tightrope we didn't ask for and don't deserve, but we have to walk it as courageously and authentically as we can. We have to keep pushing the boundaries of how much of ourselves we can bring to the world, because it's often more than we think. But it's also OK to accept that in the real world, there are limits.

In particular, we have to work on finding the people and environments that encourage us to be more authentic. We have to work on bringing more of ourselves *as we are* to the important relationships, romantic and otherwise, in our lives. We have to work on seeing the value in saying, "This is who I am" and "This is what I offer" to the important people in our lives and expecting them to do the same. Because that is the foundation of building strong relationships — with other people, but also with ourselves.

Vulnerability

If authenticity is the essential art of being your best whole self, then vulnerability is the essential art of sharing your best whole self with the important people in your life.

And like with authenticity, learning to access the vulnerability we need to form deeper and more meaningful bonds with others isn't a challenge only for queer people. But also like with authenticity, as queer men we face our own specific hurdles when it comes to learning to be vulnerable with the people we want to feel close to.

What vulnerability is — and why it's important

In short, vulnerability is expressing emotional authenticity when doing so involves a level of risk, uncertainty or emotional exposure. Being vulnerable means being authentic about what you think or feel when it really counts, which is often when opening up in that way feels difficult or uncomfortable, or when it might come at a cost.

In dating, common situations that involve vulnerability include telling someone you find them attractive, which comes with the risk of rejection, and telling a partner that you want to break up or renegotiate your relationship, which comes with the emotional discomfort of telling them something they might not want to hear.

It's that emotional discomfort that makes vulnerable situations so difficult. Most of the time, the words involved aren't complicated. "You're cute" and "I want to break up" are wildly simple sentences.

And yet, even just thinking about saying them can get your heart pumping, make your palms sweaty and leave you staring shiftily at the floor like an awkward teenager.

That's normal. It's a normal and fundamentally human response to vulnerability, to emotional risk. But relationships simply can't exist without some risk and uncertainty.

When you invite someone on a date, there's the risk they'll turn you down.

When you're getting to know someone, there's the risk they won't turn out to be the person you thought they were.

At any stage of a relationship, there's the risk that someone you love will leave you — even after years together.

So in a very practical sense, if we close ourselves of to risk, we stop ourselves from being able to form connections with others.

But vulnerability goes much deeper than that too. Anytime we're afraid of sharing ourselves more authentically with someone else, that tends to limit the depth and emotional intimacy we can create in our relationship with them.

That's because emotional vulnerability is at the heart of forming close and meaningful bonds. A lot of people assume that physical closeness — spending time together — is what helps people connect more deeply, but it isn't. It's authenticity and vulnerability.

Deep and meaningful relationships are relationships where we consistently feel seen, heard and valued as we authentically are. They're relationships where we can share the difficult, even ugly, parts of ourselves without shame or fear. They're relationships where we can show up authentically as we are, knowing that doing that won't subject us to lots of criticism or judgment.

But the key is that building relationships like that isn't just about finding people who are good at accepting us as we are. (Though sure, that is a big part of it.) It's also about being willing to share all the parts of ourselves, including the ones that open us up to hurt and rejection.

If we shut down our ability to be vulnerable — if we decide, "Yeah, sharing my deepest thoughts and feelings just isn't for me, thanks!" — we limit our ability to build closer relationships. We limit our ability to create emotional intimacy, and that tends to leave us feeling disconnected.

We can't be loved as we are if we're not prepared to be seen as we are. And we can't be seen as we are without sharing who we are more authentically. So if we want to open ourselves up to more meaningful relationships, we have to open ourselves up to the possibility of being hurt or rejected by those relationships.

I know, it sounds like a total scam. But it's true.

In fact, when a lot of queer men say they feel disconnected from other queer men, fear of vulnerability is often one of the reasons why. You might be around queer men regularly, in person or online, but if you don't allow yourself to be vulnerable with them — if you can't share what you think and feel openly — it's hard to feel emotionally close to any of them.

There are lots of reasons why queer men often struggle with vulnerability. But a big one is that, like with authenticity, we often find ourselves at a cultural disadvantage when it comes to bringing more vulnerability to our relationships.

That's because, in our sometimes-cursed society, men especially are conditioned to see vulnerability as weakness.

Queer or otherwise, a lot of men grow up learning that expressing emotion or any kind of fragility makes us weak or even unmanly. (Two things we're definitely not supposed to be.) Of course, the reality is the exact opposite — it takes a huge amount of courage and strength to share difficult or uncomfortable feelings.

But for queer men specifically, we're also disadvantaged because we live in a world that is especially good at rejecting us for sharing our authentic feelings and desires.

We live in a world where we're often *right* to be cautious about sharing what we think and feel.

For us, one of the most defining vulnerable things we have to do is "coming out" to the people we're close to.[1] Sharing any kind of not-completely-straight or not-cisgender identity is still a very vulnerable thing to do. It shouldn't open us up to risk and rejection, but it does. And like with many moments of vulnerability, the words "I'm gay," "I'm bi," or "I'm queer" aren't complicated, but as long as the basic act of existing as an openly queer person risks rejection and even abuse, saying those words will carry a high level of emotional exposure.

And as you don't need me to point out, that kind of emotional exposure still doesn't always end well. Sometimes it's met with flat-out rejection or disgust. Sometimes it's met with confusion or intense questioning or just deafening silence. And as long as we live in a society where saying something like "I'm gay" risks a response that's anything more complicated than "OK, cool!", sharing our queerness authentically with others will continue to feel especially risky, fraught or just complicated for most of us.

And as a result, just like homophobia can encourage us to shy away from authenticity, if sharing our queerness authentically often comes with rejection or even just awkwardness, that can help us conclude that that kind of vulnerability is bad, harmful or wrong. Homophobia can help us conclude that sharing what we authentically think and feel only leads to hurt and rejection — and that hiding our true thoughts and feelings is a much better strategy.

But as tempting as it can be to decide that being vulnerable is the problem, as we've seen, it's the exact opposite. As we've seen, being

---

[1] Urgh, yes, "coming out" is a concept that's long overdue for retirement. (Maybe you can feel my disdain for it in those quotation marks.) Assuming everyone is straight and cisgender then expecting anyone who isn't to announce it like it's an Ed Sheeran world tour is not a great way to go about any of this. It's also one reason some people are starting to prefer terms like "inviting in" — opening up to someone we trust about what's going on internally for us. See, for example, Sadhbh O'Sullivan, "The Phrase 'Coming Out' Harms Us More Than It Helps Us," *Refinery29* ♦ (June 16, 2021).

vulnerable with the right people is essential in forming more meaningful connections.

If we're emotionally open with our families in a way that makes them uncomfortable, the problem is not vulnerability itself.

If we express interest in someone who then snubs us or ignores us, the problem is not vulnerability itself.

If we share our feelings with a boyfriend who then laughs at us and tells us to "man up," the problem is not vulnerability itself.

The issue is that the specific people we're talking to don't see the value in vulnerability, or it's just that they're not interested in building a deeper connection with us.

If we want to build deeper relationships with the right people, we have to resist the masculine urge to hide behind a strong, emotionless exterior all the time if that's not a reflection of how we truly feel. And we have to fight the temptation to hide every possible flaw or imperfection from everyone out of fear of rejection or judgment.

Because the fact is, connection just doesn't work like that. As much as we fear we'll be rejected for our rough edges, showing the right people our rough edges is exactly what lets them connect with us. It's not just attractive — it's actively reassuring to know that someone is imperfect, fallible and human like we are. As much as we're afraid of our own vulnerability, it's one of the first things we're drawn to in other people. So we have to let other people realize that "Ohhh, that bitch has insecurities and anxieties too!" if we want to encourage them to lower their guard and start connecting with us more deeply.

Yes, that kind of emotional openness won't always be received well. Some people will reject or criticize us for it. But as painful as it can be to experience that, ultimately it's usually a good thing that we do. It shows us who is only ready to accept us on a superficial level, who is only willing to be around us if we hide the parts of ourselves that aren't always positive or perfect, or who would just rather we kept our deeper thoughts and feelings hidden. And that allows us to focus on other people who *are* ready to connect with us more deeply.

In short, that's why it feels frightening to show other people our authentic and vulnerable selves. But that's the sometimes-terrifying ordeal we have to submit to if we want to feel truly loved and accepted.

What vulnerability looks like in relationships

Vulnerability is important in basically every type of relationship, not just romantic ones. But since this is a book about dating and romantic relationships, that's the kind we'll focus on here.

In short, in relationships where vulnerability is encouraged, conversations that are risky, difficult or sensitive are welcomed and not avoided. As a result, those important conversations can happen freely, without anyone feeling shamed, shut down, or dismissed.

To be clear, vulnerability does not mean you have to share literally every thought that enters your brain with your partner. The goal in a relationship where vulnerability is valued is that difficult or emotional conversations aren't off-limits. If you're concerned about something, you feel like you can bring it up with your partner, and vice versa. If you need support from your partner, you're not afraid to ask for it, and vice versa. If you feel hurt by something your partner did, you can be open about it and don't just default to trying to hurt them back.

What's more, vulnerability is not about making uncomfortable conversations comfortable. Sometimes, necessary conversations are uncomfortable. Being in a relationship where vulnerability is valued just means that truth, authenticity and openness are seen as essential to maintaining the relationship and building a deeper connection. Showing up authentically is valued all the time, not just when it's simple or easy.

Just like with authenticity, vulnerability — or a lack of it — tends to show up in relationships in subtle ways. I've summarized a few common ones in another Insta-worthy table on the next page.

As you can see, in relationships where vulnerability is practiced and prioritized, clear and direct communication is common. Feelings

Common in people or relationships where vulnerability is valued	Common in people or relationships where vulnerability is avoided
A willingness to talk openly about the things they find challenging or painful	Saying things like "I'm fine" or "Don't worry about it" to avoid an important conversation
Confidently and directly expressing romantic interest or attraction to other people	Expressing interest in others indirectly, like by teasing or joking — or shying away from expressing interest at all
Proactively initiating difficult conversations when necessary, in the hope of finding mutually beneficial solutions	Avoiding or shutting down difficult but necessary conversations with the important people in their life
Confronting conflicts or disagreements directly by expressing their thoughts and feelings openly and clearly	Ignoring conflicts, or only confronting them indirectly, like through insults, passive-aggression or sarcasm
When one partner shares something vulnerable, the other one responds with curiosity and compassion	When one partner shares something vulnerable, it's met with judgment, blame and/or defensiveness
Prepared to break off a relationship or commitment directly but considerately if it's no longer working for them	When in a relationship that's no longer working for them, acting evasively or cagily, or in a way that encourages the other person to end it

can be expressed authentically, and problems can be brought up openly without anyone becoming overly judgmental or defensive. As a result, that allows a high level of trust to form, and conflicts and disagreements can be faced head-on in the hope of finding solutions.

Meanwhile, in relationships where vulnerability is rare, avoidance and evasion are more common. If anyone does share how they feel, they tend to communicate it in more indirect or immature ways, like through teasing or insults, or with a lot of judgment and blame. That creates a culture of low trust and low authenticity, where genuine feelings stay hidden and persistent problems are ignored. As a result, people in relationships like that are unlikely to feel especially close or trust each other that much.

Because a lack of vulnerability often causes people to keep their emotions hidden and unexpressed, in dating it's often known as *emotional unavailability*.

Emotionally available people — people who are comfortable being vulnerable — are good at identifying their emotions and expressing them to others. In dating specifically, they're comfortable showing interest in other people, and they're comfortable receiving interest from other people. They're comfortable rejecting and being rejected by others. And they're comfortable telling other people how they feel and what they want from a relationship.

On the other hand, emotionally unavailable people are often tight-lipped or withdrawn about anything emotional or personal. While they might find it easy to talk about things like their gym routine or what they did today, they might seize up if you ask them about their past relationships or try to start a conversation about where your relationship with them is going. They might try to flirt by teasing you, or even low-key insulting you to test your reaction — anything that might get your attention while letting them avoid expressing direct and genuine interest in you.[2]

---

[2] Flirting with insults is sometimes called "negging," and it's yet another technique that might get someone's attention initially but is rarely a good

Emotionally unavailable people also tend to be avoidant when it comes to relationships. They might avoid taking chances on deeper relationships altogether, or just withdraw from anyone who tries to be vulnerable with them, even though those people are often the best prepared for forming meaningful, fulfilling relationships.

Emotional unavailability is usually a defense mechanism, a form of psychological self-protection. Most people — queer or otherwise — learn to be emotionally unavailable because at some point they found that expressing raw and genuine feelings was overwhelming, or it caused them emotional harm or discomfort. As a result, their instinct was to hide their emotions to avoid that happening again in the future.

I've already talked about how just existing as queer in an often-homophobic world is enough to convince many of us that avoiding vulnerability is the best strategy. But since queer dating is often so difficult and painful, and we have a bad habit of hurting each other unnecessarily in relationships, that gives us extra reason to learn that relationships are painful and emotions are bad. It makes it even easier to think that protecting ourselves from hurt by avoiding vulnerability altogether is a good solution.

But again, unless keeping absolutely everyone at a safe emotional distance or feeling trapped in emotionally unfulfilling relationships is the goal, it's not a solution. Again, avoiding vulnerability deprives us of better relationships, more authentic connections and a stronger sense of belonging.

That means our challenge as queer men is to lean into vulnerability and seek out partners willing to do the same, despite all the rough and painful dating experiences that might have led us here.

As rough as it can be out there, the solution isn't just to withdraw. The secret to finding deeper and more fulfilling connections with other men is twofold: leaning into our own vulnerability, and finding people to build relationships with who are ready to do that too.

---

foundation for a strong and loving connection in the long term. Healthy relationships are built on respect not abuse, gurl.

How to practice being more vulnerable

Like with authenticity, vulnerability is not just a trait you have or you don't. It's a skill you practice, actively and consciously, in order to develop. But, like with authenticity, probably the biggest barrier to cultivating more vulnerability is that vulnerability often feels unsafe.

If you've spent (or still spend) a lot of time in environments where vulnerability is dismissed and discouraged, sharing how you feel more authentically can feel dangerous and even irresponsible. And sure, there is such a thing as oversharing — being excessively vulnerable with someone you barely know. That's often a rash, defensive move people make when they don't have healthier channels to be vulnerable with people they trust. The goal with vulnerability is not to share everything you think and feel with anyone, but to use it to deepen your relationships with the people who matter to you, who you've had the chance to build some trust and respect with. That's important.

Still, even with people you trust, leaning into more vulnerability usually means leaving your comfort zone. It often feels risky and uncomfortable. In the words of the world-renowned maestra of vulnerability Brené Brown, "Vulnerability often sounds like truth and feels like courage."[3] So if sharing something feels urgent and necessary but also scary, delicate or even shameful, then it likely is vulnerability.

Here are a few important ways you can bring more vulnerability into your relationships.

Bring more authenticity into conversations with the people you're already close to

If you usually answer friends who ask, "How are you?" with a default "I'm fine," at least give yourself the option of answering more truthfully. You might say, "Not too bad, but work has been kind of

---

[3] Brené Brown, *Daring Greatly: How the Courage to Be Vulnerable Transforms the Way We Live, Love, Parent, and Lead* (Avery, 2012), 37.

stressful lately" or "OK, but I'm worried about my relationship with my boyfriend," if that's more accurate.

Get used to taking even small risks in sharing what you're feeling and thinking with the people you trust. Give the people you're close to a chance to know how you're really doing. We assume that sharing will push people away, but again, with the right people more vulnerability always leads to a deeper and more genuine connection.

Get used to asking other people for support

It's great to respond with vulnerability when someone asks you how you're doing, but sometimes we need to find the vulnerability to proactively ask for support. A lot of men — straight and queer — especially struggle with this. And it sucks that a lot of queer men are often right in thinking they can't rely on their straight family and friends for support, who aren't always well equipped to understand our specific struggles. This, honestly, is a real tragedy, because when we're struggling, talking it through with someone is often enough to make us feel better, and more confident about dealing with whatever we're facing.

It can take real courage to hit up someone you trust to say, "Can we talk?" or "Hey, I'm struggling," but it's definitely something we should normalize. On the other side, it's also important we learn to be better at supporting other men who are struggling by trying hard to listen without judgment, encouraging them to talk openly about what's on their mind, and checking in if a friend or partner seems unusually distant or preoccupied.

Learn to spot shame triggers

One of the biggest barriers to vulnerability is shame, which can manifest as thinking "Actually, my problems aren't that bad" or "I don't deserve support" or "If I talk openly about how I feel, people will laugh at me or reject me."

Shame is different from guilt because guilt says "I was wrong" or "I did something bad," while shame says "There is something wrong with me" or "I'm a bad person." And this fear that if people see who we truly are they'll push us away stops us leaning into more vulnerability.

Because again, with the right people, the complete opposite is true. When they see our rough edges, when they see that we're human and flawed too, it draws them in. It helps them feel more comfortable that their life is hard sometimes too, and allows a stronger and more authentic connection to be built.

So learning to spot those voices that tell us, "If I open up, everyone will reject me," "I don't deserve help" or just "I can manage on my own" and sending them to shame-trigger jail, where they belong, is a key step in unlocking more vulnerability.

Don't be afraid if things get messy

Yes, wandering the streets at dawn in a tank top and booty shorts, trying to find the nearest McDonald's before you get a cab home is definitely one fun kind of messy. But let me also introduce you to how messy being vulnerable can be. (Even if, yes, it's booty shorts optional.)

Talking about your feelings with the people you're close to can mean struggling to get the words out. It can mean acknowledging that it's hard for you to say, but you want to because it's important. It can mean repeating or re-explaining something if it didn't land the first time. It can mean admitting you don't know or you're not sure. It can mean apologizing if the words come out wrong. It can mean taking a time-out if a conversation gets heated or anyone needs time to mull things over before they respond.

Because vulnerability often comes with uncertainty, it isn't about knowing all the answers all the time, or even getting it right all the time. It's about showing up, as we are, and seeing the value in sharing ourselves authentically, knowing that with the right people, that always creates a deeper connection in the long run.

Get used to speaking your mind and asking for clarity when you need it

One of the ways the male urge to be unemotional and unexpressive can really mess up our relationships is that it encourages us not to tell people where we stand in those relationships.

For us, our cultural baggage can make vulnerability feel especially subversive, like we're breaking some unspoken ancient rule. So let's be subversive, boys.

Let's be more expressive with each other. Let's normalize telling people we like them. Let's normalize telling people we respect them but we just see them as a friend. Let's normalize asking people how they feel, even when we're afraid of what their answer might be. (Including when we're terrified we might get the answer we want. Because, oh boy, that's definitely a thing too.)

This fear often stops us asking for clarity, but that usually only makes us more miserable because it leaves us stuck not knowing. Being vulnerable means embracing that kind of uncertainty. And as queer men, our learned cautiousness around each other can be a real barrier to connecting more deeply. We have to unlearn that.

Try journaling

Vulnerability matters most when it involves other people, but it can also be valuable to identify what and how you feel on your own before you try the difficult thing of sharing that with others.

Journaling — writing, typing or speaking aloud to yourself about how you feel — is a great way of doing that. It's possible to feel an emotion without having the words describe it, but there's power in being able to identify and name your emotions, even just for yourself.

My notes app is full of random thoughts and feelings that have come to me at different times, especially when I knew I wanted to share them with someone later. For me, it's always a powerful way of sorting through my own emotions — especially when they feel messy or complicated — so I could talk about them more clearly with others.

You can journal about literally anything that's on your mind, but in case it's helpful I've also included a list of prompts on the next page. The key is to practice connecting with how you think and feel as authentically as you can, whatever that turns out to be, and then trying to put that into words.

Like with authenticity, learning to be more vulnerable is about a ton of small decisions. So it's OK to start small, in situations that don't completely terrify you. Plus, like with authenticity, vulnerability is also contagious — so it pays to be around people who are comfortable being vulnerable, and encouraging other people to tell you the truth even when it's not necessarily what you want to hear. The best response to other people's vulnerability is always interest, curiosity and acceptance, not judgment, blame or invalidation.

At the same time, it's important to be strategic about who you share your most vulnerable thoughts and feelings with. Not everyone will have earned the right to see you at your most vulnerable, and some people will not be able to handle your vulnerability well.

In fact, one of the toughest lessons as you learn to be more vulnerable is that some people won't be ready to follow you down that path. Most people can only tolerate vulnerability in others to the extent they can tolerate it in themselves, so you shouldn't take it personally anytime you learn someone is not a great person to open up to about your deepest or most personal feelings. Being vulnerable is never about having no filters or boundaries. You get to choose how much of yourself you want to share with any specific person.

Still, despite the challenges that come with learning to be more vulnerable, the benefits are always worth it in the long run. And despite the cultural baggage that comes with being a queer man — and the way we have a bad habit of hurting each other in relationships — no bad dating experience has to become our supervillain origin story. It can just be an opportunity to unlock more of our own vulnerability and focus on finding other people who've done the same.

Journaling prompts to practice vulnerability

To use these prompts, just continue where they leave off. Try to express your thoughts and feelings as authentically as possible — including when that might feel messy, personal or uncomfortable.

- Today I feel ...
- Today I'm thinking a lot about ...
- Right now I'm concerned or worried about ...
- I feel optimistic that ...
- I feel confused or unsure because ...
- When ... happened, I felt ...
- One great thing about my relationship with ... is ...
- One challenge in my relationship with ... is ...

If you need some extra help naming how you feel, here are some common ways you might be feeling:

content	happy	annoyed
overwhelmed	confused	ignored
worried	nervous	uncertain
unheard	optimistic	unbothered
in control	hurt	sad
enthusiastic	disconnected	trusting
lonely	angry	suspicious

How to date emotionally available people

So yes, while it's true that a big part of building more authentic connections is tending to your side of the vulnerability fence, your partner's ability to be vulnerable obviously also matters. You can be the most emotionally available person in the world, but if you try to get close to someone who is seriously emotionally unavailable, you're probably not going to get the emotional intimacy you're looking for.

Because while we can encourage more vulnerability in others to an extent, like by modeling it in ourselves and being a patient and nonjudgmental listener, unfortunately there is no magic cure for low vulnerability. Patterns of emotional unavailability are often deeply rooted.[4] They're often a defense mechanism that people have built up over years, even decades, from being in environments where emotions weren't or couldn't be acknowledged. So with some people, even if the Authenticity Fairy spent all afternoon yelling "Live your truth, bish!" and "Speak your mind, king!!" at them, it likely wouldn't be enough to undo those patterns.

Often, deeply emotionally unavailable people need to learn, slowly but surely, that it's safe to express their emotions. That doesn't happen overnight, and it basically never happens without that person wanting it to.

I'll say that a bit louder for the "But I can CHANGE HIM!" crowd at the back: any kind of personal growth only happens when someone does it to and for themselves. You can encourage someone, you can love and support them while they work on themselves, but sadly, no, nope, sorry, you can't do it for them.

So anytime you identify that someone you're dating or might date especially struggles with vulnerability, it's important to recognize that that will limit your ability to get close to them.

---

[4] Julie Marks and Sandra Silva Casabianca, "How to Spot Emotional Unavailability: 5 Signs," *PsychCentral* ◆ (September 24, 2021).

And unfortunately, no, they're unlikely to wake up some day and just think, "Oh wow, I'm so emotionally available now! This is great!" So it's worth bearing that in mind when you're choosing who you want to build a relationship with.

I say that because even to some very emotionally available people, emotional unavailability can be surprisingly attractive. There are a few different reasons for that.

One is that in our culture — queer culture and in general — we often prize emotionally limited men. We see distant and aloof men as attractive. (Maybe we saw one in a movie or something.)

Another is that if you grew up in a family environment where vulnerability was avoided, there's often an attractive familiarity to emotionally unavailable people, even if you've done a lot of work to overcome your own emotional unavailability. (Yes, another scam.)

But as attractive as emotional unavailability might feel in the moment, again, it always limits intimacy and connection in the long run. And again, if you want to build deeper and more emotionally fulfilling relationships, it's important to choose partners who are as comfortable with vulnerability as you are, or at least near enough.

Spotting emotional availability in other people can be a challenge, but there are important clues to look out for.

At the extreme end, because people who especially struggle with emotional unavailability are often highly avoidant in relationships, it's worth looking out for signs someone is avoiding opportunities for intimacy or emotional closeness with you. People like that might want sex, but none of the emotional parts of a relationship. It might feel like they're always keeping you at a distance. They might even be difficult to pin down or make definitive plans with.

But emotional availability can also be more nuanced. A lot of emotionally unavailable people are lonely — because it *is* lonely when your playbook is to keep everyone at a safe emotional distance. So some are good at finding ways to be in close physical proximity to other people without ever getting emotionally close.

The classic version of this is the stereotypical "fuckboy."[5] In short, the stereotypical fuckboy might be an externally attractive man, who is physically fit, outgoing and flirty, but whose fear of vulnerability seriously limits his ability to form more intimate connections with others. Men like that are often skilled at getting the attention and validation they need — whether through people to talk to, date and/or fuck — but when any kind of relationship progression or commitment presents itself, they'll usually bail, shut down or ghost. (Often just to restart the same cycle of fuckery with someone else.)

OK, perfect stereotypes don't always exist in real life. But if you want to build a lasting relationship with someone, it's important to be able to recognize when they're telling you, either through their words or actions, that they can't or won't give you that kind of commitment.

Because if you give him commitment anyway, hoping it'll all magically turn out fine, he'll likely get what *he* wants — commitment and vulnerability from you without offering any of that in return — while you become emotionally invested and likely end up heartbroken when he cuts things off and moves on. Thus the sacred arc of "fuck around and find out" will have reached its glorious conclusion, only he'll have done most of the fucking around while you did most of the finding out.

Obviously, if someone is so avoidant they won't make plans with you, that's less of a problem. You're probably not going to end up heartbroken. Things get trickier when the clues are more subtle, like when someone is happy to communicate with you and spend time with you but can't give you the kind of emotional intimacy you want because their tolerance for vulnerability is much lower than yours.

In short, the way you learn to recognize someone else's tolerance for vulnerability is to be vulnerable around them yourself. Offer up something vulnerable and see how he responds. Someone who's comfortable with vulnerability is likely to "lean in" and respond with

---

[5] You might prefer to spell it "fuckboi" or even "fuccboi." We support all spelling variations here.

empathy, understanding, or offer up something vulnerable of their own. Someone with a lower level of vulnerability might acknowledge what you say without really engaging with it, or even try keeping you at an emotional distance by responding with criticism or judgment.

Suppose you've gotten to know someone a little, and you bring up that time you took a weekend trip to Lisbon to reconnect with an old flame but he totally snubbed you when you arrived.[6] Someone who is comfortable with vulnerability might respond with something like:

- "Ouch, I bet that hurt!" *(sympathizing)*
- "Damn, I've been there too. At least we both got good stories out of it!" *(reassuring / offering vulnerability themselves)*

Meanwhile, someone who's less comfortable with vulnerability might respond with something more like:

- "Oh, OK. That's interesting." *(acknowledging but not engaging emotionally)*
- "Well, that was dumb. How did you not see that coming?" *(judging / blaming)*

Or, if you've gotten to know someone well enough that it feels appropriate to invite him to share something more personal about himself, how he responds to that is often an even better indicator of his attitude toward vulnerability.

For example, if you ask someone about their past relationships, someone comfortable with vulnerability is likely to be happy sharing some of their relationship history. On the other hand, someone who struggles with vulnerability might respond more like this:

- "Urgh, let's not talk about it. Do you want another drink?" *(changing the subject / avoiding)*
- "What, you think I'm Adele, ready to spill about all of my exes!?" *(making a joke)*

---

[6] What, that totally never happened to me, why would you ask?? And yes, within reason I think it's good to know a bit about a potential partner's dating history. You can learn a lot about someone from how they talk about it.

- "Haha no, I want to hear about *your* juicy past!" *(shifting the focus / evading)*
- "My ex was a total dick. I'm so over it now though." *(giving an emotionally hollow or superficial answer)*

And in case it sounds like I'm telling you to do a little Dr. Freud roleplay and overanalyze every word someone says, I'm really not. Because actually, if you have a decent level of emotional availability, someone's lack of it often isn't just something you notice, it's something you *feel*.

You might open up about something personal or invite someone else to open up about something personal to them, and they give an answer that feels distancing, evasive or hollow somehow. Or in a better situation, you offer someone a chance to connect with you more vulnerably and they take it — they respond in a way that feels genuine, engaging and like it draws you in emotionally.

This isn't about "shit testing" anyone — saying something weird or unexpected to see how they respond — either. It's just about giving someone a chance to build a deeper connection with you as you try to get to know them better, and recognizing when that's a path they're not ready to come down with you.

Naturally, none of this is black and white. It's not that everyone who won't tell you every last detail about their exes is wildly emotionally unavailable. It's not that someone who doesn't want a long-term relationship right now — or isn't 100% ready to give you a commitment after three dates — is a complete fuckboy. There are plenty of very healthy reasons to want to take a relationship more slowly or not to want a commitment at all.

The key difference is that people who are comfortable with vulnerability will usually be much more open and genuine in sharing how they feel. They'll tell you they were hurt by a past relationship and don't want to rush into this one, or that they just don't like talking about their exes until they've gotten to know a new partner better. And they'll mean it: their behavior will generally be consistent and won't contradict what they say.

Emotionally available people can choose to set boundaries around what they share with others, but for more emotionally unavailable people it's not a choice. Avoiding vulnerability is usually their default. And because deeper vulnerability depends on trust, it's often not easy to spot emotional unavailability right away. It's not usually obvious on a dating profile or even on a first date. It's something that tends to reveal itself over time as you get to know someone better.

In particular, if you seem to be feeling closer to someone over time but the reverse isn't true, that's often a sign that their emotional unavailability is limiting how much they're able to feel close to you. (Assuming it's not just that they're not interested in a relationship with you specifically.) People do develop intimacy in relationships at different speeds for all kinds of reasons, so you don't have to panic if you're not on the exact same trajectory. But if the relationship is progressing emotionally for you and hardly at all for them, that's likely a sign of a major vulnerability mismatch.

What sucks is that yes, there are plenty of attractive men who struggle with emotional availability. Plenty of them are physically attractive, intelligent, ambitious and fun people. But if you've been dating someone for a while and you've identified — or you suspect — that they're not ready to bring themselves as wholeheartedly as you'd like to your relationship, you have a few different options.

A great first step is to talk to them about it — ask them what they want from the relationship, if they're sure they want to be in the relationship, or just that you've noticed they don't seem that engaged in the relationship and you'd like to talk about it. Or you could just enjoy a more short-term relationship or try a friendship with them. But if it's clear he isn't able to invest emotionally in a relationship with you in the way you want, it might just be best to move on and find someone whose emotional openness is a better match for you.

Again, it sucks to wind up feeling emotionally shortchanged after you've opened up to someone or tried to connect with them on a deeper level. But that's exactly why you want to lean into your own vulnerability early on in new relationships. Yes, it'll result in you getting disappointed sometimes, but it's always better to find out who isn't able to meet you at the level of intimacy you're looking for sooner rather than later, so you can decide what you want to do about that.

That's also why it rarely pays to play it cool in dating and relationships. It's why you don't want to hold back in telling people how you feel about them.

Sure, there are plenty of people who just won't be interested in you, for whatever reason. There are plenty of people who struggle with vulnerability so much that they'll be put off and even intimidated by your openness and directness. And sure, since flirting is a form of vulnerability, there is an art to not oversharing or coming on too strongly with people you don't know well. But if you want to build deeper and more emotionally fulfilling relationships — and find out who is ready to meet you at a higher level of vulnerability — playing it cool and holding back emotionally is never a good strategy.

To build more fulfilling relationships, we have to learn to be more vulnerable. We have to embrace emotional exposure and emotional risk. But we also have to find partners who have learned to lean into vulnerability too. We have to build relationships where emotional openness, honesty and integrity are valued. We have to build environments where being truthful all the time matters more than being comfortable all the time.

In short, we have to embrace vulnerability.

Rejection

You've heard of the game "Would you rather?" right? Well, let's ponder some fun hypotheticals.

Would you rather be able to fly or turn invisible?

Would you rather be able to listen to Mariah but never Lana, or Lana but never Mariah?

Would you rather never be able to orgasm or always be in the middle of one permanent orgasm?

Or how about this one: would you rather exist in a world where you can date literally anyone you want, but, by the same token, you're forced to date anyone who wants to date you? Or, would you rather everyone, including you, gets to choose who they do and do not want to date?

I guess you can save your first three answers for 3 am pillow talk or your next cross-country road trip, because we're really here to talk about that last one.

Let's face it, if most of us could be with literally anyone we wanted for some combination of a date, a lifetime of marriage and a lot of toe-curling sex, of course we'd say yes. Why wouldn't we?

And yet, you probably agree that if literally anyone who wanted to date, marry and/or fuck you got to do that, it wouldn't be much fun. It would be a violation of your autonomy and personal space, and would lead to some pretty unhealthy (and exhausting) relationships.

None of us would feel comfortable being in a relationship with someone we don't like, don't find attractive, or don't feel a connection with. And as fun as it might be to fantasize about hitting it off with someone we really like, it doesn't take a lot of authenticity and self-respect to realize that, really, we don't want to be with someone who doesn't want to be with us. That doesn't sound fun. Or cute. It doesn't sound like the foundation of anything but a very weird one-sided relationship.

And in short, that's why rejection — being comfortable rejecting others and being rejected by others — is so important. It's why it matters not just in dating, but in all kinds of relationships.

The value — the beauty, even — of rejection is that it keeps people who don't really belong together away from each other. It helps us avoid low-quality or one-sided relationships so we're all free to pursue the people we *do*, or at least could, belong with. So as painful rejection can feel, we're definitely better off with it than without it.

Fuck yes or no: The art of rejection

Author and self-help blogger Mark Manson has a maxim for dealing with relationships he calls "The Law of Fuck Yes or No." Mark is not the only person to write about this idea, but his version has the word "fuck" in it, so let's assume that that's why it's my favorite.

Manson's Law of Fuck Yes or No is very simple. When it comes to making relationship decisions, there are really only two options: "fuck yes" and "no."[1]

There is no "maybe." There isn't even just "yes." There is only "fuck yes," and if the answer is not "fuck yes" *from everyone involved*, then it's "no."

Anytime I've seen Mark write about this, his examples seemed pretty heteronormative. So let's look at some situations that might apply more to us.

Say you meet someone online and after a few days' chatting you decide to meet. You hit it off great. He's fun, chilled, handsome and

---

[1] For more, see https://markmanson.net/fuck-yes.

seems to like you. At the end of the date you both agree to a second, but after three tries at fixing a time with him, he's always busy with work, his family, or maintaining his poppers collection. That doesn't sound like a "fuck yes" from him, so it's a "no."

Say you've been dating someone for a few weeks, and everything is ticking along nicely. One night, after a frozen margarita or two, he shares that he doesn't want a committed relationship with you. This kind of confuses you since not only does he keep talking about longer-term plans with you, but he also seems to expect you'll cancel plans to make time for him every weekend. He's acting like he wants a relationship but consistently telling you he doesn't. That doesn't sound like a decisive "fuck yes" either, so therefore it's a "no."

But Manson's Law of Fuck Yes or No doesn't just apply to dating. It also applies to sex, marriage, and significant friendships, and at basically every stage of the relationship.

Say you've been hooking up with someone once or twice a week for a couple of months, until one day he asks you whether you want something romantic together. You say, politely, you don't, so it's a "no" on that. But it turns out he doesn't want to keep going just as fuckbuddies either. To him, it's only "fuck yes" to progressing to dating, and only "uhh, sure?" to keeping it purely about sex. Therefore there's no universal "fuck yes," either to dating or to just fucking. So sadly, it's time to wipe your dick on the bedsheet, put your pants back on and accept that, therefore, it's a "no."

Now say the guy you've been hooking up with regularly asks you about starting a romantic relationship, and your answer is also "fuck yes." Your relationship progresses to a new stage. Woohoo! You've got a boyfriend.

But now there's a problem. While the relationship is great maybe 60% of the time, sometimes your new boyfriend literally takes days to reply to your texts. And he has this habit of getting pointlessly argumentative over things like where to go for dinner. That seems a little weird because when it's great, it's really great. But it's also confusing and infuriating because you're left wondering how you get that "60% great" much closer to "100% great."

Still, to get some much-needed clarity, it's Manson's Law of Fuck Yes or No to the rescue. If it's either "fuck yes" or "no," "60% great" doesn't really sound like "fuck yes" from anyone's perspective. He doesn't sound like he's actually that happy being in a relationship with you, and that sucky 40% from him probably doesn't make it a true "fuck yes" from you, either. You probably want more consistency than that. So as good as the relationship might sometimes be, it's not truly a "fuck yes," and therefore, it must be a "no."

And that, in short, is what's so powerful about the Law of Fuck Yes or No. It stops you putting tons of time and effort into people who just aren't interested in you. It puts a stop to poorly defined "are we, aren't we?" relationships, because it forces you to pick one or the other. It gives you a solution to relationships that leave you feeling stuck or unfulfilled because it encourages you to talk about how you feel with your partner. Then, if you can't find a direction for the relationship that works for everyone in it, it reminds you that that relationship might have run its course already, and you might both be happier with other people.

Because OK, there is an argument that an undefined or unfulfilling relationship is at least a relationship, and that can have value too, right? Maybe. But usually, no.

In practice, undefined and unfulfilling relationships are usually draining. It's annoying when you don't know where you stand with someone and what you can expect from them, or when a relationship is constantly leaving you feeling shortchanged.

There's also a major opportunity cost to being in an unfulfilling relationship. You're putting time and effort into a "meh" relationship, and maybe starting to wonder whether that's all there really is, when you could be putting it into a fulfilling "fuck yes" relationship instead. And even if you met the ideal partner for you tomorrow, you'll likely have to go through an emotionally taxing breakup or readjusting process with your current partner before you're fully able to give yourself to someone new.

In a way, it's kind of like douching: you have to actively clear space for the great things you want to receive. To feel confident and ready for the relationships you really want, you have to clear yourself of the relationships you don't. (Even if, yes, no matter how well you prepare, relationships can still get messy sometimes.)

Yes, that does mean losing out on some "meh" relationships. But it also frees you up for "fuck yes" relationships. It means you end up in relationships that everyone wants to be in, that are mutually beneficial for everyone involved, that aren't draining or confusing because everyone knows where they stand. Crucially, it also means you end up in relationships where nobody has to twist anyone's arm — or tempt them with sex or money — to get them to stay.

And sure, you might be thinking, "Well, if someone's only half into me, why shouldn't I try to convince them to be fully into me? My sauciest nudes are locked and loadeddd. Someone playing hard to get is my kink!!"

Or equally, you might be furrowing your brow and wondering "Well maybe he really wants a relationship, but I don't, so is it really that bad if we still fool around once a week?"

The answers are the same, only from opposite sides. It's not fun to have to work overtime convincing someone of your worth if they can't see it on their own.[2] It's not fun — or authentic — if you constantly have to adapt your behavior so someone keeps a basic level of interest in you.

Most people don't play hard to get. We tend to prioritize the things and people we're interested in, and as we've talked about, if someone

---

[2] Actual kinks are great, obviously. Only, being interested in people who aren't interested in you probably isn't one. It might come down to low self-worth or just a fear of vulnerability — it's emotionally much safer to want people who don't want you back — but that's clearly not a sexual preference.

is playing games to make you prove you're really interested, that doesn't give the relationship a great start.

In the other situation, it's not great, or fair, to keep something going that benefits you if you know the other person isn't really into it. As those kinds of relationships continue, there's a real risk they'll lead to resentment, hurt feelings and/or someone feeling used.

That's why the Law of Fuck Yes or No is so important. It stops you being strung along by people who aren't that into you. It stops you stringing along people you're not that into. It saves you from hurt feelings since you're less likely to get seriously emotionally invested in relationships that can't give you what you need or want. And again, by saying no to those kinds of relationships, you make space for the relationships that deserve your time and energy the most.

All of that said, like most concepts in dating and relationships, "fuck yes or no" is not without its caveats and subtleties. And since it's a concept we'll come back to a few times, let's look at three important nuances that apply to making any "fuck yes or no" decision.

Every "fuck yes or no" decision is to a specific thing and can be time-limited

Saying "fuck yes" to someone isn't necessarily about saying you'll spend the rest of your life with them.

It can be "fuck yes" to a first date.

It can be "fuck yes" to being someone's vacation boyfriend.

It can be "fuck yes" to a blowjob in the back of his truck without wanting that to turn into a long-term relationship.

Often, you might be "fuck yes" to one thing, like sex, while being "no" about something else, like committing to a relationship. Equally, in longer-term relationships, "fuck yes or no" might only be about agreeing to progress to the next stage, like deciding to be committed or exclusive, or making plans to move in together. It doesn't have to mean agreeing to get married and share a mortgage by the fourth date.

"Fuck yes or no" doesn't have to be an instant decision

Despite what it might sound like, "fuck yes or no" isn't like "Red pill or blue pill, bitch!? You have ten seconds." You can take your time to decide, and "fuck yeses" often *should* be carefully considered.

"Fuck yes or no" is about simplifying relationship decisions, not rushing into them. Equally, the idea that a relationship is in trouble if someone has to be constantly persuaded to stay doesn't mean you can't change your mind over time or after talking things through with your partner. It just means that if the *only* reason you stay in a relationship is someone else's influence, that's usually problematic for the relationship in the long run.

"Fuck yes or no" doesn't work without vulnerability

Yes, a big part of "fuck yes or no" is about raising your relationship standards. But no, it is not about raising them so high you'll only accept perfection.

We'll talk more about perfectionism later, but maybe you've met (or are) a guy with unrealistically high standards. You probably know what I'm talking about, the kind of guys who say they're open to relationships, but will only even consider men above a certain height and income level, who share 98% of the same interests as them, who also have an intact foreskin and immaculately bleached asshole, and work out at least seventeen times a week. Inevitably, expectations like those usually leave you way more single than not.

"Fuck yes or no" is not about chasing perfection, because perfection doesn't exist.

"Fuck yes or no" is not about rejecting potential partners for every tiny incompatibility or flaw in the hope that if you do, the perfect Ken doll of a partner will eventually come along.[3]

---

[3] In any case, Ken dolls don't have dicks — or anything else — down there. So unless your preferred style of genitalia is "a giant perineum to nowhere," maybe even Ken dolls aren't that perfect.

Saying "fuck yes" is not the same as saying "I can see literally zero negatives about this relationship!!" It just means saying "I've weighed up both the positives and the negatives, and I really want to give this combo a shot." Again, it takes vulnerability to accept the entirety of someone as they are, and if you can't do that, "fuck yes or no" doesn't work.

Equally, "fuck yes or no" is not a perfect system for avoiding all heartbreak and hurt feelings, but it can spare you a lot of unnecessary heartbreak and hurt feelings. Again, all relationships — even short-lived ones — involve risk. There's no way to guarantee a relationship will work out exactly the way you hope it will, and if you don't have the vulnerability to accept that risk, "fuck yes or no" doesn't work either.

So if it starts to feel like you're using "fuck yes or no" to keep everyone at an emotional distance, it's worth asking yourself whether you're afraid to take a chance on *anyone*.

If you basically never meet anyone you feel "fuck yes" about, that might be because you're not open to discovering the things that are great about them. (A confident person won't be shy about their good points, but it's also your job to try to figure out what a potential partner has to offer.)

Or, if you're constantly rejecting people for tiny, inconsequential things — if they have a slight stutter, or they don't eat sushi — you might be avoiding vulnerability by trying to seize a false sense of control. You might be using "fuck yes or no" to act protectively, not selectively, which is not how it works.

In short, you want to find the sweet spot, the Goldilocks zone, to "fuck yes or no." You want to be selective enough to focus on high-compatibility relationships, while making sure you don't become so picky you overlook potentially great relationships because they're not 100% perfect, because no relationship is perfect all the time.

And when you tune it right, the beauty of "fuck yes or no" is that it lets rejection do its job. It lets rejection keep you from the people who aren't that into you, or that you aren't that into, or that you aren't that compatible with, or that you don't have compatible dating goals with, or that just aren't right for you right now.

And yes, it often leads you to fewer connections, but they're usually more promising and better-suited connections. Therefore, it usually *increases* your odds of getting what you want.

"Fuck yes or no" is also great at bringing you a lot of peace. If someone rejects you, it reminds you that of your options — to go crazy trying to show them how wrong and dumb they are, or to accept the rejection and focus on finding someone else — moving on is usually best.

"Fuck yes or no" is also a reminder that no response — or an inconsistent, confusing or half-assed response — is still a response.[4] It's another reminder that if you have to play games to keep someone interested in you, you've probably already lost. And it's a reminder that nobody is everyone's type, no matter who they are or what they look like.

At the same time, "fuck yes or no" emphasizes why it's important to show direct and unapologetic interest in the people you *are* "fuck yes" about. If he doesn't know it's a "fuck yes" from you, and he's too shy to make clear it's a "fuck yes" from him, it makes the relationship a "no" by default.

Yes, showing or telling someone it's a "fuck yes" from you does open you up to rejection, but a "no" is just rejection redirecting you toward someone else who will be "fuck yes" to your authentic, vulnerable self.

And that's something we can all say "fuck yes" about.

---

4 Not everyone has the emotional maturity to reject others directly. (That's one reason ghosting exists.) But you can have the maturity to reject someone because their inconsistency or indecision doesn't work for you.

How to deal with rejection

So yes, if great relationships come from mutual "fuck yeses," the "nos" that keep you away from unfulfilling relationships ultimately are a good thing, whatever form they take.

Still, as easy as it is to accept that rejection is both necessary and healthy on an intellectual level, things get trickier because there are emotions involved. In practice, there's no getting around the fact that rejection and the disappointment that comes with it can really fucking chafe.

In fact, as queer people, our struggles with authenticity tend to make us especially sensitive to rejection. Basically, because most of us have faced different versions of rejection from society as a whole, we become highly sensitized to it.

As we talked about earlier, even if we're comfortably "out" now, we still tend to carry the psychological scars of the closet. As a result, we become adept at scanning our environments for potential rejection. This is not only exhausting, but it also makes us susceptible to knee-jerk reactions when we are rejected, and can even make us sense rejection when it's not there.

Researchers call this **rejection sensitivity** — and it's why, for all LGBTQ+ people, romantic rejection can feel especially wounding. For us, it doesn't just hurt because being rejected or broken up with hurts, it also has a nasty habit of bringing up all the rejection we've felt *in general* as queer people. Which feels about as fun as it sounds.[5]

In turn, that means we have to be especially good at responding to rejection healthily, so it doesn't make us turn away from vulnerability, leaving us less open to building great connections in the future.

Here are some ways to do that.

---

[5] See Joseph Slimowicz, Jedidiah Siev and Paula M. Brochu, "Impact of Status-Based Rejection Sensitivity on Depression and Anxiety Symptoms in Gay Men," *International Journal of Environmental Research and Public Health* 17/5 ◆ (March 2020).

Try to see rejection as a compatibility mismatch, not a sign that you're terrible or undateable

We'll cover this properly in the next chapter, but the simple truth is, most people just won't be a good fit for you. You won't have enough in common. You'll want different things from a relationship. You just won't be able to give each other what you both need.

So even if a rejection feels personal in the sense that it obviously *is* about you and who you are, you should try not to take it personally.

I know, that's often easier said than done, but it's important to try. Again, rejection is really just redirection — so even if it hurts, it helps to trust that the rejection is just doing its job of redirecting you toward people you'll be more compatible with.

And crucially, if you aren't able to give someone what they need, that's not a sign you should change everything about yourself to give it to them. Yes, some compromise is necessary in relationships. Yes, being with someone means trying to understand each other's needs and figuring out how you can help each other get them met better. But it doesn't mean sacrificing who you authentically are and what you authentically need to keep a relationship going. It's much better to focus on finding people who are interested in you as you are — and vice versa.

Ask for an explanation if it'll help, but don't torture yourself, hun

When we're rejected, it can help us process that rejection better if we understand a bit about why it's happening.

Obviously, how you approach starting a conversation about this will depend on the situation. If you shoot someone a nice message after matching on an app and they don't respond, you probably don't want to ask for comprehensive feedback on why your "Hi, how's it going?" didn't get the response you wanted. But if you've been on a few dates with someone and they've told you they don't want to move forward, you're also entitled to ask them why they feel that way.

Of course, they're not obligated to give you a lengthy explanation — and they might not want to or even know how to. It's also possible they'll tell you something that makes you feel worse. So if you decide to spin this particular roulette wheel, you should be ready for any of those outcomes.

But either way, the best thing you can do is to focus on you. That's where the "don't torture yourself" part comes in. Yes, if you've been with someone for a while, a longer conversation about the breakup might help you find closure and move on. But if you reach a point where keeping a conversation going is more about maintaining a connection with someone before they're gone, that's more likely to prolong your pain than help it. Focusing on you means focusing on moving on and finding what you want elsewhere.

And yes, these conversations often aren't easy. He might say something critical or just mean about you. And sure, it might contain some valuable feedback about how you can show up better in a future relationship. But if he's mean enough to say something like "You're just not that cute," that's definitely not your cue to go into overdrive changing everything about your body. It's your cue to focus on finding someone who *does* think you're cute. (Or just isn't as superficial.)

Start a conversation if it might help give you closure or help you be better at dating in the future. But again, keep your focus on you — on coming to terms with a rejection and moving on from it. Nothing else.

Be kind to yourself

When Kesha sang "Your Love Is My Drug," she was actually making an important and scientifically backed point: love is basically as addictive as cocaine.[6] So coming down from the connection you felt with someone, even in a short-term relationship, really can mess with you.

---

[6] Helen Fisher, "Love Is Like Cocaine," *Nautilus* ♦ (February 2, 2016).

Even if you know intellectually that a rejection is good for you, and even if you're a full and unreserved believer in the concept of "fuck yes or no," the part of your brain that deals with attachment and connection isn't. The only thing it knows is that the warm, amorous feeling you were supplying it just got cut off — and you can guess the fuck again if you thought it was going to take that lightly.

As a result, no matter how right and necessary the rejection is, it can still make you feel terrible, even when you're the one initiating it. So anytime a rejection really stings, you have to give yourself — and the silly but very human part of your brain that's telling you that love is a lie and your life is over — time to process.

During that time, it's very healthy to try to compensate for those negative feelings by making time for the things that bring you peace, joy, and/or endorphins. That might mean spending more time with friends, spending more time outdoors, exercising, diving into hobbies you enjoy, masturbating or having more sex than usual, or whatever.

How deeply you feel a rejection or separation will depend on lots of different factors, not least how long the connection lasted. But the same principle always applies: if you felt at all attached to someone and they reject you, you'll likely need an uncomfortable period of emotionally detaching from them before you're ready to move on.

So give yourself what you need. Take a break from dating if you want to. Just get yourself back to normal so you're ready for the next person to come along.

How to reject someone gracefully

On the other side — when you're the one rejecting someone else — the challenge is to find a way to do it as respectfully as possible. Yes, it's still true that rejection is healthy and necessary. But also yes, it's still true that being rejected isn't fun, especially when you're queer.

So if we want to exist in a healthier but kinder dating culture, the way we communicate rejection also matters.

Here's how you can turn someone down more gracefully.

Be direct

Yes, there's that saying that you have to be cruel to be kind, but it's not true. (And I'm not sure who invited a low-key sociopath to start coining influential phrases, but here we are.)

In dating, kindness is not about being cruel, but it often is about being direct and upfront with someone. It's kind to let someone know what your genuine feelings and intentions are when it will help them plan their time and their life.

Sure, there are times when you don't know exactly what you want — and it's fine to communicate that. But in general, "No thanks," "Sorry, that's not what I want right now," or "Thanks, but I don't see you that way" is kinder than "Maybe," "I'll let you know" or "I guess, I'll have to think about it," if that's not how you genuinely feel.

A lot of us are indirect partly because we're worried that someone might take a rejection badly. (And yes, some people will.) But for the same reason they rip the wax from your buttcrack in one decisive yank — because it's ultimately less painful than peeling it off hair by hair — delaying or skirting around a rejection often just makes things worse.

Having high authenticity means being able to be compassionately honest about how you feel — including when it means ending a relationship or connection that isn't working for you.

...but don't be more direct than you need to be

That said, less often is more when it comes to rejection. You don't always have to be hyper-direct to the point of being brutal.

If someone messages you with "Hey sexy" and you see them as just a friend, "Hi buddy" or "Hey man" is probably a better response than "Fuck off, you horny sex pest!!"

Equally, if you're on a first date and you're pretty sure neither of you is vibing with it, it's fine to part with "It was nice to meet you — see you around" and not "Urgh, this was a no from me!"

Yes, in practice it can be tough to strike the right balance. Some people are good at reading between the lines, and some will need you to spell things out more directly. And when you barely know someone, it's especially hard to judge what the right balance is for them. So if in doubt, tell them what you think is necessary, and if they don't get it, you can turn the directness up a notch. But again, given queer men's sensitivity to rejection, less can also be more. Try to keep it kind, and try not to say tons more than is necessary.

Explain if it'll help

We've just seen this from the other side: sharing part of why your connection is ending can help someone process, especially if you've been with them for a while. Part of our rejection sensitivity is perceiving reasons for rejection that aren't there, so even a quick explanation can help stop someone falling into the trap of thinking "I suck and I fucked this up," and help them move on more healthily.

Unless someone did something that really crossed a line for you, it's usually best to focus on the issue or incompatibility and avoid pointing fingers or moralizing about anyone's behavior. So something like "I think we want different things from this relationship" or "I can't cope with doing long-distance anymore" is a good start. Though if it's true, you could say something like "I've really struggled to trust you after you lied to me about your trip."

Rejection can also be more about drawing a boundary or redefining a relationship. That might mean saying something like "I like spending time with you, but I think we'd be better off as friends." Or it might mean saying "I'm not looking for a long-term relationship right now, but if you want to be fuckbuddies, I'm open to that."

Whatever the situation is, the goal isn't to give someone a detailed autopsy of what isn't working, or every reason you don't want to move forward with the connection. Offering a brief explanation is just one way you can reject people more lovingly, and leave them feeling more respected, rather than invalidated or dismissed.

Try not to say anything too personal or that could sound judgmental

Yes, authenticity is an important part of rejecting someone directly. But authenticity also has consequences.

Rejecting someone because of a specific compatibility issue — say, you just want different things from the relationship — is often easier to put into words, because it's not really about anyone personally. But if the rejection is more personal than that (and it sometimes is) you'll want to be careful about how you communicate that.

"You're not really my dating type" is better than "I just don't find you attractive." "Sorry, I just didn't feel that much of a connection" is better than "You were boring to talk to" or "Gurl, I'm just not into you!" Again, you're trying to get to the heart of the issue that the relationship or potential relationship isn't a good match for what you want or need — not that there's anything wrong with either of you.

Plus, it's worth treading extra carefully anytime you bring up any personal characteristics people can't change about themselves. Lots of queer men have hang-ups about their bodies, so unless you're willing to foot someone's therapy bill while they undo the complex you helped give them, it's worth avoiding anything like "You're too skinny" or "You're too short." (Not least because to someone else, the same feature might be really attractive, or just not matter.)

Given our sensitivity to rejection, it's kind to avoid giving anyone any hang-ups about who they authentically are, or flaring up any of their insecurities unnecessarily.

Try to be positive too

If you want to soften a rejection even more, it can help to throw in something positive too. Even something as simple as "It was nice to meet you," "I enjoyed hanging out," or "It's been great getting to know you" can really help.

Depending on the exact circumstances, phrases like "Thanks for understanding," "I know this might be difficult to hear," "I don't want to lead you on," or a genuine "Good luck finding what you're looking for" can also help give a rejection a more compassionate spin.

You can make it clear that you enjoyed meeting someone even if they're not for you. You can tell someone you think they're great even if they're not for you. You can reject someone but genuinely respect them and want them to find what they're looking for too.

You can present your best, most authentic self to someone and vice versa and realize that you're just not that good a fit for each other. You can accept that it's not a "fuck yes," but that doesn't mean anyone should change who they fundamentally are.

All of that said, there often isn't a perfect and completely positive way to reject someone. There often isn't any language you can use that will save someone from hard feelings entirely. No matter how kind you are, some people will lash out at you, object to what you've said or how you said it, try to change your mind, or start demonizing you like you're the literal spawn of Satan. They might struggle to accept the rejection, and you might have to repeat where you stand, or in some cases, leave without them accepting it.

Still, the possibility that someone might take it badly doesn't make kind but clear rejection any less necessary.

Because really, the power of graceful rejection is that it allows "fuck yes or no" to work at its best. The "rejection" part keeps us out of relationships that aren't fulfilling, while the "graceful" part lets "fuck yes or no" do its job without creating tons of unnecessary pain along the way.

There's a saying that some queer men are only nice to the people they want to fuck. For starters, that's not entirely true. They're also nice to their dogs. And they fawn over tons of strong-willed female celebrities they'll never actually meet. But that aside, it's true that we could also be kinder when it really counts: when we have to turn someone down.

We can turn people down directly but respectfully. We can reject people with love. We can pursue the people we're interested in without leaving a trail of unnecessary misery and hurt feelings along the way. We can see what's great about someone even if we recognize they're not for us. And as a community of people who often struggle to see our own authentic value, we definitely should.

Chemistry and Compatibility

There are plenty of reasons not to trust social media algorithms, but Exhibit A might be Facebook's "People you may know" feature. You'll probably know what I'm talking about — the feature that should really be called "People you actually do know but urgh, you'd rather not connect with on here."

Still, sometimes that feature becomes "People you don't know, but ohhhh you might want to." And in some ways, we love that. It can feel great to connect with people outside of the virtual meat market that dating apps can be. Plus, meeting someone because you have friends in common is often a sign you might really click with them.

Once upon a time, I shot my shot with a cute guy some Silicon Valley algorithm thought maybe I should know.

"Hey Jake, what's up? You're friends with Jorge?" (A mutual friend.)

"Ohhhh hi!" he shot back, with three heart-eyes emojis. "Yeah, kind of. I used to see him a lot on nights out."

Jake lived in a different town, but I was due to take a weeklong trip there a few weeks later, so we made plans to meet. We did, and it was great. It was fun, it was exciting, we both enjoyed getting to know each other. In fact, it felt kind of intense — but that felt great.

Over the next couple of months we stayed in touch. We talked about one of us visiting the other, but firm plans never materialized. Then, as luck would have it, work sent me back to Jake's town.

Inevitably, plans were made. More heart-eyes emojis were exchanged. We were both really looking forward to it.

This time, though, things were kind of weird. In fact, things were awkward. Hanging out felt nothing like it had only a few months before. Surely neither of us could have changed that much? So how was this low as intense as the high of before? And why did it feel so confusing?

This was my lesson in chemistry and compatibility — and why a solid relationship needs both.

Attraction is important — but attraction alone is
not enough

Chemistry — romantic chemistry — is the feeling of being attracted to someone. It's the butterflies in your stomach when you think about them. It's seeing their latest post and feeling warm inside. It's walking around with a smile on your face because you're seeing them tonight.

Chemistry is the hormonal, instinctual feeling that someone is or could be good for you. It's the literal chemicals in your brain giving you a "fuck yes" feeling about someone.

The feeling of romantic attraction — in the short term, at least — is usually based on chemistry. But chemistry is not the only thing that's needed to make love work.

Compatibility is the state of being well matched with someone logically, even logistically. It's having shared values. It's having some shared interests. It's being able to spend time together without disagreeing or falling out over tons of tiny things because you're fundamentally very different people.

Unlike its cousin chemistry, compatibility often doesn't feel very exciting. In fact, it can feel about as exciting as ticking boxes on a passport application. It can feel as exciting as finding the right lid for a Tupperware container. But just like matching the right top with the right bottom — in Tupperware but also other things — compatibility is important in relationships too.

That said, what makes dating interesting is that there's often no obvious correlation between having lots of chemistry with someone and having lots of compatibility with someone. You'll meet people you have one with, but not the other. You'll meet people you have neither with. And, when you're lucky, you'll meet people who you have both with.

Like many important things — sexuality, gender, the number of hot dogs you can fit inside your asshole — chemistry and compatibility exist on a spectrum. But for the sake of discussion, let's not think too much about hot dogs, and simplify chemistry and compatibility into two states, "high" and "low."

That gives us four theoretical boxes a partner might fit into for you:

High chemistry, high compatibility	**High chemistry, low compatibility**
Low chemistry, high compatibility	**Low chemistry, low compatibility**

And sure, every relationship has its own quirks and charms. But relationships that fall within each of these four theoretical categories often have surprisingly similar dynamics.

The simplest relationships to talk about are low chemistry, low compatibility relationships. They're relationships with people you're unlikely to pursue romantically, because, um, why would you? If you don't feel emotionally attracted to someone, and you guys have wildly different values and virtually nothing in common, you're probably not going to show much interest in them. Fin. End of play.

High compatibility but low chemistry relationships are interesting because, if you consider all of human history, they're probably the most common type. That's correct: being with someone because you actually like them, never mind love them, is a pretty modern idea. How lucky we are.[1]

Once, you might have been a handsome prince with his own heart and mind, but if daddy decides your relationship with some foreign *princesa* could end the Great Pointy Stick War of 1800 BC, then that's probably a done deal. Or, even a century or two ago, a woman might prioritize marrying a wealthy man not out of love, but for safety and security, and so she could comfortably raise a few kids.

Then or now, these are relationships that might be logically feasible and built on plenty of shared values. They might involve some genuine love and affection. But they're relationships that are mainly expected to function, and not necessarily expected to be much fun.

In the opposite corner, high chemistry but low compatibility relationships are often intense and fun but short-lived. They're typically exciting at the start but tend to burn out pretty quickly, often leaving you with a painful comedown, wondering what went wrong.

They can be relationships that involve great sex, crazy adventures and time spent together that just seems to fly by. But without a solid foundation to build the relationship on — common interests and common values — cracks in the relationship start appearing, and what began as a strong attraction can end up feeling surprisingly hollow.

An example of this kind of relationship might be when a young woman ends up infatuated with some Casanova who's only looking for his next fling. Or it might be when some guy leaves his partner of twenty years for someone younger, but quickly realizes that the new relationship doesn't fulfill him anything like his last one did. (Whoops.)

---

[1] See, for example, Stephanie Coontz, "The Radical Idea of Marrying for Love," *The Sun* ◆ (September 2016).

They're the type of relationship that a lot of people fantasize about — the hope that someone hot, charming and intriguing will just sweep us off our feet and everything will magically slot into place. But in reality, these relationships prove that, on their own, attraction and infatuation are not enough.

And finally, that brings us to the pinnacle, the apex, the ne plus ultra of great relationships: those that have both high chemistry and high compatibility.

These are relationships where there is not just genuine love and attraction, but also shared values, shared interests, and two ways of seeing the world that slot well together. That doesn't mean you have to date your identical twin — even if it can feel like plenty of queer men do, shout-out to all the boyfriend twins — it just means that you have enough in common that you can build a happy and fulfilling life together, not just a romance.

Yes, you get excited when your phone buzzes and it's them. Yes, your world feels a bit brighter when you're in the same room.

But also yes, you have things to do together that you both enjoy. Also yes, you rarely struggle for something to talk about. Also yes, being with each other and making decisions together is not painful or tedious because you're similar enough that things generally just flow.

Sure, there's no such thing as perfect compatibility (or chemistry). You won't agree on everything. You'll have to negotiate and deal with conflict sometimes. But since there's high chemistry, you'll want to, and since there's high compatibility, you'll be able to.

How to spot high-chemistry, high-compatibility partners

So if a big part of building fulfilling romantic relationships is trying to connect with people who you're likely to have a high level of chemistry *and* compatibility with, how do you do that? How do you spot potential relationships that aren't likely to work out, and what exactly do you have to sacrifice at the altar of St. Faggotré to attract people you likely have lots of potential with?

Well, the good news is that you mostly don't need to worry about low-chemistry relationships. Anytime you meet someone you don't have much chemistry or compatibility with, you probably won't show much interest in them. And most queer men don't tend to pursue high-compatibility partners they don't feel much chemistry with either. While that kind of relationship could bring some benefits in theory, in practice, most of us would rather stay single than chase someone we're not that excited about.

The trickier relationship categories, then, are the ones with high chemistry. And in practice, there are two common traps you'll want to avoid.

The first trap is falling into a high-chemistry but low-compatibility relationship, believing that the strong if sometimes confusing feelings that come with it are a sign the relationship has promise. Despite the common belief, infatuation isn't supposed to feel like an emotional rollercoaster. And lots of us aren't great at spotting low compatibility early on, then applying the "fuck yes or no" principle so we can focus on more compatible partners.

The second trap is rejecting potentially great partners too soon because you have high compatibility but only OK chemistry at first. Because while compatibility is often more or less fixed — unless one partner sacrifices a lot of authenticity — chemistry definitely isn't. Chemistry is not always instant and often grows over time. Yep, the way Walt Disney personally taught us that to be in a great relationship we should instantly feel "the spark" is not helpful. And it's easy to overlook a potentially great partner if you don't know that.

And for us, one key reason we can fall into either of these traps is our common queer nemesis, instant validation.

Let's look at some of the subtleties here.

The lure of high-chemistry, low-compatibility relationships is that they tend to feel good instantly. They feel promising instantly. And so, a lot of us are prone to charging into relationships with people we think are hot but actually have very little in common with.

We go all in, believing that it's deeper attraction or even love, but quickly the cold, hard reality of the lack of compatibility starts to show itself. We run out of things to talk about. Or we end up arguing over tons of small, even petty things. Or the initial physical attraction just fades until the early excitement we felt becomes the painful reality that the relationship might have always been a nonstarter.

The key to avoiding this trap is learning to ask yourself the simple but normally very unsexy questions that help you, as you're getting to know someone, determine your level of compatibility with them:

What can you enjoy doing when you're together? What can you talk about? Would he get on with your friends, or would putting them together cause issues? Are you looking for similar things in a relationship? Would you want a similar amount of independence from each other?

Are you financially compatible — do you have similar ideas about how to spend money, or are your values (or paychecks) so different that it would become an issue? If you don't live in the same town (or even if you do), how easy is it to find time or ways to get together?

And yes, because it's also important: are you sexually compatible? There's more to sexual preferences than "top seeking bottom" and "bottom seeking top." For starters, a lot of queer men are at least a bit versatile, and some are "sides" who don't enjoy or want penetrative sex at all. But beyond that, sexual compatibility isn't just about how you feel about penetration. It's also about factors like how often you want sex, whether you're more adventurous or conservative when having sex, and whether you care about sexual exclusivity in your relationships or not. And if having fulfilling sex is an important part of a relationship for you, then low sexual compatibility is eventually going to create relationship hurdles.

Sometimes the answers to these questions will come instantly — but often they won't. Some will only be revealed as you get to know someone better. And as you do, if your answers are mostly "no," "not much," or "not sure," you probably don't need me to wheel out Carlos the Compatibility Koala to tell you that you might struggle to sustain a longer-term relationship with that person. When you give yourself honest answers to these questions, any big gaps in compatibility usually become pretty obvious.

Still, let me come back to one key detail: there's no such thing as perfect compatibility. Two people, and especially two highly authentic people, will not see eye to eye on everything. Part of making a relationship work is learning to manage your incompatibilities, including when that means accepting you're just going to see some things differently. (Yes, that also means if you wait for "the one" — your perfectly compatible soulmate — you'll be waiting a long time. There is no "the one," only the occasional "wow, you're (mostly) great!" you can build something exciting with together.)

All the same, you set yourself up for relationship success when you begin with a foundation of high compatibility. That means that there aren't any absolute deal-breakers — you might be a hard no on dating someone who smokes, or who makes zero effort to get on with your friends, or who wants a completely different type of relationship to you. But assuming there are no deal-breakers for anyone, being mostly compatible is enough to build something great.[2]

On the flip side, our need for instant validation can also screw us over when we meet someone we have high compatibility with but don't feel instant chemistry with.

Yes, chemistry is usually more about feelings while compatibility is usually more about facts. But again, chemistry can grow — like love can. And chemistry doesn't have to be passionate and intense: it can mean finding someone's company fun and comfortable, not just wanting to tear all their clothes off the second you first see them. Plus,

---

[2] You might wonder how compatible "mostly compatible" is, and there isn't really a definitive answer. But if you want a figure, let's say at least 80%: if at least 80% of the things that matter to you both won't create significant compatibility issues, that's a solid foundation for a long-term relationship.

some people are naturally more shy or cautious around new people, so they might need to get to know you better before they're ready to open up and be more fully themselves with you.

So again, if you insist on needing to feel "the spark" right away, you're likely pushing away some potentially great partners. If you're used to thinking "um, no chemistry, NEXT!" about every connection you make that isn't instantly exciting, you're likely sabotaging your chances of finding a high-chemistry, high-compatibility partner.

Plenty of queer men I know who are or have been in happy, long-term relationships said they didn't necessarily feel an intense initial attraction, just a desire to keep getting to know someone better. Their relationships grew out of more of a slow burn than a spark.

Maybe that flies against your every instinct, but it's how it works. Feeling comfortable around and intrigued by someone on a first date is often the only sign you need that there's room for even more chemistry to grow between you.

That means one deeper solution to this trap is recognizing what you want more authentically — especially longer-term — from your relationships. When you're used to focusing on passing validation, it's easy to overlook the signs that there's potential for a relationship with someone to grow and deepen over time.

But there's also a more immediate solution, and it's much simpler: stop hoping to feel "the spark" on a first date. Focus on whether you feel comfortable around someone. And if you do — even if you don't feel besotted just yet — offer them a second or third date. Give the connection chance to develop, then see how you feel a few dates in.

Of course, if you get to know someone better and your attraction toward them hasn't grown, if the chemistry still isn't there, then that's fine too. That's when you break things off, or ask if they'd be interested in a friendship.

Because that's part of the deal with these relationship categories. It's not that relationships are inherently bad for us unless they have high chemistry *and* compatibility. High-chemistry, low-compatibility relationships might make a fun vacation romance. Low-chemistry, high-compatibility relationships might lead to a great friendship, or give you a new fitness buddy or roommate.

It's about casting, darling. It's about who you invite into the different roles in your life. It's about who is likely to be a good fit — who can give you what you need — in the different roles in your life. (And vice versa for him.)

But it's also about recognizing that attraction, on its own, is not enough.

Because that was the simple truth with Jake and me. We may have been attracted to each other. In a way, we may have even loved each other. But without a solid foundation to build a relationship on, there was nowhere for it to go.[3]

In this case, we found that out the hard way. If we'd thought more about compatibility we might have figured it out sooner. We might have decided to enjoy the chemistry for what it was all the same. But we could have done it without most of the confusing highs and lows.

---

[3] I'll also add that distance and the internet can make high-chemistry, low-compatibility relationships look more promising than they are. If you don't spend much time actually together, it's easy to get seduced by the chemistry and for the compatibility issues to take longer to reveal themselves. So I'm not saying definitely *don't* move your entire life to Argentina to live with your internet lover Ignacio, but maybe get to know him IRL at least a little first.

Unconditional Relationships

Love can be complicated. Love can be hard. And truthfully, not every kind of love is healthy, or even really love at all.

The key to which kind we're likely to cultivate in our relationships — healthy, fulfilling love versus harmful, draining love — often comes down to our relationship with love itself.

Love, but with conditions

It might sound obvious, but I'll say it anyway: every relationship exists because the people in it get something from each other. Maybe one reason you love your best friend is because through thick and thin, she's always supported you. Maybe one reason you love your parents is that they cancel their plans to spend as much time with you as possible when you visit. Maybe three reasons you love your boyfriend are his sense of humor, his kindness, and that thing he knows how to do with his tongue.

And that's great.

The trouble is, when a relationship is mostly based on the ways someone benefits you, things start to get problematic. If you maintain a relationship with a friend because you know she'll always pick up the phone every time you have personal drama but you usually avoid her calls, that's not great. If you mostly keep a close relationship with your parents because if you don't, you're worried they'll stop paying half of your rent, that's not great. And if you're only still with your boyfriend because he gives you easy access to sex four times a week, that's not ideal either.

These are **conditional relationships**, or **transactional relationships** — relationships that exist mostly because of what the people in them can take or extract from each other.

The foundation of these relationships isn't that two people like each other and enjoy being together. The main reason the relationship exists is that the people in it can take certain benefits from each other.

And that's the big problem when a relationship becomes especially conditional — it stops being a personal relationship at all. It becomes a relationship that's really about benefits, and not the fact that two or more people have a genuine, human connection or admiration for each other.

If you have a relationship with someone mostly because they give you money, you don't really have a relationship with them, you have a relationship with their money. If you have a relationship with someone mostly because they give you sex, you don't really have a relationship with them, you have a relationship with their body, with how good your glands make you feel after you've come on their chest. The person willing to have sex with you is kind of irrelevant — it's the fact that they're willing that counts.

And that's why conditional relationships usually don't feel very fulfilling. It's hard to feel good about a relationship when we know, or sense, that someone doesn't really care about us, only what we give them. And it's hard to feel good about ourselves when we're trading part of ourselves for part of someone else, and not really allowing that person to form any kind of connection with us as people.

Let's look at one scenario where this issue can come up. Maybe you'll recognize it.

Ash is at home. His phone buzzes with a notification.

"Looking?" it says.

"Yeah, into?" he replies.

"Top vers, you?" the guy shoots back.[1]

"Bottom. You're close. Wanna meet?" Ash sends his location. "6B. Top floor."

"Sure. 20 mins."

Forty minutes later, the guy is downstairs. Ash buzzes him in. They fuck. It's fun.

"Sorry," Ash says as the guy is leaving, "what's your name by the way?"

"Kam. See you around..." he replies, halfway out the door.

Kam is gone. Ash carries on with his day feeling not that much different than he did an hour ago, before this story even began.

Casual sex like this is easily available to a lot of queer men, and casual sex — like sex in general — can be really great.

But even if scenarios like this one feel sexually fulfilling on some level, many queer men find that they're not actually that emotionally fulfilling. In fact, lots of queer men end up leaving this kind of experience feeling emptier and *more* disconnected than they did when it started, even though they might have put themselves in it to try to feel the exact opposite.

And why is that?

It's nothing to do with sex itself. And it's not really to do with the fact that the sex in this scenario is without strings. It's not even really to do with the fact that these two men might never see each other again and don't know each other's names.

The reason this experience can be emotionally disconnecting and even alienating for the people in it is because it's pretty much the definition of a transactional exchange.

If we enter into a relationship purely because I like fucking buttholes and you like having yours fucked, and because you think my body is hot and vice versa, and because the app on our phones says

---

[1] OK, he probably actually wrote "top vers u" but I wrote out "you" in full and included some punctuation because in this book we hold ourselves to different grammar standards.

we're two hundred feet away, that sounds a lot like a relationship built purely on the exchange of sexual benefits. (And probably fluids.) And if that relationship is really only about our bodies, that sounds like a relationship that conveniently bypasses the fact that there are also actual people inside those bodies.

And again, this isn't just about sex. It's not about slut-shaming. There are no walks of shame, only walks of glory.

I can have a relationship with you as a person while knowing you only as "flirtycumdump69," and that relationship can last just thirty-five minutes one Thursday afternoon. (Yes, a short-lived connection is still a kind of relationship.) But what matters is the "as a person" part. What matters is that we're also both people, not just sources of sexual gratification for each other.

Even if we joke about you being "just a hole" and you spend most of the time we're together lying naked on your back with your legs in the air, when it comes down to it, you're not "just a hole," but also an actual, complete person.[2]

Part of the challenge here is that sex and erotic desire are often heightened by mystery and emotional detachment. That's partly why guys who fit the "fuckboy" or "bad boy" stereotypes can be attractive. (And why once we've had sex with someone new — and some of the mystery has gone away — we're often less inclined to do it again.)

But if that emotional detachment goes too far, there's the risk you're only using me and my body to get your needs met, and I'm only using you and your body to get my needs met. Without some sense that we're also both people, there likely is only an exchange of sexual benefits. (And probably fluids.) We're likely both bypassing each other's humanity or humanness in the pursuit of getting our needs met. So if we end up feeling used and a little dehumanized, maybe it shouldn't be that surprising. It might be basically what just happened.

---

[2] Yes, you can be an actual, complete person who happens to have a hole (or pole) and strong feelings about what you like to do with it. But that is different.

And sure, there are times when it's fun to be feral and fuck like animals. Anonymous, dehumanizing or even degrading sex might authentically turn you on, and if it does, that's great.

But if you find yourself mostly having sex that feels empty and transactional, what can you do about it? Should you always get dinner before you fuck someone? Should you only fuck your nearest and dearest friends?

No, this isn't about always getting dinner first. And no, I'm not going to recommend you have regular sex with your friends. (Though some queer men happily do.)

The key to avoiding an excessively transactional relationship here is to create opportunities to get to know — and see if you even like — someone before you get too preoccupied with the specific benefits they might bring you.

That might mean starting with dinner or a coffee.

It might mean chilling in your living room for a while before you invite him into your bedroom.

It might mean acknowledging that as fun as sex can be in itself, sex is usually more emotionally fulfilling when you have it with a person, not just a body you found on the internet. (It might also mean avoiding environments like hookup apps that are centered on facilitating quick, transactional connections.)

Yes, starting with people over benefits can mean it takes longer for the relationship to reach a point where you receive those benefits. But it usually feels more emotionally satisfying — and authentic — when you go about it that way.

Because whether they're based on sex, money or other benefits, the basic underlying issue with transactional relationships is that they're inauthentic. They're not personal relationships that exist for the only authentic reason: that two complete, authentic people like each other as complete, authentic people. And in turn, that inauthenticity tends to limit the trust, intimacy and connection that can develop within the relationship.

So if we want to form more authentic connections, what matters is that we focus on building relationships that exist between people, not just between people and benefits.

Why queer people are especially susceptible to conditional relationships

Conditionality isn't just an issue in queer relationships. All kinds of people can find themselves in conditional relationships for all sorts of reasons. But partly thanks to the extra challenges homophobia creates for us around authenticity, queer people can be especially susceptible to conditional relationships.

Queer or otherwise, the simplest reason a lot of people relate to others conditionally is that a lot of people around them do too. It sounds lazy to blame everyone's adult behavior on how they were raised, but because childhood is where we form our first relationships, if you watched your close family relating to each other conditionally, there's a good chance you picked up some of those dynamics too.

There are a few different ways our immediate families can model conditional love and help us internalize the idea that "If only I do this, I will be accepted and loved." Some kids learn to gain acceptance by getting good grades or being impeccably behaved. And some kids never see their parents disagree or stand up for themselves, and conclude that if you want to be loved, raising your voice or directly asking for what you need are both definite no-nos.

That can be true for anyone. But as usual, growing up queer adds extra layers to all of this.

As we've talked about, as a queer kid you almost certainly learned the powerful lesson that it's a good idea to deny or hide parts of who you are if you want to be loved and accepted, not just by your family but by society as a whole. Even with a generally loving and accepting family, you'll likely have learned to be careful about not acting a certain way, or dressing a certain way, or saying certain things in order to feel loved and accepted. That's about as conditional as love can get.

And even today, in the year of our Lordt twenty-whatever, as a queer adult you might feel like your acceptance in society is still conditional. Because it often is. For all the progress we've made, queer people still have to think twice about public displays of affection, and try not to act "too gay" at work, and casually omit key details about our personal lives when our straight friends and family ask. We do this because we understand that we'll be transactionally accepted by society as long as we avoid gaying it the fuck up in a way that might make any straight people uncomfortable.[3]

And psychologically, this isn't great. You might even describe it as "an absolute mindfuck."

In short, queer people are encouraged to accept conditional love as the best kind we can hope for. We're incentivized and expected to deny our authentic selves in order to be tolerated by a straight-centric, cis-centric society. Yes, like we've also discussed, that affects our self-image and self-esteem. But what's more, it can deeply affect the models we internalize for what a healthy relationship should be.

We get used to conditional acceptance from the society we live in, because we have to, to survive. But then we tend to model this shitty approach to relationships by acting the same way to each other. We're prone to building relationships on such questionable foundations as "I will love you, but only if you stay in shape," or "I will love you, but only if you let me fuck you whenever I'm horny," or "I will love you, but only as long as you earn a lot and buy me things." And we can get used to thinking "If I don't give him what he wants, this relationship will be over and I'll be alone."

And sure, not every queer relationship is like that. But because so many queer men learn to attach these conditions of worth to other

---

[3] There's much more on this in Alan Downs's *The Velvet Rage*, especially in the earlier chapters.

queer men — as well as themselves — conditional relationships can be difficult to avoid.

We've found ourselves in an ecosystem where conditional love can feel like the norm. We've helped to normalize the idea that being in a relationship can mean "I will love you, not necessarily as an entire person, as long as you fit this specific mold and give me what I want." And conversely, a lot of us end up tempted to think "I crave your love and attention enough that I'm willing to give you what you want, even if you don't care about me as a person."

And unfortunately, when you're comfortable with these kinds of transactions, you're more likely to accept being treated badly in your relationships. Specifically, if the relationship I have is mostly not with you but with the sex or social status you bring me, I'm likely to tolerate you treating me poorly as long as I'm still getting the sex or social status I really have the relationship with.

That's one reason why these transactional, tit-for-tat relationships usually aren't that fulfilling. It's also why they tend to misfire, or burn out, or actively feel draining or invalidating.

In pop psychology, unconditional relationship dynamics are sometimes described as being between people who are "raised on love" (who love the people in their lives mostly because they like being around them), while transactional dynamics are described as being between people who are "raised on survival" (who learned to use other people to get their needs met).

But however you were raised, if you've read through this chapter and thought "Yep, that sounds like me and a lot of my relationships," the good news is that it's always possible to break these patterns. Like with most long-standing relationship dynamics, it's not necessarily easy. But it's always possible.

How to cultivate more unconditional relationships

Conditionality in relationships is not black and white. Again, all adult relationships exist because someone (and ideally everyone) benefits from them. So the goal is never to tell someone, "Bitch, I'm never doing anything that could benefit you again to make you prove you love me for me!!" That's not what this is about.

In healthier relationship dynamics, though, the benefits are offered more freely, for their own sake, and without the expectation of a specific benefit being received in return.

So if you want to identify whether a relationship is especially conditional, the way to do it is to ask yourself how the relationship would change if the specific relationship benefits changed.

If your friend didn't want to go on nights out with you all the time, would you find other ways to hang out or would that effectively end the friendship? If you didn't rely on your parents to help with your tuition, would you be as close? If your boyfriend went through a period of wanting less sex, would you break up?

Or, to frame it through some especially conditional relationships that queer men often find themselves in:

Would you keep dating an older man if he stopped sending you money? Would you still want to hang out with your friend if he lost his high-paying job and couldn't afford his luxury apartment? Would you drop your fuckbuddy — or even a friend — if he put on a little weight?

Because if losing the benefit means you wouldn't want much to do with that person anymore, that sounds like a relationship that's highly conditional.

Again, there are subtleties here. If you have a sex-only relationship with someone and they've decided they don't want sex with you anymore, you could try to turn the relationship into a friendship. But if you don't really want any new friends, you're not the asshole of the year if you just wish them well and end the relationship.

But if a change in the benefits someone gives you would radically affect *what you fundamentally think about them as a person*, that's not a good sign. And if that's true of a lot of your relationships, it sounds like you're used to transactional relationships and might be treating a lot of the people in your life as disposable.[4]

Of course, for a relationship to be unconditional it needs to be unconditional on all sides. And with other people it can be harder to judge whether they're more interested in you or the benefits you bring them. But that's another good reason to ask for what you want and say what you feel in your relationships. You won't get everything you want all the time from any relationship, but if being vulnerable or telling someone no seriously harms your connection with them, it likely wasn't that respectful of a relationship in the first place.

And if you've identified that a relationship in your life is especially conditional and want to change that, you have a number of different ways to deal with it.

The simplest way — and often the best or only realistic option — is to end the relationship. Focus on finding people who want to have sex with you who also respect you as a person. Focus your time on friends who'll support you no matter what life throws at you and no matter what specific perks you can offer them — and vice versa.

Otherwise, it's often an option to try renegotiating or restructuring a relationship. You can invite your friend who isn't into clubbing now to do something else with you. If someone giving you money is making you feel uncomfortably obligated to them, you can respectfully decline their financial support. You can focus on finding opportunities to spend time with someone for the sake of spending time with them, not just for the benefits they might give you.

---

[4] Queer men suddenly dropping other people when it turns out those people won't give them exactly what they want is its own subgenre of "men are trash." It's also why it's important to pay attention to the way a new partner responds the first time you tell him "I can't" or "I don't want to."

In short, you can say no to the aspects of a relationship that feel transactional or inauthentic to you, while embracing the aspects that feel more unconditional.

That said, adjusting a conditional relationship can get difficult. Just because you've decided you don't want to be in a relationship that's subject to certain conditions, it doesn't mean the other person will have done the same.

As a result, they may push back on the changes you've proposed to the relationship. And if someone is used to getting their needs met through conditional relationships, any threat to the relationship might be seen as a threat to them getting their needs met. So often, people like that will respond in the only way they know: by going into bargaining mode.

Obviously though, submitting to transactional bargaining won't fix what was making you feel uncomfortable about the relationship in the first place. Someone offering you more money or sex or other perks doesn't help when the money or sex or perks are essentially the problem. And as tough as it can be to resist that kind of negotiation if you're used to seeing relationships as transactional, it's obviously important that you do.

If you want to build stronger and more authentic relationships, it's important to build relationships primarily with people, not benefits. And it's important that benefits are given reciprocally — freely and without specific expectations, from all sides.

That said, love has to come with boundaries. Unconditional love is never about giving someone what they want if doing that hurts or exhausts you. (Even and especially in your closest relationships.)

You can have unconditional love for a partner and still tell him you sometimes need time alone. You can have unconditional love for your friend who's struggling with alcohol while you help him into a recovery program, and limit your time with him if he's being abusive or violent. You can accept someone unconditionally while knowing you have to keep them at a distance.

Unconditional love does not mean putting up with abuse. It does not mean giving unconditional tolerance or unconditional access. It can mean limiting who you give your time, energy and attention to. It just means building reciprocal, not transactional, relationships. It means building personal relationships where people are valued for who they are, and not just for what they give.

In reality, there's room to value both who someone is and what having them in our lives brings us. And no adult relationships are 100% unconditional — they're conditioned on being satisfying and fulfilling for the people in them. But in our most important and most intimate relationships, unconditional love is what we should strive for.

The healthiest kind of love accepts us and the people we love as we are. It doesn't apply conditions we have to meet to be deemed worthy. It doesn't diminish anyone's authenticity. It only encourages it.

PART II:
SEX

Sex Is Great

Sex is powerful. Sex is consequential. It can unite kingdoms. It can get a president impeached. It can give you an infection that makes it hurt to pee.

But most importantly, with the right people and for the right reasons, sex is great. Fucking great. Literally.

And yet, sex can be complicated. It can be awkward. It can feel weird. It can be good for our glands but bad for our hearts.

Why is that? Why do we get weird about sex sometimes? And what can we do about it?

These are the questions I'll try to answer in this chapter.

Some reasons sex is great

For starters, sex is physiologically good for you — it can lower your blood pressure, it can improve your immune system, and it can help you sleep better.[1]

One of the fun things about orgasms — which aren't the same as sex, but are obviously often part of sex — is that they release a cocktail of endorphins that help put a smile on your face, love in your heart, and a warm feeling in your general perineal area.

---

[1] Elizabeth Scott, "How Does Sex Relieve Stress and Anxiety?," *Verywell Mind* ◆ (May 18, 2022).

But sex isn't just about physiology — it's psychologically important too. It can improve your self-esteem. It helps to reduce depression and anxiety.[2]

With the right person and in the right circumstances, sexual intimacy is also a powerful way of connecting with someone you care about. Being physically desired is also often part of how we feel loved and wanted by others.

You might have heard of Maslow's Hierarchy of Needs — a popular way of categorizing our very human needs created by psychologist Abraham Maslow, ranging from basic physiological needs at the bottom to more advanced "esteem" and "self-actualization" needs at the top.

Self-actualization Needs
Realizing your full potential,
e.g. through creative activities

Esteem Needs
e.g. respect, status, recognition

Belonging Needs
e.g. family, friendships, intimacy, connection

Safety Needs
e.g. shelter, security, financial stability

Physiological Needs
e.g. food, water, sleep, a good fuck

MASLOW'S HIERARCHY OF NEEDS

[2] Cindy M. Meston and David M. Buss, "Why humans have sex," *Archives of Sexual Behavior* 36 ♦ (2007), 477–507.

Well, as it turns out, sex is right there on the bottom rung, next to food, water and rest.[3] Whatever some people might think, wanting to have sex is a natural, hormonal need most humans have.

And sure, there are plenty of reasons some people abstain from sex, either temporarily or in general. But if you do have sex, and you enjoy sex, there's no hiding from the fact that sex is *good* for us.

And that's great.

Some reasons sex gets complicated

Still, sex isn't always happiness and rainbows. Sex can be used to manipulate or take advantage of someone. Sex without consent is a serious violation of personal boundaries. Sex can hurt, physically and emotionally. Sex can feel complicated. Sex can feel shameful.

Yes, some queer men have a habit of using sex to hide from emotional vulnerability. (It's often easier to show someone your naked body than your naked soul.) But all sex — even a seven-minute hookup — involves some vulnerability and risk.

There's the risk it'll be disappointing. There's the risk you'll regret it. There's the risk someone's body won't perform in the ways you hope it will. (Bodies are like that sometimes.)

But one reason a lot of us — and queer people especially — have a complicated relationship with sex is because of the way we're conditioned to think about it.

As usual, the problem is that we mostly inherit our values and beliefs from the people around us, especially when we're growing up.

So depending on who you listen to, that might mean you picked up ideas like "sex before marriage is wrong," "sex isn't something we

---

[3] Maslow actually said the exact list of physiological needs is open to interpretation, though sex is often included. But that's enough evidence for me that he implied that if you're eating, sleeping and fucking regularly, your body will be grateful for it. There's a good introduction to Maslow's hierarchy at https://www.simplypsychology.org/maslow.html.

should ever talk about," or even "having lots of sex makes you more of a man."

And if you're queer, it might mean internalizing ideas like "sex is between one man and one woman," "what your body wants is wrong, gurl," or just "BUTTS ARE NOT FOR FUCKING, Y'ALL."

We've talked before about how, as queer men, one of our biggest tasks as adults is to figure out which parts of us are truly authentic, and which parts we created to fit in, or to protect us from shame and rejection. This is true in general, but it also applies to what we believe about sex.

Importantly, that doesn't mean all of the values and beliefs you inherited about sex are wrong. It just means that if you haven't done the work to figure out the values and beliefs that are authentic to you — based on what's important to you, what makes you tick, or just what turns you on — you likely won't have a relationship with sex that's as fulfilling and healthy as it could be.

So for starters, you can throw out any hard-and-fast rules about what sex is and isn't, or should and shouldn't be. "No sex on the first date" is not an indisputable law of the universe. "Relationship sex is always better than casual sex" is not a universal truth. "It's not sex unless someone comes" is not built into the very fabric of space and time. (Or space-time, whatever that is.)

And in practice, these unchallenged beliefs about sex tend to push us to one of two different but equally shitty extremes. Some of us hold on to unhelpful beliefs that make us feel ashamed about having or wanting sex, and that tends to stop us having, or just being open to, the sex we really want to have. At the other extreme, we can respond to these beliefs by having lots of sex that doesn't honor what we truly want or need. And that can be limiting and harmful too.

Sex is not just a form of self-expression. (Though it is, and that's important.) It's also a unique way of connecting with ourselves and our inner emotional world. It feels limiting to deny our sexual desires, so there's power in feeling zero shame about connecting with, or even just discovering, what turns us on. There's a special joy in pursuing what makes us feel sexually fulfilled.

But because most of us live in sometimes-cursed societies that cling on to ideas like "sex is shameful!" and, especially for men, "it's more impressive to have lots of sex, even if it's not good sex," a lot of people don't explore their sexual desires with as much authenticity as they could. Or if they do connect with them, they might still feel ashamed to tell their partners what they found out, so their sexual liberation ends up being more theoretical than practical.

But what does it mean to become more sexually liberated? How do you find the relationship that you want to have with sex and get better at communicating what you want when you're getting it on?

The seven sex commandments: How to figure out what sex means to you

Probably the best thing about sex is that there's no intrinsically right or wrong way to think about it. It really is all about how you're wired and what turns you on — and that's different for all of us.

And importantly, sexual liberation is not necessarily the same as "try to fuck everyone who'll let you." Nope. Sexual liberation just means finding a more authentic relationship with sex so you can pursue having it in a way that truly honors you, your body, and your sexuality as a whole.[4]

To help you do that, I'm going to share with you seven powerful ideas about sex. Think of them as the seven sex commandments, if you like, and you can use them to draw your own conclusions.

That means that, despite the name, the seven ideas are not "the gospel according to Brad, the secret but sexy thirteenth apostle." It's more of a "choose your own adventure" expedition into what gets you off.

---

[4] And, if appropriate, as a hole.

With that in mind, let's go adventuring.

1. Sex is normal, natural and human

Yes, some people are asexual, and experience little to no sexual attraction to others. Yes, some people are abstinent, and decide not to have sex, for all kinds of reasons. But again, many, even most, people have not just sexual desires but hormonal, sexual needs they're trying to satisfy, whether they're good at openly admitting that or not.

And good for them. Whether they do it for the physical benefits, the emotional benefits, or, um, just because it's fun, wanting to have sex is a normal, natural, and potentially very fulfilling part of being human.

2. You get to decide what you do with your body

On the one hand this is about consent — you get to say yes or no to what happens to your body, and your partners get to decide what happens to their bodies, too. On the other hand, it means that what you do with your body isn't really anyone's business but yours and whoever you're getting busy with.

Slut-shaming? I don't know her. Bottom-shaming? She doesn't go here.[5] Kink-shaming? I met her once but I was not a fan.

Because again, a lot of the "truths" we've learned to accept about sex are just inherited cultural beliefs.

Relationship sex actually isn't, on average, better than casual sex. Sex does put you at risk of catching certain infections, but driving comes with a much higher risk of serious injury or death than sex

---

[5] We'll go into gender roles properly later, but can we talk about the idea that bottoming makes you somehow more feminine for a second? I mean, what could be more masculine than a MAN having arguably the MANLIEST part of another MAN inside him? Unless you're comparing gay sex to straight sex (which it isn't) so being the receptive partner makes you more like a woman (which he isn't), surely bottoming just makes someone MORE masculine...?

does.[6] (And last time I checked, we don't tell people to abstain from getting into a car or shame anyone who ends up in a traffic accident for being a dirty steering-wheel slut.)

Yes, having a healthy relationship with sex means being prepared to draw boundaries — including with yourself — around what's a clear no for you. But your body is your body, and you get the incredible power and responsibility of deciding what to do with it, and what serves you sexually.

3. Sex can be lots of different things

Maybe the best thing about sex is that sex is not just one thing. It's not just eggplant emoji plus peach emoji aaaaand done. It can be sexting, it can be oral sex, it can be frotting, it can be fingering, it can be playing with sex toys, it can be getting dressed up, it can be masturbating furiously to NPR podcasts on a Sunday afternoon. It's natural and very human to want to try different things, and you won't always know what you're into until you try it.

Queer men put a lot of effort into labeling our sexual tastes and preferences. And there's value in recognizing what, with experience, you know you do and don't like. There's value in having words to figure out the basics of sexual compatibility. But the best sex isn't just about labels. It's about flow. It's about going where your curiosity and the connection with your partner(s) leads. In the right circumstances, you might even enjoy something you weren't sure you were into.

Sure, there are situations where trying something new might put you at risk of lasting emotional or physical harm. And that's different. Boundaries are necessary in sex to keep us safe.

But if the worst that can happen if you try something is that you realize it's not for you, then there's probably not a lot to lose. Most people wouldn't feel ashamed if they woke up one morning and

---

[6] For more on all these facts — yep, they're all true — see Terri Conley, "We need to rethink casual sex," *TED* ♦ (undated).

wanted to try tennis or a new restaurant for the first time. And that's a great attitude to have about sex too.

4. Sex isn't just about physical desires — it's about emotional desires too

Contrary to popular belief — at least, one belief many queer men hold — completely emotionless sex doesn't really exist. Even the most transactional sex is driven by feelings like desire and curiosity. But whether the sex is mostly about a physical connection or an emotional connection, most sex involves some of both.

One fun thing about being human and having needs is that our needs are varied and sometimes contradict each other. Yes, part of your brain just wants to eat and fuck everything it can. At the same time, part of your brain realizes that doing that all the time probably isn't a great idea. And while both of these signals might be valid in their own way, it's our job to find healthy ways of balancing them.

And with sex specifically, navigating these potentially conflicting signals often means balancing what you want physically from sex with what you want or need emotionally. For example, if you're driven more by the physical side of sex, you're more likely to enjoy fucking someone without needing to connect with them emotionally. Equally, you might need to feel an emotional connection with someone to be interested in them sexually — or just to feel safe having sex with them.

We're all wired differently, and what we want and need sexually can change, even day to day. But understanding your sexual needs isn't just about figuring out what you like to stick where. It's also about realizing what turns you on emotionally. It's about pursuing sex that honors your emotional needs, not just your physical ones.

5. Good sex needs good communication

It's dreamy to think that someday you'll just wind up naked with someone's son and you won't have to speak because you'll know exactly what he's thinking from the smokin'-hot look in his eyes.

But in real life, no one is a sexy mind reader. No one knows for sure what you're thinking unless you tell them, and you can't be sure what someone else is thinking unless they tell you. Unfortunately, sexual shame often stops us verbalizing what we want and how we feel because it can feel wrong to just come out and say it. But if that stops us having the sex we'd enjoy most, that's no fun.

Yes, there is room for nonverbal communication. Yes, grunts and moans and sultry glances all play their role in a good dicking down. But so does looking him in the eye and saying, "Wanna **** my ****?" or "Can I **** your *******?" or "I'd love it if you ******* my *** with that copy of *People* magazine." When someone knows and isn't ashamed about what turns them on, it's really hot. And often, if you don't ask, you don't get.

6. *Your relationship with sex will change over time*

How you feel about sex, what you want from sex, what kind of sex you're interested in — and with whom — can change over time.

It's normal to be in more of a hoe phase sometimes. It's normal to be in a "no sex, just focusing on me" phase sometimes. It's normal to want sex without strings sometimes. It's normal to crave sex with strings sometimes. And sometimes, there are plenty of reasons why your body will dictate what you can or want to do sexually.

Sexual liberation or enlightenment does not mean meditating under a tree for fifty days until you realize "Oh, sex is *this*" and calling it done. Having a deeper and more authentic relationship with sex means understanding that what drives you sexually and emotionally will change over time. And being open to those changes will help you recognize and pursue what you need as it shifts.

7. *Above all, go with what feels like freedom*

In our weirdly puritanical society, it *is* hard to have a healthy relationship with sex, whatever your sexual identity. It is hard not to internalize the harmful message that sex is shameful or wrong or dirty. Then add to that the ways queer men are stigmatized for who and how we fuck, and things get even more complicated.

Sexual shame is a complex topic, and as I've said, it can manifest as different emotional blocks that seem to contradict each other. It can stop you having the sex you want because it feels wrong. It can also push you into sex you don't really want but you have because it validates your queerness or softens the shame you feel about being attracted to other men.

It can be hard to tell whether you're being motivated by sexual freedom or sexual shame since the things they motivate you into doing can look very similar. You might know you enjoy kissing as many people in the club as you can, and you might know you like being fucked by seventeen different guys in the space of one weekend. But it can be harder to know whether you're enjoying it out of sexual liberation, or out of thinking "The more people that want me, the more valid and loved I feel."

The key is finding your answer to the question "Does it feel like freedom?" Is the sex more about fun and exploration, or about having to be or do something to feel worthy?

Because, like any kind of authenticity, sexual authenticity should feel freeing. If sex honors you, it will feel like a true, free expression of what you want and who you are.

Yes, you are valid as a queer person if you've never had sex. You are valid as a queer person if you don't want or don't like sex. Still, for many queer people, finding self-expression and connection through sex is an important part of how we explore and validate our queerness. And if the sex you're having does either of those things, then it's probably sex worth having.

Again, sexual freedom isn't just about celebrating the word "slut" or having as much sex as possible. It's about something broader but somehow simpler: it's being able to have the sex we want, with the other consenting adults we want, without feeling fear, shame or embarrassment.

And in a culture that can have very specific views on what sex should and shouldn't look like, doing that can feel like a revolutionary act. It *is* revolutionary to accept that sex can be many different things, for love or just for fun, and nobody has the right to weigh in on or feel threatened by what two (and sometimes more) consenting adults do with their bodies in private spaces.

Sex is great. Fucking great. Literally.

But sex is especially great when it honors who you are and what you need. Above all, sex is great when it makes you feel free.

...And Consent Is Sexy

Sure, sex should feel like freedom. But sex should feel like freedom for everyone involved. And a big part of making that happen comes down to the tricky art of navigating personal boundaries.

In general, personal boundaries are based on the idea that we all have the right to decide what we allow into our personal lives. If you're my friend and you have a habit of blowing secondhand smoke in my face, I'm entitled to say, "Bitch, please don't." If we're in a relationship and I want some alone time this weekend, I'm entitled to have it without feeling guilty or like we need to be together every fucking second of every day.

Because I am not you and you are not me, what is right for you is not necessarily right for me. So I'm entitled to choose what I am — and am not — willing to allow into my personal life. And vice versa.

Consent — sometimes called sexual or bodily consent — is about the boundaries that relate to our bodies. So naturally, I get to decide what I do with my body because it's my body, while you get to decide what you do with your body because it's yours.

And should we decide to do something with our bodies, say, together, that's also great as long as we're both up for that specific thing. Otherwise, it's not very ethical — or sexy — if we go ahead.

Two of the most extreme violations of bodily consent are rape and sexual assault, where someone has sexual activity forced on them against their will. And needless to say, both tend to cause lasting psychological (and sometimes physical) harm.

But consent issues can also arise in much subtler ways. There are situations where someone thinks they have consent for something but they don't, or where someone feels pressured into doing something they don't really want to do, or where someone is too drunk or high to be able to give clear consent in the first place. And these situations are obviously also harmful in their own ways.

Unfortunately, a lot of queer men see these kinds of boundary violations as OK, and normal even. But they really aren't.

No, it's not cool to grab some guy's butt in the club unless you're sure he's open to that. No, somebody agreeing to hook up with you in an app conversation doesn't mean they're obligated to it if they get to your place and aren't feeling it. No, just because some queer men are pretty open-minded about who they have sex with, it doesn't mean every queer man is automatically up for everything with everyone.

And sure, I know. Consent might not seem like the funnest thing to talk about when you're getting a lil' amorous with someone you like. But the problem is, not talking about consent is often even less fun.

It's not fun if something happens to you you're really not cool with. It's not fun feeling guilty because you did something to someone that he really wasn't cool with.

But most of all, navigating consent isn't about stopping anyone having fun. In fact, it's a big part of making sure that the sex is fun for everyone involved. That's why consent is sexy. And it's why we should talk about it more, not less.

With that in mind, let's look at some ways you can give and receive consent when you're thinking about getting it on with someone cute.

How to get clear consent

Consent is often framed as "What does each person agree to?" But as long as the sex involves more than one person, consent is really more about "What do we want to do together?"

Because yes, consent is just another dimension of "fuck yes or no" in relationships. It's not hot if you're into it but I'm not. And it's not hot if I'm into it but you're not. Unless it's something everyone is into doing or trying together, it's exploitative on some level. And that doesn't sound that sexy.

That also means consent isn't just about saying, "Sure, let's do whatever" or "No, no sex today please!" Consent can mean saying yes to some things but not to others, and it can mean saying yes to something at one point before deciding you've had enough and changing the yes to a no.[1]

Because consent is specific and can change, it's another reason clear communication is so important in sex. And with consent, there are two main types of communication.

One is **verbal consent** — like answering "yes" or "no" to "Can I kiss you?" or "Can I suck your dick?" or "Do you want to fuck?"

The other is **nonverbal consent** — actions like nodding your head, taking your shirt off, making noises to show you're enjoying something, or directing his hand to a specific part of your body.

The big advantage of verbal consent is that it's really clear. If you ask someone if you can kiss them and they say, "Um, nope," it's hard to misinterpret that. But one disadvantage of verbal consent is if you have to stop every ten seconds to ask "Can I lick your titties like this?" then "How about this!?" then "And this!?" that might kill the vibe a little.

The big advantage of nonverbal consent is that it often feels sexier and more intimate if you can communicate some things through body language or encouraging sounds alone. There's a specific kind of intimacy that comes from not needing constant yes or no answers to sense how the person whose company you're enjoying is feeling. But

---

[1] And if you were wondering, that's why people who say, "So what, I should just get every partner to sign a consent waiver before we fuck!?" are missing the point. That's because a) that'd be a really fucking weird thing to do, and b) if consent can be withdrawn at any time, it would be meaningless anyway.

the obvious disadvantage of nonverbal consent is that it's nearly always open to interpretation.

Someone might have winked at you because they think you're sexy. Or they might just have something in their eye. Someone might seem really into it while you make out, but that doesn't give you clear confirmation that they want you to touch their dick.

That means, in practice, consent is usually given through a mix of verbal and nonverbal signals. It means you should keep a lookout for nonverbal cues, but if you have any doubts, you can communicate verbally to be sure.

Verbal consent is often seriously underrated. The first time a guy straight up asked me, "Can I kiss you?" his directness knocked me off guard a bit, but the trust and respect it created felt great. But equally, if you've been out to dinner with someone, he was happy to come back to your apartment and you've been cuddling on the couch, and as you turn to face each other he maintains direct eye contact with you, then as you gently lean in to kiss him he leans in as well, it's likely he's happy to kiss you too. (Though if he pulls away or says no at any point, then you'll know he's not.)

So in practice, consent is partly about judging the vibe someone is giving you, then if you're not sure — or if that vibe doesn't feel clearly enthusiastic — asking them about it.

People sometimes get a bit tongue-tied starting conversations about consent, but it doesn't have to be complicated:

- "Do you want to ... ?"
- "Can I ... ?"
- "Would you like it if ... ?"
- "What would you like to do?"

You can use whatever words or phrases express what you want to ask. The goal is just to find out whether something is a "fuck yes" for someone, and if it's not, then you know it's a "no."

That said, like with most things in relationships, there are some important subtleties to bear in mind here.

Can they even give clear consent?

You can't really take someone's consent at face value if they're not in a good position to give it.

For starters, if someone is below the age of consent — the age we collectively decide they have the maturity to make decisions about what they do with their body — then no, they can't. If someone isn't legally old enough to give consent, a "yes" from them can't be a "fuck yes," and you should act accordingly.

Similarly, if someone is blind drunk, half-asleep, clearly under the influence of drugs or especially emotional after a breakup, you can't really take their "yes" as a "fuck yes" either. It can't be a "fuck yes" if they aren't in a good enough state of mind to decide that, so it has to be a "no."

These situations can be hard to judge. There's no one one-size-fits-all solution for navigating every scenario. But applying the "fuck yes or no" principle to consent means that enthusiastic consent — a clear, freely given and enthusiastic "fuck yes" — is really the only kind you can interpret as a green light. So if there's any doubt that it even *can* be a "fuck yes," that gives you your answer: "no."

When you're reading nonverbal cues, context matters

It's much easier to read nonverbal cues with a regular partner than someone you're having sex with for the first time. Similarly, if you're relatively inexperienced with sex, you probably won't be as good at reading other people's body language as you'll be with more experience.

If your partner is relatively inexperienced — if he's a lot younger than you or doesn't seem that confident about sex, or if there's some kind of power dynamic in play — it's a good idea to rely on clear verbal cues more than you might otherwise to be sure he's comfortable.

The environment you're in also matters. Of course you'll think about consent differently sitting opposite a cute guy on the bus versus meeting someone at a sex party. But just because someone is present at an orgy, or someone turned up to a gay club in a tank top that says "Kiss me, sluts!" that doesn't give you an automatic license to do whatever you want with them. (Despite all the unwanted touching and kissing that goes on in a lot of queer spaces.) In short, judging nonverbal consent is about more than just body language. It's also about the context, the whole situation you're in. And like always, the same principle applies: if you're not sure you have enthusiastic and freely given consent, then ask. Just ask.

Again, consent is not just a one-time thing

Sex is not just a carousel that goes from cuddling to kissing to heavy petting to oral to buttfucking in that exact order, but whatever you end up doing together, you want to be sure there's mutual consent at every stage. Again, someone being happy to kiss you does not give you an automatic invitation to do whatever you want to their butthole.[2]

Plus, communication doesn't end once you've both taken off your last item of clothing. "Do you like that?" or "Is that sexy?" or just "How is that?" are great questions to find out if he's still having a good time. And if he starts giving you ambiguous cues or his body language changes mid-fuck, asking something like "You don't want to?" or "You're not feeling it?" is a great way to find out for sure.

Yes, some people like being more submissive or passive in sex, and if he's been clear he specifically wants you to be more dominant, that's great. But there's a lot of value in checking in with each other while you're partaking in a bit of adult naptime together to make sure you're still enjoying it.

Ultimately, making sure there's mutual consent is largely about creating trust and intimacy. Yes, it might be sexy when a cute boy has

---

[2] Actually, in case it needs saying: penetrative (anal) sex is something most queer men will *always* ask for verbal consent for. ("Can I fuck you?" or "Do you wanna fuck me?") Not every queer man is into anal sex, and even if he is, you probably don't need a reminder that nobody is up for it all the time — for all kinds of emotional and bodily reasons.

his dick in your mouth. But it's even sexier when you know that cute boy cares that you're enjoying yourself, that he respects your bodily autonomy, and that he doesn't want you feeling taken advantage of. And it's sexy to know that if you said you wanted to stop anytime, he'd respect that.

That's why checking in is important. Yes, too much verbal consent can be a bit of a mood killer. But not enough verbal consent — and all the ambiguity it leaves you with — can ruin the mood even faster.

Because that's the thing — consent isn't just about making sure no one's body feels invaded or trespassed upon. Consent is about making sure that sex is enjoyable for everyone involved. Consent is about making someone feel safe enough with you that they can have fun.

Consent is about building intimacy, trust and respect. And there's nothing sexier than that.

How to give clear consent

In a perfect world, we'd live among sprites and unicorns, and nobody would try to do anything with our bodies unless they were sure we were into it.

But — as you might have noticed — we don't live in that world.

That means it's important to be able to give clear signals about what you do and don't consent to, whether you're specifically invited to or not.

Because, whatever situation you end up in, that doesn't change the fact that you are the only person who gets to decide what you do with your body. And I hope you don't need me, Beyoncé or the gayest subsections of the Geneva Conventions to tell you that.

Beyond that, there are two important parts to expressing consent: deciding what you do and don't want to do, and then communicating that to other people.

Sometimes, it's the deciding part that's hardest. As we've seen, sex can get complicated, and often you might recognize that part of you wants to say yes to it but part of you doesn't. There are also situations where queer men aren't directly pressured into sex, but end up doing something they're not fully into either because they think it's just "what queer people do," or they're afraid of being rejected by someone if they say no.[3] That can be especially true with younger or less experienced queer men, who sometimes don't realize they can say no, whatever age or power dynamic is in play.

Ultimately, only you can decide what is right for you, but as usual, "fuck yes or no" will probably give you the answer. (And for the record, "Part of me wants to, but actually let's not," and "I'm not sure, so let's not rush into anything," are both legitimate types of answer.)

From there, it's about being able to express what you authentically do and don't want to do with someone. In theory, this shouldn't be that complicated, though in practice it can be.

Because queer people are prone to rejection sensitivity, it can make it harder for us to be assertive if it might lead to conflict or a relationship breaking down. But if saying no creates conflict or ends a relationship, you're probably better off without that relationship.

Expressing you don't consent to something is as simple as saying "no," "I don't want to" or "We should stop." If you do want to say no, it's usually expressed most clearly and directly verbally, but if you want to respond nonverbally, you could gently push someone away or withdraw.

Of course, you might want to consent to something, in which case "Yes," "I'd love that" or "Fuck me, daddy!" work great. For nonverbal consent, nodding your head or even just letting someone carry on while you maintain eye contact work great too.

---

[3] PrEP (the medication that stops HIV-negative people getting the virus) has changed the equation on the spread of HIV. But before PrEP was widely available, a fear of rejection was one reason queer men would consent to risky, condomless sex they weren't necessarily comfortable with. See Katie Wang and John E. Pachankis, "Gay-Related Rejection Sensitivity as a Risk Factor for Condomless Sex," *AIDS and Behavior* 20/4 ◆ (April 2016), 763–67.

Since enthusiastic consent — "fuck yes," not just "yes" — really is the only kind of consent, it's also worth making sure you're giving off either a clear "fuck yes" or a clear "no," and not something in between. So a clear "Not tonight," "What if we did this instead?" or just "I like you, but I'm not ready for this yet" will work great.

In an ideal world, your partner would hear an unenthusiastic "yes" and take it as a "no." But you also protect yourself and help your partner understand how you feel if you hear your own unenthusiastic "yes" and turn it into a clear "no" or "not right now."

Similarly, it's worth being mindful of the nonverbal cues you might be giving someone. No, wearing a revealing outfit doesn't give anyone the right to do what they want with you. But equally, if you're giving off plenty of nonverbal signals that might suggest you're interested in someone even though you definitely aren't, that's not really helpful for anyone.

If he cooks you dinner but you're not really feeling a romantic or sexual connection, that's fine. But he might misread your intentions if you take off your shirt and offer him a back rub on the couch afterwards. (As great as free back rubs can be.)

They key to managing consent is really just good communication. It's about expressing how you feel and what you want, and inviting other people to do the same. And if you've done that, that's basically all you can control.

Of course, you can't guarantee someone else will take what you want or how you feel seriously. Some people have a pretty low bar when it comes to implied or explicit consent. They might not really ask you for it, they might try to change your mind after you've said no, or they might essentially carry on trying to get what they want even though you've clearly said no.

Because consent is dynamic, your "no" can become a "fuck yes" after a conversation if you want it to. But like with any personal boundary, with some people you'll have to be firm about enforcing what you do and don't consent to. Sometimes it's necessary to repeat a "no," or say something like "I mean it, not tonight" or "Baby, I said no."

That said, if someone needs telling over and over before they respect or even acknowledge how you feel, that's not great. It doesn't exactly scream "It would be great if I let this person do very intimate things with my body!"

In other words, if someone repeatedly won't or can't respect your consent boundaries, often the best response is to withdraw from that relationship altogether. You can just stop having sex with them. You can stop putting yourself in situations where they can stomp all over your boundaries, and try to get your sexual needs met elsewhere.

Sex is intimate. Sex requires trust. And one important way you can honor your emotional and sexual needs is to be prepared to withdraw if someone proves they won't or can't respect you and your body.

Expressing a consent boundary can feel intimidating or scary because, ultimately, it's a form of vulnerability. It can feel vulnerable to talk to someone else about what does and doesn't turn you on, and if communicating a boundary might end or alter a relationship, it's normal to feel nervous about it.

But like with any kind of vulnerability, that's exactly why you should do it. It helps you identify disrespectful partners who have boundary issues. It helps you identify who probably cares more about what they can get from you, sexually or otherwise, than about you as a person.

Sex is supposed to be fun, and if you're lucky enough to have some mindfuckingly amazing sex once in a while, that's great. But most of us also have a need to feel seen and respected. And being prepared to express strong consent boundaries doesn't just mean you're more likely to have sex that you enjoy, it means you're more likely to have sex that leaves you feeling respected and emotionally fulfilled as well.

DTF? Or DTL?

The thing that's really wild about the prejudice and stigma queer men face is that it's weirdly specific. Often, it all comes down to sex.

It's not really that queer couples hold hands. It's not really how queer people dress. It's not even really that queer men sometimes live together.

It's that hand-holding might be a sign we're fucking each other. It's that we might be dressing to look attractive to each other. It's that we might be — *astonishingly* — fucking each other in our own homes.

What we do for work, how we spend our free time or who we're friends with isn't important. Historically, most homophobia stems from who we fuck, and how it makes us "unnatural" or "deviant."

And this isn't just about baselessly calling drag queens "groomers" or child abusers. (Though it is also about that.) The specific cause behind a lot of the stigma we face affects all of us. And it can affect, among other things, how we think about sex and love.

We're more than just who we fuck

Why is it that there can be lots of interesting and important things about our lives, and yet the one thing that defines us to some people is who we have sex with?

Why do some straight people feel entitled to ask, "So who is the woman in the relationship?" — usually meaning the sexual part of the relationship — when a couple is made up of two men?

And while we're at it, why does a straight man sucking one dick make him gay, but a gay man experimenting with a woman doesn't make him straight?

These are the subtle biases that often come with homophobia that have real-world consequences for us. They stop lots of us having a healthier relationship with sex. They make some of us shy away from our sexuality because we — rightly — don't want to be defined solely by it.

But worse, it can make us internalize other people's discomfort about who we fuck to the point that we don't realize we can love other men. We're so busy wrestling with that sexual stigma that we forget a lot of us are hardwired for love and emotional intimacy first, and sex and physical intimacy second.[1]

In other words, as much as it's possible to enjoy sex just as "fun," a lot of us find sex that's part of a loving relationship fulfilling on a deeper level. A lot of us crave emotional connection — or even just physical touch — as much as we crave sexual connection. (If you've ever thought "I think I prefer cuddling to sex," that might be why.)

But because of the stigma about who and how we fuck, a lot of us either feel pushed into having lots of no-strings sex to assert our freedom and liberation, or we just plain don't realize that we *can* love.

What's more, when so many of us are pushed into thinking that way, it creates a network effect. Because when it seems like sex is easy to access but lasting relationships aren't — like it does for many queer men — it's understandable that some of us conclude that longer-term same-sex relationships aren't realistic or even possible.[2]

---

[1] For more on the psychology of this important topic, see the chapter "Are Gay Men Homosexuals?" in Walt Odets, *Out of the Shadows: The Psychology of Gay Men's Lives* (Penguin, 2019), 19–59.

[2] Yes, it's often the same homophobic people who hate us because of who we fuck who also condemn us for being "promiscuous" and "sex-obsessed" — even though that discrimination is a major factor in what pushes us toward casual, no-strings sex in the first place. Make it make sense.

That's not helped by the fact that long-term queer relationships still aren't that visible. We don't see nearly as many queer people in happy and thriving long-term relationships as we do straight people, though those relationships definitely exist. So it's easy to think that queer men are good at connecting only physically, not emotionally.

As you know, you get to decide what sex means to you. You get to decide what you do with your body, and who you do it with. But given that our culture is often so focused on sex, it's worth asking yourself: do you even see love as an option?

DTF? Or something more?

Sex is great. Sex is fun. Sex is freedom.

But so is love.

And sex with someone you love is, honestly, top-tier.

So when it comes to figuring out the relationship you want to have with sex, it's worth asking yourself: are you just down to fuck? Or are you open to something more?

Are you down to connect? Are you down to bond? Are you down to *love*? Are you down to *be loved*?

And if you decide you are, it's not about putting "DTL" or "DTBL" on a dating profile instead of "DTF." It means asking yourself whether the way you're acting is more "DTF" or more "DTL" and "DTBL."

Are you only working on making yourself sexually attractive to other men, or are you also working on being romantically attractive?

Are you only talking to potential partners about your sexual preferences, or are you having conversations about your emotional needs too?

As much as there's no rule that says "no sex on the first date," if your end goal is romance, it's worth thinking about whether you want to lead with sex or an emotional connection. Though a sex-only relationship definitely can grow into a romantic one, in practice, turning a hookup into a boyfriend can get complicated. A strong sexual connection can make it harder to judge — or even see — the potential in a romantic connection.

In fact, when one group of researchers studied 192 friends-with-benefits relationships, including plenty of queer ones, that was exactly what they found. Of the couples who wanted to go from being fuckbuddies to steady romantic partners, only 15% — less than one in six — managed to do it successfully.[3]

And so, as boring and heteronormative as it might sound, if you're looking for love, you'll probably have more success if you focus on getting to know someone and letting sex become part of the relationship organically. In the long term that tends to work out better than rushing to get naked with someone and then figuring everything out once the dust — and your dopamine level — settles.

Again, sex is great. We absolutely should chase it. We absolutely should want it. But for many of us, sex is not the only thing we want. And who we have sex with is always just one part of who we are.

Whatever anyone else might think of us, as queer men we don't have to be just homo-sexuals. We can be homo-romantic, homo-enamored and homo-loving too.[4]

And if we care about love and not just sex, we definitely should.

---

[3] Yes, I also love that people are actually paid to find these things out. See Laura V. Machia, Morgan L. Proulx, Michael Ioerger and Justin J. Lehmiller, "A longitudinal study of friends with benefits relationships," *Personal Relationships* 27/1 ◆ (March 2020), 47–60.

[4] See Walt Odets, *Out of the Shadows: The Psychology of Gay Men's Lives* (Penguin, 2019), 29–30.

PART III:
REALITIES

Abs

Statistically speaking, it'll have been roughly 4.6 days since the last Great Twitter Abs Debate of [Whatever Fucking Year It Is Already].

In it, people will have raised all kinds of important questions.

Is being pro-abs body-shaming people without them? Is being body-positive abs-shaming people who have them? Are all queer men with abs former bullied fat kids? Are all queer men without abs just jealous? Are abs something to lust over shamelessly in all of their loin-arousing glory, a drain on our community — or somehow both!?

Truthfully, the answer to most of these questions is "no, maybe, kind of."

The answer is that no, there's nothing fundamentally wrong with anyone's body — though as queer men, it's really fucking easy to feel like there is.

In fact, a 2017 study of more than 5,000 queer men found that 59% of them said they felt "unhappy" or "very unhappy" with their bodies.[1] In 2023, an even bigger study of 34,000 young queer people discovered that among the thirteen- to seventeen-year-olds they surveyed, a shocking 88% of them — yes, two eights — didn't like the bodies they were in.[2]

---

[1] Samuel McManus, "More than half of gay men say they are 'unhappy' with their body," *Attitude* ◆ (February 1, 2017).

[2] Joe Ali, "Nearly nine in 10 young LGBTQ+ people unhappy with their body, eye-opening study finds," *PinkNews* ◆ (January 31, 2023).

And then, the more dissatisfied queer people are with their bodies, the more likely they are to attempt suicide or self-harm — or just go to extreme lengths to alter the way they look.[3]

Clearly, we live in an era of feeling a lot of pressure about the way we look. Clearly, being happy in the body you're in is radical these days. While abs and buff bodies might have a hypnotic power over many queer men, our fascination with how we all look clearly has a dark side. And we should talk about that.

Before we do, though, let me just be clear about one thing: ***the last thing any of us should do is feel ashamed about who we're attracted to.***

The root cause of a lot of homophobia, as we've just talked about, is that some people think that anytime two people of the same gender find each other physically attractive — and could therefore have sex together — crops will fail, the sky will fall in, and society as we know it will collapse.[4]

As we've also talked about, physical attraction is hormonal, human, and totally normal. It's cute queer hormones flooding your cute queer brain when you're exposed to certain kinds of stimuli — someone's scent, someone's flirty messages, or yes, someone's bare torso. And evolutionarily speaking, I guess our species' survival has always depended on around half of us feeling a hormonal desire to be impregnated by tough, virile men from time to time. So if you also harbor a desire to be impregnated by a tough, virile man from time to time, that's great. I fully support you in that.

But seriously, because physical attraction is hormonal, it's not something we can control. That's true of all of our emotions. But like

---

[3] Ben Hunte, "The gay men risking their health for the perfect body," *BBC News* ◆ (January 29, 2020).

[4] Queer people — and same-sex animals, for that matter — have been fucking for millennia, Deborah, and the sky is still there. Maybe we could focus on making some actually meaningful improvements to society, not on getting heated about who is consensually fucking whom.

with all of our emotions, it's not always a great idea to act on them the moment we feel them in the first way that comes to mind.

So the crux here is that no, there is no shame in finding anyone — including anyone's body — attractive. You just want to make sure that acting on that attraction isn't having lots of unintended or undesirable consequences.

With that in mind — and with a little help from the Authenticity Fairy — let's try to unpack some of what's going on here.

For starters, a lot of us are too good at measuring our own and others' worth based on our bodies

Some of us say we're into fitness, but we're actually more into working out to look hot. Some of us rave about how authenticity and acceptance are important, but are suspiciously good at dating, befriending or insta-following people who all look a similar way.

And sure, there are tons of great reasons to have health and fitness goals. Looking after your body is definitely important.

Pursuing a fitness goal (or any goal, for that matter) because it's important and meaningful to you is great. Working out or playing a sport because you enjoy it, because it's good for your mental health, because it's good for your skin, because you like the community of people you meet while you do — and even because *you* like the effect it has on your body — are all great and authentic reasons to stay active. They're the sort of motivations that would make the Authenticity Fairy be proud to say, "You go, gurl! Live your best life!!"

But if you're chasing a fitness goal because you care more about the validation you get from having a hotter body, that's less ideal. That's because, as usual, the danger in relying on external validation is that you're putting your self-worth in other people's hands.

In fact, if you're mostly working out because you're terrified that if you don't, you'll get absolutely zero dick in Puerto Vallarta this summer, that can actually make you feel worse about your body. There's a chance it'll only reinforce any fears you have that you need to look hot to be lovable, and won't help you feel confident that you're worthy of love and respect however you look. And in that case, you can bet the Authenticity Fairy wouldn't be shy about saying, "Bish, you hate the gym, you don't even LIKE half the people who thirst over you for your body, and boo, I wish you cared less about other people's opinions of you. External validation is a trap, babe!!!"

Still, I get why many of us fall into that trap sometimes. When you're queer and you feel shame just for existing, being — or being around — someone physically attractive can feel soothing. It can make you feel a little more worthy of being here. And as a result, lots of queer men *are* very good at rewarding each other for being physically attractive. But inevitably, that comes with a catch.

It helps create a culture where we're disproportionately good at giving people attention, validation, and status based on how they look, not who they are. It helps create a culture where lots of us have very conditional relationships with our own and others' bodies. And in turn, that tends to complicate the way we love and build relationships. It creates barriers to more authentic and healthy connection.

There's this joke that a lot of queer men think that maybe all of their problems — including finding a partner they like — would be solved if only they got a little bit hotter. It doesn't work like that at all, obviously, but trying to look as hot as possible is definitely one way some of us try to compensate for the shame or inadequacy we feel. Understandably, it's one way some of us try to gain control of our situation.

And so, a lot of us focus on bulking up or working out more, hoping it'll help us find better relationships. Only, working out, on its own, never made anyone better at being in relationships. If anything, it just helps you attract hotter people to be bad at relationships with. Learning to be better at relationships is a whole separate thing.

But that's the outcome when your dating pool puts too much importance on physical attractiveness. It incentivizes us to focus on becoming fun to look at over becoming actually better partners.

And if we want to change that, no diet plan or workout routine can help — only a more balanced understanding of what it means to be an attractive man will.

Social media and dating apps aren't helping either

The reassuring news is it's not just being queer that makes many of us more superficial — the internet is playing its part too.

On the apps, we're faced with so many decisions about who to chat to — and looking for easy, efficient ways to decide — that we end up making those decisions super quickly, often in less than a second. And more often than not, a photo is what makes the fastest, strongest impression.

In fact, a Michigan State University study in 2021 found that physical attractiveness and race — *ouch* — were the main factors people used to decide who to talk to online. Other things like personality or even what kind of relationship someone wanted hardly factored into it at all.[5] So it's not surprising that spending time on the apps can make us feel extra pressure to look attractive: we sense that's what we're being disproportionately judged for there.

And on the smoke-and-mirrors machine that is social media, it's easy to get a wildly distorted view of what "normal" bodies look like. Most of us are good at only sharing our best sides online. We post the photos that make us look cutest or where the lighting showed off our bodies the best. And then the algorithms, being designed to keep us on the apps, are good at shoving the most popular profiles and content in our faces — which, for queer men, tends to include a lot of lean and muscular torsos.[6]

And so, even if we know logically that most queer men have more than 6% body fat, by exposing ourselves to idealized body types too

---

[5] "Online Dating: Super Effective, or Just... Superficial?," *Neuroscience News* ◆ (March 7, 2021).

[6] Erin Heger, "The sneaky ways social media can sabotage your body image — and 3 easy tips to help you break the cycle," *Insider* ◆ (May 19, 2022).

much we teach our brains to think that those bodies are the norm. A lot of us start out with the hunch that we need to look super hot to find a partner we like, so seeing the online attention ecosystem reward people for looking like that — and also being on a boat, for some reason — only tends to amplify that hunch.

That's not helped by the fact that, for every "embrace the journey, not the destination" post, social media is really good at focusing our attention on the results, not the process. It's not a place we have many conversations about how much our body types are influenced by things like age, genetics and lifestyle.[7] And since talking about steroid use online still seems taboo, that can create a false impression about the kinds of bodies that are achievable for most of us.[8]

The point is not that social media is bad, or that anyone sharing their bodies online is bad. The curse of the internet is that it distorts reality. Many queer men are already prone to body dysmorphia — an obsession with every potential flaw they see in their appearance, even if they already look great. And the real or perceived pressure to look good online can easily make that worse.

There's just way more to life — and happy relationships — than hot bodies

OK, sure — insanely hot bodies have their perks. They're fun to look at. They're fun to wake up next to. They're fun to have. (I'm told.) But again, you don't form a relationship — at least, not a healthy one — with a body. You form a relationship with a person.

---

[7] Yep, some people can just build muscle and lose body fat much more easily than others. See Ashwin Rodrigues, "Six-Pack Abs Are Mostly Genetic," *Elemental* ◆ (December 18, 2019).

[8] To be clear, I think it's everyone's personal choice whether they use steroids or not. But it's definitely harmful that we don't talk about it more. See Lindsay Dodgson and Rachel Hosie, "Steroids are rampant among fitness influencers, trainers and bodybuilders say. Most use in secret, claiming their gains come from workouts and diet plans," *Insider* ◆ (February 3, 2022).

And when you care about how a potential partner looks without thinking about much else, it's easy to end up in an emotionally unfulfilling relationship with someone who isn't right for you.

Put it this way: abs don't ask you how your day was. Huge muscles don't cook you dinner when you're sick. A low body fat percentage doesn't encourage you to book that trip or ask for that raise or follow your dreams — or make you feel safe and respected in a relationship.

And maybe worst of all, like we saw in the chapter on conditional relationships, if your relationship is really with someone's body and not with them, you're much more likely to look past the ways they might actually not be a great person to date.

If you're dating a guy you have hardly anything in common with, either of you having abs doesn't fix that. If you're dating a guy who's unreliable or insecure or outright mean to you, none of that changes because he has huge biceps. If you're dating a guy who's kind of racist, the racism doesn't suddenly disappear because he's hot and you like having sex with him.

It's not true that every man with abs is boring, superficial or mean. That's a stereotype that also belongs in the trash can. But when we value physical attractiveness above everything else to the point that it actively leads us into unfulfilling and even harmful relationships, then no, that's not great. There are probably lots of men you might find physically attractive but who wouldn't be a great fit for you in a relationship in other ways. And if you aren't good at recognizing that, it's easy to fall into relationships that aren't that fulfilling.

And sure, this is just another example of how chemistry and compatibility are important. But if chasing partners based on looks and not much else keeps tripping you up, all you have to do is expand your attractiveness criteria a bit.

When you find someone you think is hot, get used to thinking, "Great! But what else do I like about them?" Sure, acknowledge you like the way they look, but also ask yourself how much they might be a good fit for you in other ways. Because again, you're not just dating someone's body. You're also dating their personality, their values, and their emotional intelligence, among other things.

It's definitely OK — and very human — to care about the way a potential partner looks. But physical appearance is just one factor. If you're interested in a longer-term relationship with someone, the depth and success of that relationship will always depend more on things like emotional maturity, empathy and self-confidence than what anyone in the relationship happens to look like.

In any case, this isn't just about how we date. It's also about trying to create a culture where fewer and fewer of us are adding the way we look to the list of reasons we feel unworthy or inadequate.

It's about judging each other less for our bodies, and seeing our bodies more as the containers we're in — the vessel that contains the people we are, not the people we are.

It's about actively validating or complimenting other queer men not just for being handsome or hot, but also for being kind, friendly, dependable, honest, or for building a life that's meaningful to them.[9]

It's about being better at accepting the bodies we're in — *all* the different bodies we'll be in throughout our lives — as valid in their own ways. And it's about remembering that if someone is especially judgmental about other people's bodies, or just constantly talks about their own or others' bodies, that often stems from their own insecurities that they need to have a certain body type to be acceptable.

Body positivity is not about celebrating unhealthy living habits. But it is about finding a more balanced definition for what a healthy and attractive body can be.

---

[9] And if you do want to compliment a queer man for his athletic body, you could always compliment him for his persistence, his dedication or his commitment to his goals. (Not least because plenty of very athletic queer men feel hyper-conscious about their bodies too. Our never-buff-enough culture impacts us all, gurl.)

Because the funny thing is, once you actively look for beauty in more body types, you start to realize how arbitrary (and restrictive) our learned attraction to certain body types is. And in turn, you help free yourself from our often wildly unrealistic standards for what an attractive man is supposed to look like.

And online, as much as the social media companies are good at shoving certain types of content in our faces, "like" and "follow" buttons don't click themselves. Ultimately, we all vote for what makes a person deserving of attention and social status, online *and* off. We decide whether that's, say, being kind, living authentically or helping other people, or just having a lean, muscular torso.

And in case it needs saying, if your social media diet (more than your actual diet) is helping you internalize unrealistic body standards, then there's plenty you can do about that.

Unfollow any accounts that don't make you feel good about who you are. Get online fitness advice from people who say things that actually help you, not just from people you think are hot. Or focus on using social media more to keep in touch with people you have a healthy two-way relationship with, and less on thirst following people who will literally never know you exist.

Ultimately, we don't live in a bubble. Every time one of us decides that someone is valuable and worthy of attention because of their high muscle mass and low body fat percentage, we encourage other queer men to do the same. Every time we let the abs economy, or the youth economy, or the looks economy in general determine a queer man's inherent worth, we encourage other queer men to do the same.

But it works the other way too.

Whenever we choose more accepting and authentic attitudes about our own and others' bodies, we encourage other queer men to do the same. And whenever we decide that the body someone is in is just one tiny part of what can make them attractive, we encourage other queer men to do the same.

If we want to live in a more body-positive culture, we can. If we want to liberate ourselves from the tyranny of unrealistic body standards, the tyranny of buffness, we can.

Stability, Variety and Open Relationships

One fun thing about relationships is that there are lots of different types of them. One messy thing about relationships is that we're all driven by different needs, so figuring out which type is right for you can sometimes get complicated.

To explain what I mean by that, let me introduce you to two friends of mine, Rahul and Vincenzo.

Rahul and Vincenzo: A tale of two temperaments

First, meet Rahul.

If there's one thing to know about Rahul, it's that he loves a routine. He works 9 am to 5:30 pm at an advertising agency in his medium-sized town. He does CrossFit before work every Monday, Wednesday and Friday, basically without fail, trying to lift something a bit heavier than last time, or whatever the ultimate goal of CrossFit is.

Rahul spends his weekends either relaxing at home or out with his closest half a dozen friends. They'll usually go out for brunch or to someone's house to watch a movie. He and his friends try to take a vacation together every summer, usually to one of the same three resort destinations they know they'll enjoy.

Rahul knows some people think his life is kind of tame. But he's comfortable with that. He likes what he knows.

Now say hello to Vincenzo.

For Vincenzo, variety and novelty are his raisons d'être. (Like me, he likes using fancy foreign words to prove how cultured he is.)

Vincenzo is a freelance interior designer. He enjoys working with different clients on projects big and small. And he loves having the freedom to take on work when he wants it and turn it down when he wants to take a vacation or have some time off.

Vincenzo is always trying out new restaurants and loves getting to know new people at work, in bars, or at parties. Every few weeks he'll find himself in a surprisingly deep conversation with someone he just met on the subway. His schedule is a bit unpredictable, but he's happy to squeeze in a workout or yoga class when he can. He travels a lot for work and for fun, and always prefers an adventure somewhere new.

His work is stressful sometimes, and his friends tell him he might be happier with something more regular and stable. But Vincenzo isn't interested in routine. He wants newness and novelty.

For what it's worth, Rahul and Vincenzo are both single. I thought about setting them up one time, before realizing that would probably be a terrible idea. That's because, you won't be surprised to hear, what they want from a relationship is very different.

Rahul is looking for a life partner. He's been in a few long-term relationships, lasting from a couple of months (which counts as long-term in gay relationship time) to three years (which counts as forever in gay relationship time). Even though those relationships ran their course, he loved getting to know his exes well — who they are, what makes them tick, what they want from life. He goes on dates every now and then, but if he doesn't see a future with someone, he finds it really hard to invest in them emotionally.

Vincenzo goes on five or six dates a month. Most of them are first dates. And for now, Vincenzo is cool with that. It's not that he can't deal with commitment, he just likes getting to know new people at this point in his life. And since he's away a lot, he's not sure he could offer anyone a serious commitment anyway. He doesn't really like random hookups, but every few dates he'll end up spending the night at the guy's house, and for Vincenzo that's enough to keep him happy.

And OK, you got me: I made Rahul and Vincenzo up. Gay men are nowhere near as good at organizing an annual vacation as I implied, and in this economy, basically none of us are turning down good work.

But maybe you can see where I'm going with this.

In real life, we're sometimes a lot like Rahul: we appreciate the routine, the familiar, the things and people we know well. It's fun to wake up every morning and not have to start from scratch with a whole new schedule, new friends and a new job we're still figuring out how to do.

But sometimes, we're more like Vincenzo: we get bored of our routines. We need a healthy dose of variety, novelty — risk even — to feel alive. Comfort zones might be comfortable places, but the most interesting things rarely grow there. Sometimes we have to venture beyond what we know to find out what else is out there.

And that brings us to relationships.

Because sure, in real life there are people who are quite clearly Rahuls and quite clearly Vincenzos. But in real life, a lot of us aren't just Rahul or Vincenzo. We're a mix of both.

And these two poles, stability and variety, are in many ways the two poles that define how we approach relationships. They're two important factors that inform the kinds of relationships we're likely to be open to at different points in our lives.

If stability is most important in your life, you'll probably want to find one person to build a longer-term relationship with — to get to know, to grow with, to rely on.

If variety is most important in your life, you'll probably be happier dating around and even building relationships with multiple people at once. You're more likely to enjoy the freedom that comes with breadth rather than depth in relationships.

But if a lot of us are part Rahul and part Vincenzo, that means choosing one particular relationship style can feel limiting.

There are advantages to being happily monogamous. But there can be a cost too — a life wondering, even only slightly, how things might have turned out with someone else.

There are advantages to forming relationships with lots of different people, whether that's having multiple committed partners or lots of commitment-free ones. But there can be a cost too — a life where you're always splitting your time and energy between so many people you won't be able to connect as deeply with them as you would if you focused yourself entirely on one person.

So, naturally, most of us build relationships to try and get these different needs met.

That might mean having a monogamous partner for stability but a wide circle of friends for variety. It might mean having a small, close-knit circle of friends for stability and deciding not to settle into longer-term relationships for variety. Or it might mean entering into a nonmonogamous relationship to get your needs for stability and variety met that way.

There are a few different styles of nonmonogamous romantic relationships. Some are polyamorous relationships, where three or more people enter into a relationship as more-or-less equal partners, but especially common among queer men are open relationships.

Open relationships can work in different ways, too. Some are fully open, where two people decide to build a longer-term relationship together but also give each other the freedom to form shorter-term romantic or sexual relationships with other partners. Some are "monogamish," where two people form a mostly exclusive longer-term relationship, but occasionally seek out other partners, together or individually. Some relationships are open purely to manage a specific incompatibility or to help one partner get a specific need met — like if, for example, one partner mostly tops in sex but occasionally wants to bottom, and the other partner only wants to bottom.

All of these relationship styles are different ways people — and not just queer people — can find the balance of stability and variety that's right for them. And one of the best things about living in a world where heterosexual monogamy definitely isn't the only kind of relationship style anymore is that we have the freedom to build the kinds of relationships that are most likely to fulfill us: monogamous, mostly monogamous, polyamorous, or otherwise.

Some people have some strange thoughts about nonmonogamy, believing it's immoral or always just a sign of a fear of commitment. And if nonmonogamy is not for them, or you, or anyone else, that's great.

But there's no automatic reason that monogamy is always the "best" relationship style. Monogamy is only held up as the default because it's the type of relationship most of us see regularly.[1] There's nothing immoral about any personal relationship two or more adults willingly enter into. And plenty of open relationships involve just as much commitment as many closed ones do. (So you can stop projecting, Justin.)

Most people don't struggle with the idea that they could love two parents equally, or love multiple friends easily, or love multiple kids, nieces or nephews equally. It's also a bit insane to think that "true love" means never feeling even the slightest attraction to anyone else. We're not hormonally wired like that, at all.

So a lot of open relationships are built on the idea that committing to a longer-term relationship with one person, sometimes called a "nesting partner" or "primary partner," is not mutually exclusive with pursuing other partners to get other needs met. And some might be built on the idea that, um, some people think open relationships are just more fun and fulfilling.

Because if we're honest, a lot of supposedly closed relationships actually aren't that closed anyway: they're open relationships by stealth or deception. When people cheat — when they pursue another

---

[1] Sure, maybe monogamy was historically normalized so children could be raised by their biological mother and father. But plenty of kids are raised by single parents, stepparents, adoptive parents or their wider family — and they usually turn out just fine.

partner while in an exclusive relationship — it's basically because the thrill of the novelty they think they'll get from a fling with someone else outweighs the benefits they see in the stability and depth they get from having one longer-term partner.

Of course, people who are emotionally aware and comfortable with vulnerability don't cheat because they have the maturity to start a conversation about it before they do anything that could hurt their partner. They're mature enough to recognize that their needs aren't being met by the relationship and they'll work with their partner to find a solution, whether that's exploring ways to get those needs met within the closed relationship, opening it up, or (if necessary) ending it entirely.

Again, open relationships are not for everyone. As we'll talk about, they take work and negotiation. And that work usually isn't worth it unless it gets you the kind of relationship you want.

But people in happy and successful open relationships get, to them, the best of both worlds: the stability and intimacy of a longer-term relationship with someone, plus the freedom to find variety and novelty in other relationships with other partners. They satisfy their inner Rahul and inner Vincenzo — and don't see the two sides as mutually exclusive.[2]

That's why blanket statements like "Open relationships aren't real relationships" or "Opening up a relationship is just cheating with extra steps" just aren't fair. (Or accurate.) How long a relationship lasts and how exclusive it is are not the only measures of a successful relationship, Brenda. I'm just spitballing, but maybe how happy the relationship makes the people in it should be the most important factor.

---

[2] One great resource on everything from the intricacies of managing different relationship styles to arranging orgies with twenty of your closest friends is Janet W. Hardy and Dossie Easton's *The Ethical Slut: A Practical Guide to Polyamory, Open Relationships, and Other Freedoms in Sex and Love* (Ten Speed Press, 2017).

"Happily ever after" and monogamy "'til death do us part" are only two ways of thinking about relationships.[3] Whether they're right for you or not depends on how you're wired and what you want and need from your relationships. And one part of building more authentic relationships is understanding your needs and the relationship styles that work for you, then trying to build the kind of relationship you want with people who also want that type of relationship.

That said, there are great and not-so-great reasons to enter into an open relationship. So to help you decide whether nonmonogamy is right for you and your partner(s), we should talk about them.

Why, why not and how to be in an open relationship

One common assumption about open relationships is that they involve less commitment, which means they don't need as much emotional maturity as an off-the-shelf monogamous relationship might. But often, that's not how it works.

First, many open relationships *do* involve as much commitment as most monogamous relationships. Lots of open relationships are about committing to building a life with someone, and the fact that the relationship is not 100% exclusive changes literally nothing about that.

And second, designing your relationship style from the ground up usually involves *more* emotional maturity, not less. It demands more authenticity and better communication than adopting a prepackaged relationship style that comes with clearer expectations.

---

[3] Something like 40 to 50% of marriages in the US aren't "happily ever after" anyway, and that doesn't make all of those relationships a mistake or a waste of time. Plenty of people's lives feature several happy longer-term relationships instead of a single "life partner," and that can be great too. See Belinda Luscombe, "The Divorce Rate Is Dropping. That May Not Actually Be Good News," *Time* ◆ (November 26, 2018).

The exact relationship style has to be negotiated. Boundaries have to be agreed on. Expectations have to be set. As that song in *Team America* taught us, freedom isn't free.

And if you decide that freedom is worth fighting for, there are three fundamentals an open relationship typically needs in practice.

1. Everyone in the relationship should be happy with it being open

Yes, this might sound obvious. Yes, this is basically just "fuck yes or no" for relationship styles. But the main difference between ethical nonmonogamy (also called "ENM") and unethical nonmonogamy (also called "cheating") is mutual awareness and consent. And like with every kind of consent, opening up a relationship is only consensual when everyone involved freely agrees to it.

It's not even necessary for every partner to have the same needs — and because they're different people, they often won't. That means there are ethical open relationships where one partner pursues other relationships but others don't. And that can work, as long as everyone is comfortable with the arrangement. (Though sure, in many open relationships both or all partners do seek other connections.)

There is nothing intrinsically unethical about any relationship style. So the exact relationship style usually matters less than the fact that everyone agrees on what it is, and happily consents to it.

People don't get hurt in established relationships purely because they're open. People get hurt when their partner pursues outside relationships without their knowledge and/or consent. It really is that simple.

2. Everyone in the relationship should be able to communicate well and ready to negotiate a relationship style that works for everyone

Sure, all relationships depend on good communication. But in nonmonogamous relationships that's often especially true.

The beauty of open relationships is that your relationship ground rules can be literally anything. Maybe you play with other partners but only together. Maybe you play with other partners separately but never in your shared home and never with the same guy more than once. Maybe every other Thursday it's open season to lick, suck and fuck whoever you want, but only if it's also a full moon and Ariana Grande has at least one song in the iTunes Top 100.

But crucially, those ground rules only work if you all agree on them. And you can only agree on those ground rules if you can all talk about them without anyone feeling invalidated, insecure or jealous.

Truthfully, that's difficult for a lot of people. A lot of people don't like to talk — or even think — about their partner potentially getting busy with someone else. But being able to do that is essential if you want the open relationship to work.[4]

3. Everyone in the relationship needs to have a high level of trust in each other

Agreeing on ground rules or expectations is great, but it doesn't mean anything if one or more of you is just going to do whatever you want anyway. That's not the foundation of a healthy and mutually respectful relationship of any kind.

Again, it's not nonmonogamy that hurts people, it's breaches of trust and expectations. So an open relationship can't work if the people in it can't trust each other to follow through with what they've agreed to, or can't at least start a conversation about their needs or concerns before breaching that trust.[5]

---

[4] For a more detailed guide to negotiating rules and expectations in an open relationship, see Daniel Vaillancourt, "The Gay Male Couple's Guide to Nonmonogamy," *HuffPost* ◆ (January 20, 2012).

[5] Speaking of trust and openness, no, you don't have to share every detail of your primary relationship with other partners. For a connection that everyone understands is casual or no-strings, you might not even mention it. But if you're pursuing someone who might want a longer-term monogamous connection and you can't offer them that, it's good to be upfront about it.

Equally, if you've all agreed on some expectations but one partner feels they need to check what another partner is up to all the time, that's going to be a source of tension too. If someone agrees in theory to an open relationship but can't really trust that what was agreed to is going to be upheld, that doesn't sound like a "fuck yes" to opening up a relationship, so it should really be a "no."

Open relationships aren't always easy. For an open relationship to work, everyone in it needs to be secure enough in themselves and the relationship that they don't feel threatened by outside partners or the freedom in the relationship itself. Again, freedom isn't free. It takes extra work, communication, and trust to access the freedom that a nonmonogamous relationship can bring. And if you or any of your partners struggle to find the self-assurance to make nonmonogamy work, then an open relationship might just not be for you.

All that said, some open relationships aren't so successful. Some people enter into open relationships for not-so-great reasons, or without having the trust or communication skills needed to make nonmonogamy work.

Let's look at some of those common scenarios.

1. You want the freedom of an open relationship but aren't comfortable giving your partner(s) the same

Every person in a relationship is different and will have their own individual needs. So again, it's not impossible for a relationship to be open in theory for everyone in it, but open in practice for just some of the people in it. In that sense, it's OK for the partners not to be equal.

The kind of inequality that causes problems is when one partner tries to dictate what happens in the relationship without anyone else having their say, or expects different rules to apply to different people. Crazy as it may sound, there are people in this world who want the freedom of an open relationship for themselves, but really can't stand the idea of their partner getting railed by — or even getting a drink with — someone else.

As always with "fuck yes or no" in relationships, it has to be "fuck yes" from all sides, or it's a "no." It can't be a healthy relationship if one person's needs always take priority, or if anyone feels pressured into something they don't want or don't think is fair. Some people really do expect their romantic partners to slot perfectly into their life and give them what they want all the time, but that's not how relationships work. At all.

Yes, many people in open relationships feel jealous or possessive sometimes. That's normal and it's something you can work through, often just by talking about those feelings with your partner. But if one partner only really cares about molding the relationship to make it more self-serving than mutually serving, that's usually a sign that that person has some work to do to see relationships as less transactional.

2. You hope it'll be a quick fix for a relationship that's having problems

One good reason to be in an open relationship is that it's one way to manage any fundamental relationship incompatibilities. It *is* a lot to ask one person to fulfill every last one of your relationship needs — to give you companionship and belonging, while pushing all of your spiritual, sexual and intellectual buttons — at all times. Basically everyone relies on more than one friend to get their companionship needs met, so through that lens, nonmonogamy is just a way to get your sexual and romantic needs met by multiple people.

That said, while nonmonogamy might ease a few relationship incompatibilities it's not going to fix low compatibility altogether. Opening up a relationship is rarely a quick fix if the relationship is fundamentally not working for you or your partner.

If you find yourself in a relationship that's not working for you, a great first step is to talk about that with your partner. Try to explain what you need but you're not getting, and see if you can work together to find a mutually beneficial solution.

Maybe there is room for the relationship to be flexible to accommodate your needs better. Or maybe you can get what you need within the relationship once your partner understands better what you're missing out on. Or maybe by opening up about your unfulfilled needs, you'll learn that your partner(s) or your relationship can't adapt to fulfill those needs better, and it's best to end the relationship.

But whatever your situation, just opening up the relationship and hoping for the best usually isn't a good fix. Having a conversation about what's not working, then trying to find specific solutions to the problem is usually a much better bet.

3. You want an exclusive relationship in theory, but you don't believe queer men are capable of them

Yes, queer relationships can be especially challenging. Trying to find a stable and fulfilling queer relationship in the age of the internet can feel mindfuckingly exhausting. But challenging is not the same as impossible, and exhausting is not the same as "GIVE UP, GURL! Satisfying queer relationships DO NOT EXIST!!!"

As much as I hate to be the boring voice of reason — it's more fun to be an outrageous voice of reason, for starters — let's be clear on a few things:

Satisfying queer relationships do exist.

Satisfying open queer relationships do exist.

And yes, satisfying monogamous queer relationships do exist.

To put things into perspective, a 2020 survey of over five hundred gay men in San Francisco found that about 30% of them said they were in relationships that aren't fully monogamous.[6]

So if you're monogamously inclined — and even if you're not — there *are* plenty of other queer men who'll be interested in the same kind of relationship style as you. Even if it can feel like no one wants monogamy these days, that's definitely not true.

---

[6] That number might also be dropping: a similar study back in 2010 found that about 50% of the gay men surveyed were not fully monogamous in their relationships. See Matt Baume, "30% of Gay Men Are in Open Relationships, According to New Study," *them.* ♦ (January 15, 2021).

Like in any aspect of relationships, you get to decide what you do and don't want, what you could compromise on with the right person, and what's a definite deal-breaker to you. So be upfront about your expectations and be ready to say no to a relationship that doesn't work for you. With time and patience you'll find what you're looking for.

4. Truthfully, you and your partner(s) value stability over variety

We'll come back to this idea in different ways later, but the truth is, stability often *is* great.

A lot of us enter into relationships because we want to feel special to one person, or to have someone we can rely on whatever happens, or to feel like we're not sharing our emotional or sexual intimacy with anyone else.

And though open relationships can seem attractive in theory, in practice all of the extra communication and negotiation it takes to make one work — and manage the hurt feelings and possessiveness that can come up when an open relationship doesn't — are not for everyone.[7]

It's healthy to want both stability and variety in our lives. But there are lots of different places we can get both of them from. For some people, a stable life partner gives them the security they need to chase more adventurous or risky things in other areas. Or they're just happy finding variety in new friends, a new trip, a new hobby, or something else that doesn't involve fucking people who aren't their primary partner.

---

[7] That said, monogamy isn't necessarily one thing anymore either. So if you decide to be "exclusive" or "committed" or "boyfriends," it's worth making sure you have the same expectations about what that means. Can you keep the apps on your phones to chat and make friends? Would one of you commenting a fire emoji on another guy's photo — or even watching porn — create friction in the relationship? It's likely a simpler conversation than deciding on open relationship ground rules, but it's an important conversation all the same.

Ultimately, like so much in relationships, it's about authenticity. It's about figuring out what your needs are and what you want from your relationships. Then it's about finding partners who are most likely to be able to give you that, whatever that is for you.

One of the best things about being queer is that lots of us don't feel the weight of expectations about the arc our lives are "supposed" to take as many straight people do. Being queer, we already don't fit the mold of what a lot of people think a "regular" adult life is supposed to be, and that can make us feel a lot freer in how we build our lives and relationships.

We of all people can let our relationships and our lives grow more organically. We can build the relationships we actually want, not just the relationships we think we're supposed to have. We especially can build the relationships that authentically fulfill us, not just the kinds we see other people having, or the relationships we think anyone else expects us to have.

As for how you make that happen, there's not a lot you don't know already: you figure out your needs and you talk about them with your partner(s). You talk about what you do and don't want in your relationship. You explain which needs you have that aren't being met properly. And as long as it doesn't turn out you're fundamentally at odds in terms of compatibility, you try to work together to build a relationship that can meet everyone's needs as well as possible.

And if your partner tells you your relationship isn't fulfilling them the way they'd like it to, the best thing you can do is grant them the same privilege you'd want in return: you listen. You try to understand. You try to respond with curiosity, not blame or judgment. And if they propose a relationship style you're firmly against, that's OK. You're entitled to draw boundaries around the kinds of relationships you don't want — and if a partner suggests opening your relationship up, that's never a sign that you don't deserve the love and commitment you want.

Open relationships are not for everyone. Closed relationships are not for everyone. Some of us are more like Rahul, and some of us more like Vincenzo. But again, trying a different relationship style often isn't the fix people hope it will be anyway. Sometimes someone just wants to feel more heard or respected in the relationship. Sometimes they just need some more stability or variety in their life in general, and it could come from a few different sources.

But whatever your situation, the key is always communication. It's understanding your own needs and finding the vulnerability to communicate them to others. It's finding the courage and authenticity to work on building a relationship style that works for everyone in it.

"It's Just a Preference"

One of the best things about the internet is that it gives us so much *choice*. You want a takeaway? Uber Eats and DoorDash have hundreds of options. Want a fluffy poop-emoji cushion for your couch? Amazon has loads to choose from. Want to meet cute single guys near you? Oh, hello, dozens of apps and hundreds, maybe thousands, of guys' profiles right there in your pocket.

And with so much choice, it's inevitable that you start to value some choices over others. It's smart, even, to focus on the choices you know are likely to bring you the most happiness and fulfillment.

Most of us have tastes and preferences in dating too, and that's not necessarily a bad thing. There are certain things, logical or not, that attract us to some people over others. But the truth is, all preferences in dating were not created equally. Some dating "preferences" aren't really preferences at all.

And we need to talk about that.[1]

---

[1] This chapter owes everything to all the queer people of color who shared their experiences and hopes for how we can do better with me as I researched and wrote it, as well as to Writing Diversely LLC, who provided a sensitivity reader whose advice and perspective were invaluable. As a white person I obviously can't and won't speak directly for any person of color, but not discussing racism and prejudice in a book about queer dating felt like a massive dereliction of duty. So that's why we're here. Finally, if you're a person of color and the last thing you want is to listen to some white guy talking about all of this, you are obviously welcome to skip ahead.

Preference versus prejudice

A preference is liking one type of thing over another where most things of that type are similar. You can say you prefer oranges to bananas because you love the sweet, citrusy taste of an orange while the mushy-ass texture of a banana really isn't for you. And that makes sense because even without having tasted every orange and every banana that ever existed, you can be pretty confident that all oranges and all bananas are similar. It's a useful thing to think if, as far as fruit is concerned, you want to live your best life.

Prejudices, on the other hand, come from false equivalences. They come from connecting two things that aren't connected, especially in a way that's unfair or damaging to someone or some group of people. So deciding that you don't date Black people because your Black ex cheated on you and you've since concluded that every Black person will be unfaithful eventually is, well, a lot of things, including a wild prejudice. Or worse, deciding that you flat out "don't date dark-skinned guys" or "don't do Asians" because "they're just not attractive to me" is outrageously prejudiced. Ruling someone out based purely on who you assume they are because of their race or ethnicity is the literal definition of prejudice — *pre*-judging someone based on the racial or ethnic group they're part of.[2]

Because that's the problem with comparing groups of people like that in dating: the people in literally any racial, ethnic or national group are vastly different. Whatever group you pick there are men of every body type, every personality type, every level of extroversion,

---

[2] Later we'll get to some ways race and ethnicity can affect who we are, but culturally we make a *way* bigger deal out of race than science says we should. As little as 0.1% of our DNA determines our race or ethnicity — the other 99.9% all people share. In fact, an ethnically Asian person and an ethnically European person might have more genes in common than two ethnically European people. See Vivian Chou, "How Science and Genetics are Reshaping the Race Debate of the 21st Century," *harvard.edu* ◆ (April 17, 2017).

kindness and reliability. There are men in all kinds of careers and with every kind of relationship with their family and who have every imaginable hobby from quad biking to knitting to *Call of Duty* to racquetball to sex parties to stamp collecting. So concluding that all, say, darker-skinned men are just like each other creates a false equivalence, and therefore a prejudice.

But so what? Why can't people just date who they want to? Didn't I write a whole chapter about how rejection is essential in dating? And if some narrow-minded queer men are unnecessarily limiting their dating options, is that really a big deal?

Well sure, it is strategically dumb to reject a potential match for a questionable or unsound reason. Queer dating is already hard, so restricting your dating pool even further based on a false equivalence isn't exactly a boss move, Aaron.

And yes, rejection is important in dating. It is supposed to help you sort through all of your potential dating options so you can focus on the ones that seem most promising for you. But rejection only does its job when it's based on sound reasoning — when you're turning someone down based on a fundamental mismatch or incompatibility. Rejection based on prejudiced, messed-up reasoning definitely isn't healthy, productive rejection. Not even giving a potentially great connection a chance because of some pretty outrageous mental gymnastics — which is what false equivalence boils down to — is not smart or helpful.[3]

But obviously this isn't really about some queer men restricting their dating options unnecessarily. It's about how those prejudices hurt the people on the receiving end of them.

The reasons prejudice hurts are complex, but they essentially all come down to one thing: it hurts to be rejected when you don't deserve it. It hurts to be rejected for something about you that isn't a

---

[3] For more on this "fair chance" principle of dating, see Mohammad Harith Aslam Khawaja, "Are Racial Preferences in Dating Morally Defensible?," *Episteme* 30 ◆ (2019), 35–46.

legitimate reason to be rejected. And it *really* hurts if it happens in lots of different parts of your life and you're basically powerless to stop it.

That's because, again, prejudice is not healthy or reasonable rejection. It's injustice.

And actually, you know this. You know this already because as a queer person you're subjected to at least one kind of prejudice, whatever your race or ethnicity. You can't always be yourself in public for fear you'll face abuse. You might be subject to laws that treat you as less deserving of basic rights because of who you are.[4] You are rejected by the society you live in for something about you that isn't rejectable at all, a trait that's just one normal thing some people are on the spectrum of all normal things human beings can be.

When people talk about prejudice, they often focus on racial prejudice — racism — but prejudice can be based on almost anything. Whether it's someone's race, ethnicity, nationality, gender, sexuality, age, socioeconomic status, religion, body type, skin color, disability, you name it: if it's a thing someone can be, it's a thing some small-minded fuckwit can create a prejudice about.

And the problem of experiencing constant but even low-level prejudice is that it sensitizes you to it. You become acutely aware that it can turn up and ruin your whole day at a moment's notice. (That's basically where queer men's rejection sensitivity comes from.)

And so, even if you don't experience prejudice every second of every day, or even every day at all, growing up in a culture where you've learned to expect it can disproportionally affect you. You can spend a large proportion of your life feeling on guard. You can become sensitive to even *perceived* prejudice, anything that even slightly smells of discrimination or mistreatment.

---

4 Yes, a lot of countries have equal marriage laws now. And so they should. But people in same-sex relationships are still not treated the same as straight people in some legal matters even in some socially very advanced countries — as you might know if you've ever tried to adopt children or write a will.

Being subjected to prejudice hurts all the more when it doesn't feel like just a one-off or a chance encounter with a "bad egg." If there are enough bad eggs around the henhouse, every time one cracks its sorry ass open in front of you you're not just experiencing the smell of one bad egg. You're facing the psychological burden of all the bad eggs that have ever crossed your fucking nostrils.

And again, you know all of this because you experience it at least for being born queer. And for people who were born queer *and* a person of color, that means the ways they can experience prejudice are only multiplied.

And if you are thinking "But is racism really that bad still? Didn't, like, slavery end a long time ago...?" then, Brett, I have news for you: racism is still bad. Prejudice is still widespread around the world — including within the LGBTQ+ community.

Something like *half* of queer men of color say they've experienced discrimination from other queer men — though some reports say it could be as high as 80%.[5] Lots of the apps have taken steps to fight overt racism on their platforms, but you still occasionally see queer men include things like "No Asians, sorry" on their profiles.[6]

But racism can be much subtler than that too.

Plenty of us still act like whiteness is the epitome of male beauty, that paler skin is inherently more beautiful, or just the "norm" we should judge all other skin tones against. Equally, some of us continue to fetishize people of color — to show interest in queer people of color because of their "different," even "exotic" features or skin, not because of the people they are. And sure, you might think that sounds better than outright saying "no Asians," but it's still dehumanizing because

---

[5] One study by Stonewall found that 51% of queer people of color in the UK have experienced racism from other queer people. See Louis Staples, "Racism is widespread within the LGBT+ community, Stonewall research reveals," *indy100* ◆ (June 28, 2018).

[6] Owen Jones, "No Asians, no black people. Why do gay people tolerate blatant racism?," *The Guardian* ◆ (November 24, 2016).

it's a prejudice based on someone's race or ethnicity, not an attraction to that person as an individual.

And this is at the heart of why, when people try to justify their attitudes to race in dating, saying "But it's just a preference..." tends to miss the point entirely.

For starters, often it flat out isn't a preference at all. Excluding a whole racial or ethnic group as "not for me" — prejudging everyone in it based on that identity — is, again, the literal definition of prejudice. So you can call it "just a preference" or "the love you never received from your father" or "the unrepentant corpse of Ronald Reagan" all you want, but that won't make it any of those things.

But what causes a lot of the backlash when people wield the phrase "but it's just a preference" is that it's not really about anyone's genuine tastes in dating at all. It's about the overall culture of discrimination that still exists within the queer community — and how people who use that phrase are often blissfully unaware of (or just don't care about) the harm that even a soft or subtle prejudice can cause.

People who use that phrase might be defending their right to date — or fuck or marry or unceremoniously ghost — the people they want to. (Which, sure, is their right to defend.) But they're also acting like they have no idea how lots of queer people of color spend more time than they deserve wondering "Was I just rejected for who I actually am, or did he reject me because of who he thinks I am based purely on my race?"

In short, tackling prejudice is not about your right to date who you want. It's about *your responsibility to date who you want in a way that doesn't cause unjust and unnecessary harm to other queer people.*

It's not about saying, "If looking at a scrapbook of your exes' headshots would be like peering into a bag of mint imperials, then you, sir, are an irredeemable racist." It's about saying, "If you can't recognize how queer people of color face specific extra challenges in dating, not to mention life in general, then maybe you should, sis."

Because, honestly, it will never not be wild that most queer men can recognize the prejudice they face, but many can't see that other minority groups face their own shitty flavors of prejudice too. It will never not be wild that we are part of an excluded and stigmatized group, yet plenty of us can't recognize the ways we often exclude and stigmatize others within our group. Make *that* make sense.

If we want to move forward, it's not about telling ourselves we can and can't date certain types of people. We should date — and fuck and love — the people we're attracted to and the people we're compatible with. But we should also be mindful of our prejudices in dating. We should be frank with ourselves about the ways we might have internalized racial biases from the societies we grew up in. And we should commit to making sure our biases aren't causing us to rule out any potentially great relationships.

But even more importantly, we should commit to making sure our biases aren't causing us to make any queer environment a place where whole groups of queer people feel they fundamentally don't belong.

How we dismantle our biases in dating

Biases can show up in lots of different ways, and some cause more harm than others. Telling someone "You're really hot for an Asian guy" — implying Asians aren't usually attractive — is not the same as systematically refusing to date Black people or make Black friends.

That also means recognizing biases in dating isn't really about splitting everything into just a "preference" or a "prejudice." It's more about trying to recognize how much prejudices or assumptions might be influencing our choices and behaviors.

Unfortunately, like with anything when it comes to human feelings and motivations, this quickly gets complicated.

If I tell myself I'm just not attracted to someone, is it genuinely because of their features and personality or is it because of their race?

If I reject a person of color, can I ever be sure I'm doing it because I don't think we're compatible, or because at some level I've internalized that white people are more attractive?

If, over a year, I end up dating people from only one or two racial groups, is that subconscious discrimination in action? Do I have a subconscious bias toward what's familiar to me, or is it that most of the people in the social spaces I hang out in look like me? Did it just come down to chance? Or is it a combination of all of the above?

These can be difficult questions to answer, even for the most self-aware people. And that's a big reason talking about prejudice gets so fraught. It's not just that people lie — though we do — it's that many biases are subconscious, so we're not always aware of them.

What complicates things even further is that while race is a category that humans essentially made up, culture isn't. And some of the things that are connected to what we understand as race but are actually related to culture — like where and how you grow up, and the experiences you're exposed to because of that — do affect who you are.

To use a really simple example, if you grow up in a warmer climate, you're statistically more likely to grow up friendlier, more outgoing and more open to new experiences.[7] So if having an outgoing partner is important to you, statistically speaking you're more likely to click with someone from Brazil than Norway. And if you find yourself dating more people with certain backgrounds or ancestries, that's not automatically a prejudice.

Equally, because we live in a racially biased society, it's not accurate to say skin color has no impact on who we are culturally. It *does* affect how we experience the world and therefore how we think and behave. So if a person of color ends up experiencing prejudice from three white partners in a row and decides, for their sanity, it's

---

7 Yep, that's what some scientists discovered. See Angela Fritz, "Our personalities are shaped by the climate we grew up in, new study says," *The Washington Post* ♦ (November 27, 2017).

just easier to focus on dating other people of color, that's probably not a prejudice either.

In each of these cases, the key is to consider each person as an individual, and not automatically rule anyone out. Obviously there are shy Brazilians and outgoing Norwegians, and some white people are more sensitive about racism than others. And if you're making dating decisions based on who someone is — which isn't defined by their ethnicity or nationality but will probably be influenced by it — then that likely isn't a prejudice.

More generally, a lot of this is just about being aware of the ways our biases might be influencing our decision-making — in any areas of our lives. Because again, racism isn't just about splitting every thought or act into either "so, so racist" or "nah, you're good." Racist acts exist on an enormous spectrum from setting up a four-hundred-year slave trade to thinking "We're really still talking about racism? Surely everybody is equal by now!?"

And because we exist in a society where racial biases are widespread, most people still hold on to some unjust or harmful beliefs they once internalized — especially if you're white and don't experience racism firsthand.[8]

That means creating a fairer and more equitable society isn't just about being not racist. We make progress by actively being *anti*-racist. We make things better by actively taking a stance against racial biases in ourselves and others.

Inevitably, there are lots of ways to do that, but let's look at a few that apply specifically to queer dating and relationships.

Because prejudice and discrimination exist on a spectrum, I'm going to talk about three categories of behaviors that range from "um,

---

[8] Yes, white people, the people least likely to understand racism because they're not subjected to it, usually have the most work to do here. We have to fight our white fragility — the desire to put our comfort above the uneasy task of examining racism and how we're likely contributing to it — too.

definitely not" to "OK, maybe, in the right circumstances" to "model anti-racist behaviors people of color would really like you to do."

Let's start with some absolute red-flag behaviors. These are behaviors that are especially hurtful to people of color, and that are basically indefensible. You also don't really want to be dating, fucking or maintaining a friendship with anyone who insists it's their right to do them.[9] And if you ever feel tempted to do any of them, it's worth giving some serious thought to what's motivating you there.

BAD: Ruling out a relationship with someone purely because of their race

Not even giving someone a chance because of who you've decided they must be based on their race is textbook racism. There is literally no justification for writing or saying things like "no fats, no fems, no Asians,"[10] "I don't date Black people," or "whites only." And if you find yourself thinking them, you'll want to figure out why.

It's not wrong if someone's values or cultural background mean they're not a great fit for you, but it is obnoxious and wildly prejudicial not to give someone a chance solely because of their race or skin color.

ALSO BAD: Being particularly interested in someone purely because of their race

Sure, that might sound like a positive kind of bias — like working harder to give opportunities to people from underrepresented communities. But saying you like Black men for their big dicks is not like encouraging a coworker of color to go in for a promotion, Ryan.

For starters, a person's race doesn't guarantee they'll have any specific physical feature. But more importantly, this kind of bias is damaging because it's fetishizing — taking an interest in someone's

---

[9] You can't really be anti-racist if some of the people you're closest to keep acting out of prejudice and don't look like they'll stop anytime soon — just like your straight best friend isn't much of an ally if she's dating a homophobe.

[10] I also missed the memo about when a "fat" became a type of person. I can only assume this trend was started by an ignorant or a dumb.

physical features because they're "exotic," or just different to the arbitrary "norm" of whiteness.

That's hurtful because when someone senses the primary reason someone else is interested in them is their body, it's dehumanizing. And that's especially true for people who are used to being judged negatively as a person because of the body they're in.

ESPECIALLY BAD: Suddenly losing or gaining interest in someone when you find out more about their race

Many queer people of color experience this kind of live-action prejudice when someone's opinion of them drastically changes when they learn more about their ethnicity. For example, there are still queer men who'll find a guy attractive when they think he's Latino, but quickly lose interest when they discover he's actually Filipino. (I was shocked to learn how common this still is.)

The reason this is especially damaging is that if you're just not interested in someone, you might have many reasons for it. You could reject them (kindly) and that person won't necessarily feel judged for it. But if you lose interest in someone suddenly when you find out more about their race or ethnicity, how can that not be a prejudice? If your impression of someone changes purely because you found that out, even though that person hasn't changed at all, that is the literal definition of a prejudice or bias, and it's likely to be felt as such.

OBVIOUSLY BAD: Using language that's insensitive, stereotyped or flat-out racist

Language matters, and there's more to being anti-racist than just never using the N-word.[11] It also means it's an absolute hard no on phrases like "no chocolate, no curry, no rice" — somehow the only phrase that could be worse than "no Blacks, no Asians" — or any language that stereotypes people of a particular race or ethnicity.

---

[11] John McWhorter, "How the N-Word Became Unsayable," *The New York Times* ◆ (April 30, 2021).

At worst, it's outright offensive, and at best, it's subtly degrading. The literal only exception to this is when a marginalized community reclaims a word for its own use — which is why a queer man can caption a social media post "Brunch with my favorite faggots," but if a straight person uses that word it's likely to come across as a slur.[12]

Next, let's talk about some yellow-flag behaviors — behaviors that might not be flat-out racist, but could be perceived as racially insensitive. They might be OK in some circumstances, or with people who know you well enough to trust that your intentions are sound. But they're the sort of thing you'll at least want to approach carefully, especially if you're a white person speaking to a person of color.

BEST AVOIDED: Stating a positive racial preference on a profile or in a conversation

It's true that prejudices tend to exclude (like "no Asians"), while preferences are often more inclusive ("I love confident guys"). But when race is involved — like "Asians to the front of the line" or "dark-skinned guys are so sexy to me" — it can open a whole Pandora's box of racial insensitivity, even if it's intended as a compliment.

That's because phrases like these can come across as fetishization — that you're mostly interested in someone because of their race, not because of who they are. And the softer language doesn't undo that.

Again, when someone is regularly on the receiving end of prejudice they can become sensitized to it, so something that sounds like a prejudice can still cause harm, even if that's not your intention. Preferences are great when they're about values or personality — "I tend to click with guys who also love the outdoors" or "I prefer more introverted guys." But making a big statement about liking people because of their race or skin color, no matter how generous or open-minded you think it is, still has the potential to come across as hurtful.

---

[12] I'm talking about the word "faggot," obviously. Though for what it's worth, I'm also proud of the ownership queer men take of the word "brunch."

NOT GREAT: *Rejecting or taking an interest in someone because of a physical feature that could be connected with their race*

Looks often are one factor in why we find someone attractive. But you wouldn't tell a Jewish guy you're not interested in him because of his "Jew sideburns." Even without linking it to someone's ethnicity, it's mean to say something unnecessary that could make someone self-conscious about the way they look. Equally, even if you think you're being complimentary, telling someone you love their "cute Indian nose" or "beautiful Black skin" can easily come across, at worst, as fetishization and, at best, racially insensitive.

Yes, compliments are great. They're an important part of flirting. But because many people of color get used to being judged by their physical features, even a positive comment that connects the way someone looks with their race can land badly. Sure, someone who knows and trusts you might take something like that as a genuine compliment. But it's often better to leave race out of it anytime you pay someone a compliment, especially if you don't know them well.

NOT SMART: *Throwing an entire group of people under the bus based on a cultural assumption*

Again, it's true that culture is a thing. Where and how we grow up does affect who we are. But prejudice can seep into how we think about culture too.

For example, for all kinds of different cultural reasons, Spanish people might rightly have a reputation for being more spontaneous and less punctual on average than, say, Japanese people. But it's not great to reject someone because "Spanish guys are so fun, if they ever turn up!!" or "You're Japanese so you're probably kind of boring."

That's not exactly a huge prejudice. But aside from the fact you might be rejecting someone who fits hardly any of your assumptions about who they are, it is the kind of bias that can make you sound narrow-minded and a bit of a dick.

That brings us to the green-flag behaviors. These are things we can do to make the LGBTQ+ community more welcoming and inclusive, and make sure we're not rejecting anyone unjustly or unreasonably in dating and relationships.

IDEAL: Take an interest in people, not the categories they fall into

At the heart of undoing prejudice and bias is learning to make conclusions about individual people as individual people, not based on the groups they belong to. If you think someone's cute, maybe they're cute and it's basically nothing to do with their race or background. If someone's not a good fit for you, maybe they're just not a good fit for you and it's nothing to do with their race or background.

Yes, culture influences us. Yes, in a society where racial biases still exist, race isn't meaningless. But by committing to appreciate and understand people as individuals, we stand a much better chance of figuring out who they genuinely are, and not who our biases or assumptions might try to convince us they are.

HELPFUL: Question your own biases in dating

When you find yourself making assumptions about potential partners based on the groups they belong to, whether racial groups or not, it's worth trying to identify where your assumptions come from. Sometimes they're internalized from the society we exist in. Other times, like if you got stood up by two Indian guys two weeks in a row, connecting a behavior with a race might be a (kind of fucked-up) method of self-protection.

As humans, we're all prone to connect dots that aren't connected — we try to make sense of the world by connecting things within a larger trend or narrative — and that's what makes us susceptible to biases.[13] But biases thrive on ignorance and denial — they stop being unconscious biases once you're aware of them. So a key part of being anti-racist is staying open to the fact that any observations or assumptions we make about a group of people might be completely wrong.

ALSO HELPFUL: Get to know people who are different to you

If biases thrive on ignorance and denial, one reason a lot of (white) people don't understand how racism affects people in marginalized groups is that they don't have much direct contact with people in those groups. And because people of color are underrepresented in many environments, both workplaces and social spaces, it often takes a conscious effort to do something about that.

I'm lucky that I work remotely and can often do it from various parts of the world. Like every white person should, I'm still conscious of undoing my biases, but being able to travel to different places and make friends who aren't like me has given me a lot of opportunities to do that.

That said, doing the work is not just about making friends who don't look like you. "I sometimes hang out with Jaime and he's Black, so we're good, right!?" is not enough. You have to listen to people of color talk about their perspectives and experiences in order to understand them, and then reflect on how your actions or behaviors might be perpetuating racism toward anyone.

Still, while many queer people of color are happy to share their experiences with racism — and many have spoken or written about it publicly — it's not their responsibility to educate others about it. So it's good to be careful about bringing it up, and respect that if someone isn't interested in talking about racism with you, that is their choice.

---

[13] See Shahram Heshmat, "What Is Narrative Bias?," *Psychology Today* ◆ (December 12, 2016).

IMPORTANT: *Call out racism and discrimination when you see it*

Finally, the most important weapon we have to combat racism is making it wildly socially unacceptable anywhere. And that means challenging it when you see it, whether it's someone writing "only white guys" on their dating profile, or someone on a first date insisting that "No, ALL lives matter," or a white friend who happily says, "I just don't think I could date a Black guy" without shame. (Or, apparently, self-awareness.)

And importantly — and I'm gonna speak up a little for everyone in the back — it means challenging racism *whether it directly affects you or anyone you know, or not.*

A substantial amount of racism continues because the people who perpetuate it don't understand the damage it causes, and so a key part of being anti-racist means doing what you can to make them aware of it. That might be a quiet conversation, that might be a loud "hell no," it might mean breaking off a relationship with someone who refuses to reflect on or change their behavior.

This is difficult work. It's especially difficult if you're someone who experiences racism. But it's work we all have to do if we want to make our community — and our society in general — less racist.

All of that said, it's important to note that no part of anti-racism is about stopping you from getting what you want in dating, including pursuing the people you're interested in. It doesn't mean forcing yourself into relationships with people who are different to you to prove a point. It doesn't mean you're a terrible person if you mostly date white people. It just means you should go about getting what you want in a way that doesn't fuel — and ideally, helps to undo — the prejudices that still exist within the queer community.

You can pursue the people you're attracted to *and* work to dismantle your own racial biases.

You can have genuine preferences *while* trying to figure out if any of your preferences are more like prejudices in disguise.

You can date people who look like you *while* understanding how prejudice affects people who don't. It's not either/or.

And if you want to explore anti-racism in more depth, Ibram X. Kendi's *How to Be an Antiracist* and Layla F. Saad's *Me and White Supremacy* are both great resources.[14]

Throughout history, queer people have banded together to make the world a better place. We've fought for our legal right to marry. We keep fighting for our right to exist as peacefully and happily as straight people in our societies. We've played an outsized part in stopping epidemics like HIV/AIDS and mpox in order to protect not just ourselves and our communities, but the population in general.

The fight to eliminate prejudice and racism from our communities is just one more battle we can win if we all play our part. We can work to understand the impact prejudice has on some parts of the queer community. We can resist the urge to categorize and label each other in ways that perpetuate harm or injustice. We can call out racism and injustice when we see it. As a sometimes-excluded and stigmatized group, we can fight to make sure we're not excluding or stigmatizing any of our own.

---

[14] Ibram X. Kendi, *How to Be an Antiracist* (One World, 2019) and Layla F. Saad, *Me and White Supremacy: Combat Racism, Change the World, and Become a Good Ancestor* (Sourcebooks, 2020).

Straight Acting

Let's face it: "straight acting," "masc4masc" and "masculine only" are three phrases that some queer men still love to spread around like they're poppers at a circuit party.

But what's the deal there?

How did some of us learn that acting "straight" — which, it brings me great pleasure to remind you, we are not — is the ideal way a queer man should behave?

Who decided that being like straight men — the group of people historically responsible for, like, all of the world wars and most of the economic crashes — is the standard we're supposed to aspire to?

Because, as it also gives me great pleasure to point out, in at least one important way, none of us are straight acting. In fact, we do just about the most *gay* acting thing a person could ever do: we take a considered interest in dating, loving and/or fucking other men. (And again, I love that for us.)

So anytime we feel the urge to be perceived as "straight" — or just "masculine" — what is that really about?

Often, it's partly about homophobia. And often, it's about what we decide it means to be "a man" in the first place.

As a concept, masculinity is having a bit of a rough time these days. Nobody really knows what it is anymore. Some (straight) men started doing most of the childcare. Some even started wearing makeup, for fuck's sake. And that's left many (straight) men some combination of lost, directionless and turning to literally some of the worst male role models ever to find ways of filling the void where their more straightforward masculine ideals would have been fifty years ago.[1] But this definitely isn't just about straight men. It's about us too. Whatever the reason men care about being seen definitively as men, lots of us do. And whenever our definition of masculinity becomes especially narrow — "act exactly like this, or you're bad at being a man, bro" — that tends to cause more harm than good.

Put it this way: it's kind of sad that there are queer men who can have their entire week ruined by someone telling them their voice sounds a bit effeminate. And it's kind of sad that lots of us feel an urge to avoid doing anything that might make us look even slightly "feminine" — no matter how "masculine" we might be in other ways — to be attractive to each other.

Because that's often the thing here. Often, this isn't really about celebrating the good things about traditional masculinity. (Of which there are plenty.) Often, it's about avoiding femininity at all costs.

As queer men, we somehow wound up in a culture where saying "straight acting only" or "masc only" — or "not into girly fellas" or "I'm allergic to fairy dust and I don't have time for queens!" — can be more about showing everyone else you're "not that kind of gay," and you're against femininity in men, period.[2]

And OK, you got me. How do you objectively tell the difference between a "masc4masc" that's giving "authentic dating preference!" versus a "masc4masc" that's giving "I am objectively terrified of being associated with femininity and therefore being seen as less of a man!" on an app profile?

You can't. It's not that simple. But that's not really the point.

---

[1] Pankaj Mishra, "The crisis in modern masculinity," *The Guardian* ◆ (March 17, 2018).

[2] John Ersine, "Masc4Masc: What's with gay men seeking 'masculine only' partners?," *Matter* ◆ (December 11, 2015). I wish I could tell you I made the "girly fellas" and "fairy dust" examples up, by the way. They're both from real app profiles I found screenshotted online.

What matters is that as men, we often feel pressure to conform to a "masculine ideal," and that pressure isn't doing any of us any favors. That's why this "performative masculinity" exists. It's why lots of queer *and* straight men make a big deal of behaving in ways that signal they're pro-"masculinity" and anti-"femininity" so other men will accept them as "real men," whatever we think one of those is.

We live in a society that still often thinks "real man = masculine man = straight man," and if we just think "OK, cool! I see no problem with that," that's the standard we're going to measure ourselves against. And through that lens, it makes any queer man's mission to prove he's as "straight acting" or "masculine" as possible look like just another way we try to avoid shame for being queer.

As it turns out, the more conscious queer men are about living up to traditional "masculine" ideals, the *more* shame we're likely to feel about being queer, the more insecure and inadequate we're likely to feel about ourselves in general, and the more we're likely to struggle in romantic relationships.[3] In short, according to Ryon McDermott, a psychology professor at the University of South Alabama, "Research shows consistently that men who are more flexible in their gender roles tend to be healthier at nearly every level."[4]

And from an authenticity perspective, that makes sense. Anything performative — anything we do more for someone else's reaction than because it's part of who we really are — is inauthentic. It might help us get accepted by those people, but it also sends a signal to ourselves that we aren't acceptable unless we behave in a specific way.

The reality is that pretty much all of us authentically are traditionally "masculine" in some ways, and traditionally "feminine" in others. We all — queer men *and* people in general — have

---

3 Francisco J. Sánchez, Stephanie T. Greenberg, William Ming Liu and Eric Vilain, "Reported Effects of Masculine Ideals on Gay Men," *Psychology of Men & Masculinities* 10/1 ◆ (January 2009), 73–87. (Yes, there really is a journal called *Psychology of Men & Masculinities*. We are fascinating.)

4 Gabriel Arana, "Gay Men's Obsession with Masculinity Is Hurting Their Mental Health," *them.* ◆ (August 23, 2019).

"masculine" sensibilities and "feminine" sensibilities, and in a better world, none of us would feel any shame about expressing any of them. Because why shouldn't we express them?

Why shouldn't we throw heavy things around the gym in painted nails if we want to? Why shouldn't we puff out our chests to tell a homophobe to fuck off as comfortably as we hug a close friend and call him "sis" if we want to? And if it's authentic, why shouldn't we ditch the baggage of both time-honored gender roles and identify as nonbinary or genderfluid or any other gender nonconforming identity, like many queer people do?

What's more, any fear we have of coming across as too "feminine" tends to hurt us especially when it comes to vulnerability.

Because sure, plenty of queer men authentically exist toward the more "masculine" end of the spectrum. There are queer men who love beer and the great outdoors and actually tune in to the Super Bowl for the Super Bowl, not just the halftime show. But even for queer men who are authentically more "masculine," one reason it's helpful to have a more flexible attitude to gender roles is that it often creates a healthier, more balanced kind of masculinity. It allows for a masculinity that celebrates the best traditionally "masculine" qualities, like strength and perseverance, while making room for more traditionally "feminine" qualities too, like emotional openness, sensitivity, and seeing the value in community.

Because in short, one big reason most of the worst "men are trash" stereotypes exist is basically just unchecked masculinity. It's strength without the sensitivity or compassion to use it well. It's wielding power without understanding how it affects other people. It's being so focused on getting what you want, you don't stop to see how pursuing it is damaging your mental health or your relationships. That's when this kind of unchecked masculinity becomes especially dangerous. Urged on by a fear that acting in any kind of "feminine" way will be seen as weakness, lots of men feel the masculine urge to bottle up their emotions and hide their vulnerabilities and, as you know, that usually comes at a cost.

Ultimately, the solution to this femmephobia — the disdain for any "effeminate" qualities in men — is to take on the culprits that usually cause it: unchecked masculinity and internalized homophobia.

Because again, homophobia is not just something that happens to queer people. It's something queer people can wield against each other. That's where the term internalized homophobia — regular-brand homophobia's crafty, self-destructive cousin — comes from.

Unless you've spent your whole life living with gay penguins in Antarctica, you'll have grown up around some form of homophobia, and likely internalized at some level that being queer is bad.[5] OK, sure, you've probably changed your mind about a lot of that since then. But homophobic beliefs, like racial biases, often end up deeply embedded, and there's definitely a chance those beliefs still affect you sometimes, even if they harm you personally.

In fact, internalized homophobia can manifest in all kinds of subtle ways, from seeing a man swish his hips a bit while he walks and thinking "Urgh, what a faggot," to thinking queer sex is unnatural or kind of disgusting at some level, even if part of you also gets off on it.

Because crucially, internalized homophobia isn't like gonorrhea — something you have or you don't. Internalized homophobia is more like herpes — something that lurks within you and flares up in nasty but different ways sometimes.

And despite the cognitive dissonance that comes with internalized homophobia — that being queer is bad, and yet we are queer and don't really believe we're bad — the problem is that it has a habit of flaring up unexpectedly. It rears its ugly herpes-like head when we get triggered by something we think is "too gay," or not the kind of "gay" we personally think is acceptable. (Because we've appointed ourselves the queer acceptability police, or whatever.) And even worse, it can help push us into rejecting people, not because "He's great, he just

---

[5] And yes, one day these gay penguins and the lesbian mountain goats I mentioned earlier will meet, and their friendship will be *electric*.

isn't my type," but for reasons like "Urgh, he's way too effeminate to be a 'real man.'"

That's the thing about terms like "masc4masc." Some people may genuinely use them to express a personal preference. If you are a more traditionally "masculine" queer man, you might genuinely click best with other more traditionally "masculine" queer men. You might feel more comfortable around other men who are more emotionally reserved or more athletic or whatever. And that's great.

But when you exist in a community where internalized homophobia is definitely a thing, and femmephobia is definitely a thing, and performative masculinity is definitely a thing, using terms like "masc4masc" also contributes to a culture where even the tiniest bit of "femininity" in men is looked down on, which ultimately limits all of us.

And as it turns out, lots of us already agree. A 2016 study found that when queer men include femmephobic language like "real men only" in their online profiles, other queer men tend to judge them as less intelligent, less sexually confident (as if they were compensating for something), and therefore less dateable in general. And whether the queer men surveyed were looking for friendship, dating or sex, they were overall less likely to want to meet up with someone who used that kind of language online.[6]

So in short, for every queer man who insists it's important to be "masc" at all costs, there are plenty of queer men who have a more nuanced view of gender roles. Plus, if your preference genuinely is for more "masculine" partners, you could still filter for that like you would any other trait — by only chatting or swiping with people you find attractive — and avoid all of the negative consequences of openly declaring something like "no fems" on your profile.

---

6 Brandon Miller and Elizabeth Behm-Morawitz, "'Masculine Guys Only': The effects of femmephobic mobile dating application profiles on partner selection for men who have sex with men," *Computers in Human Behavior* 62 ♦ (September 2016), 176–85.

Ultimately, nobody knows for sure how much gender roles come from biology and how much societies just make them up.[7] But either way, none of us are obligated to cling to how society thinks a "man" or a "woman" is supposed to behave any more than we want to. We can focus more on being good *people*, on our terms, than anything else.

And yes, if you're used to measuring yourself according to other people's rules, casting them off can feel kind of frightening. But it can also be wildly liberating, especially when you're queer.

So as the Authenticity Fairy might say, "Be a bit fem, sis! Or be a bit masc, bro! Or be a bit fem, bro, or a bit masc, sis. Whatever works for you, I don't care!"

Because wherever you happen to sit on the vast continuum of gender, it's much better to do what's right for you, and expect other people to do the same for them.

And if that means giving yourself or the people you date more permission to be "gay acting" or "queer acting" — or just "proud to be who we authentically are" — then you should do it. Because that's always a much better standard to measure ourselves against.

---

[7] See Olivia Goldhill, "Scientific research shows gender is not just a social construct," *Quartz* ◆ (January 28, 2018).

Ghosting

Once upon a time, lovers sent letters. Penmanship was all the rage. People wrote things like "Thine butt-cheekes are like warme autumn breezes" on faded parchment with joyous abandon. Communicating took effort. Conversations happened over weeks. It was a simpler time, yes, but a time of its own many charms.

Today, communication is basically effortless and virtually instant. We can connect with hundreds, thousands or even millions of people a day. We can flirt with dozens of people, get into a heated political argument with someone called FreedomFighter87032, and publicly shame a transphobic celebrity — all before breakfast.

Which sounds bloody great.

Only, sometimes it isn't.

Because with the bar of entry so low today, communication often means less. When you have to spend an hour on a Sunday penning an elegant, thoughtful note to your beloved, you really have to like them to make it worthwhile. Today, you can shoot off "hey handsome" to a dozen different people in about thirty seconds.[1]

And so, while simple, near-instant communication has made our lives easier in many ways, it's also made our lives more complicated. We communicate with far more people than we ever could have before

---

[1] While we once might have courted one distant beau, today it's much easier to entertain many distant — or nearby — heaus.

— and far more than our brains evolved to handle.[2] A lot of us expect near-instant replies in a way that was unthinkable even twenty years ago. And that's created its own culture of communication.

Which brings us to ghosting.

Why ghosting hurts — and how to respond to it

Ghosting is when someone suddenly stops communicating with someone else without warning or explanation, and just disappears. It can happen after you've been chatting online, or after a few in-person dates. In some especially obnoxious cases, it can happen after you've been in a relationship with someone for years.

But ghosting isn't just about conversations ending.

We're left feeling ghosted when our relationship with someone feels substantial enough that we expect an explanation or just an acknowledgment that someone plans to stop communicating with us. Because once we've built up a connection with someone, it feels disrespectful — even like a betrayal — if they flat out disappear. It tends to create an emotional disconnection.

That's why it's usually not that upsetting if someone messages you on an app to say, "Hey, what's up?" and you reply, "Not much, you?" but they never respond to tell you what indeed is up. Yes, they stopped communicating with you suddenly and without explanation, but since you won't have had chance to form much of an emotional connection with that person, it's unlikely to hurt when they didn't reply.

That's also why there's no strict point at which withdrawing from communication officially becomes ghosting. Some people have a stronger need for closure and clarity in relationships than others. So some might feel ghosted if an app conversation ends, while some

---

[2] We probably have the capacity for about 150 meaningful connections, including friends and family, and as few as *five* close friends. So if you interact with more than 150 people online, you're already stretching your brain's limit. See Allie Volpe, "The case for fewer friends," *Vox* ◆ (June 6, 2022).

people might not get a text back from someone they've been on three dates with and just shrug it off as part of dating in the twenty-first century.

Still, when ghosting hurts, it hurts. It's normal to feel disrespected when someone you think you have a connection with disappears instead of being direct with you about ending the connection.

On one level, ghosting hurts for the same reason that any breakup hurts. You have to process a relationship that didn't go where you thought or hoped it would, and any rejection can trigger feelings of unworthiness in even the most self-assured people — and especially when you're queer and more sensitive to rejection.

But ghosting isn't just about rejection. It's rejection with a silent cherry on top. It's rejection that says, "Not only is it a no, but if you thought I was going to take any time out of my day to tell you that, you can guess again, bitchhh." It's rejection that says, "I guess I could make the effort to break this off cleanly and directly but nah, Imma just keep you guessing!"

So even more so than direct rejection, ghosting is especially good at triggering any insecurities or unworthiness we might feel about being rejected. And in queer dating specifically, it often reinforces the general disconnection and hopelessness many of us feel — and the fear that we can't rely even on our own community to be basically kind to us.

Because that really is the key difference between ghosting and more direct styles of rejection. Ghosting creates an emotional disconnection, via a breakdown of communication. Kind but clear rejection tends to create a moment of emotional connection, even if it means everyone accepting that a relationship has run its course.

And so, even if your self-esteem and emotional resilience are normally pretty high, it often does hurt more to be ghosted. When someone you felt a connection with suddenly disappears, the chances you'll end up thinking "Maybe I do deserve to be dropped like that," or "Dating men is a waste of time and I really am going to die alone with my cats!" will be higher than they are when you're rejected in a more direct and communicative way.

People ghost for different reasons. And some of them might be legitimate. Some people might be messaging — or even dating — more people than they could ever hope to communicate with properly. They might have rejected someone before who responded angrily or wouldn't take no for an answer, and so they decided to avoid that scenario in the future.

But often, ghosting comes down to some combination of a lack of consideration and a lack of vulnerability. It happens when someone didn't get the memo that there is value in open communication, even when it involves rejection. So they choose the easier, less vulnerable way out. They avoid the discomfort that sometimes comes with clear communication — especially when it's necessary to tell someone something they might not want to hear — and just disappear.

They might not have the language, the emotional resilience, or just the thoughtfulness to be able to tell you clearly where they stand, so they ghost instead.

Still, if you end up feeling disrespected or let down by someone disappearing, it's important to separate how you feel about being ghosted — or rejected in general — from what that says about your inherent value or worthiness as a romantic partner or human being.

Because, as Eleanor Roosevelt said, "No one can make you feel inferior without your consent."

OK, it's debatable whether she actually said that. If we're making up first lady one-liners, at this point I might as well have just quoted Martha Jefferson's famous motto "Ghosters gon' ghost, sweetie. And that's on THEM!" Still, those words that Eleanor Roosevelt may or may not have said do contain a valuable truth: how someone treats you is usually more about them than about you.

This is another situation where boundaries matter. Part of understanding boundaries is understanding that, as a rule, you are responsible for the choices you make, and other people are responsible for the choices they make.

Nobody ever has infinite choices. We're always constrained at least a little by situation and circumstance. But ultimately, we choose how to respond to the situations we find ourselves in. So I am responsible for deciding how to respond to my circumstances, and you to yours.

So if someone's situation is "This relationship isn't working for me and I want to end it," and their chosen response is "I'll just do that by disappearing, even though direct communication would be helpful and kind!" then that is their choice.

Because ultimately, that's all ghosting is: an uncommunicative way to break up with someone. It's a way to say something other than "fuck yes" to someone, and therefore a signal that that person has chosen (an easy if kind of shitty way) to say "no."

And equally, if your situation is "Damn, I'm actually kind of hurt someone vanished on me suddenly when they totally could have told me directly," you get to decide how to respond. Though we can't choose our emotions, especially in situations we don't like, we do choose how to respond to our emotions.

So sure, it can be tempting to keep trying to get their attention to get some kind of response. It can be tempting to send them a long message about how you feel sooooo disrespected and if they aren't interested all they had to do was fucking say that.

But my honest advice is, don't.

My honest advice is, respect the dead. Let them transition to ghosthood. Hold a short funeral for them if you want to. Pity them that they couldn't treat you better, then focus on finding someone willing and able to communicate with you more directly.

Because, sure, there are times people just miss messages. There are times people genuinely intend to reply but forget. But in the cases where someone's lack of vulnerability was limiting their ability to communicate with you, it was probably also limiting (or would have limited) their ability to form a deeper connection with you in other ways too.

So as much as being ghosted can suck, and as much as getting ghosted can be a shitty way to find out you've been rejected, it's usually a net positive that you *did* find out.

That's not to say respecting the dead will instantly make sure the ghosting doesn't hurt. It often hurts when people we care about leave our lives for any reason. And when someone turns out not to be who we thought they were, it can make us question our values and judgment. (Though if that helps us reassess what kinds of behaviors — and what kinds of people — we're willing to allow into our lives, that ultimately is a good thing.)

So if the ghosting hurts, take the time to process the rejection like any other, if you need to. Sit with the feelings of disappointment and disconnection, if you need to. Be as mad as you want about receiving the rejection in the way you did. But for your own sake, try to accept the message of the rejection all the same: that this relationship, fortunately or otherwise, is a no go, and that this person, fortunately or otherwise, isn't able to communicate openly with you in the way that you deserve.

That said, there is one major caveat to all of this: make sure someone has actually stopped communicating with you before you conclude you've been ghosted. People sometimes don't see messages or calls. Technology breaks or gets lost. And despite what our hyper-online world can feel like sometimes, people have other things going on in their lives and aren't on their phone all the time.

So despite what you might have heard, double texting — following up with a second message if someone didn't reply — is fine. With the right person, double texting is always fine.

If someone has been super communicative before but isn't now, hitting them up with a "Hey, just wanted to check in" or just "Hey, how's it going?" is definitely a good idea.

Our rejection sensitivity can make us perceive rejection when it's not there, so if in doubt, send that double text. You'll either confirm that they're intentionally not responding, or that they didn't reply because you're not much of a priority — or you'll find out that actually, they were busy or got distracted this time around.

Yes, it's important to know when to respect the dead. But in this hyper-connected, hyper-online world, sometimes you have to shake someone a little to check whether they've genuinely become a ghost or they've just dozed off.

How to avoid becoming a ghost yourself

So sure, maybe it's partly true that we ghost a lot now because the internet helped make things that way. But whether we're talking about how we communicate online or deciding to unicycle naked around Times Square for TikTok views, "The internet made me do it" isn't really the great justification it sounds like it should be.

Though seriously, if you're thinking about ghosting because you think it'll spare someone's feelings, or because "No response is a response," or because you think "I don't owe anyone anything!" let's look at that reasoning for a hot second.

Ghosting doesn't usually spare anyone's feelings. It often just confuses people and leaves them feeling more rejected. No response might be an appropriate way to reject someone after a couple of messages on a dating app, but it'll likely hurt someone you've built a bit of a connection with.

And sure, none of us owe anyone a date or a relationship. That's definitely true. But saying, "Bitch, I don't owe anyone anything!" like it's some kind of sociopathic badge of honor is not exactly giving "I'm a great person to date."

Call me crazy, but I think we do owe the people we date at least basic kindness and consideration — not least because we might be the one on the receiving end of being ghosted some other time.

And in any case, in my experience most queer men *do* respond well to honesty, and *do* appreciate clear communication. Most of us would rather be told unwanted news directly than be left on read until the heat death of the universe.[3]

So clear and direct communication, even and especially when it's difficult, is usually the best choice. It's usually the choice that makes dating a better experience for everyone in the long run.

To avoid ghosting, you can use phrases like these:

- "I'm really busy right now and unfortunately I don't have time to see you. If you want, you can try me again in a few weeks."
- "It was great getting to know you, but this isn't what I'm looking for in a relationship right now. Good luck finding what you're looking for."
- "I enjoyed spending time with you but I've met someone I've really clicked with and we've decided to give it a shot."
- "I'm sorry, this isn't working for me anymore. Thanks for understanding."

As with any rejection, the exact language you use will depend on your exact circumstances. And as with any rejection, there often isn't perfect, completely risk-free or hurt-free language you can use. It usually does feel uncomfortable when you have to tell someone something they might not want to hear.

And yes, there are situations where cutting off communication with someone without explanation is completely justified. If they've been abusive or seriously disrespectful to you, you are entitled to cut things off with them abruptly. And plenty of casual relationships do fizzle out without anyone officially ending them.

But none of those situations really counts as ghosting. Cutting off communication for your safety is not ghosting. Telling someone that you want to cut off communication and then doing it is not ghosting.

---

[3] That's what one survey by dating app Hinge found too. When they asked their users, 85% of them said that sure, being rejected stings, but they'd still rather know. Logan Ury, "Ghosting," *Medium* ◆ (September 3, 2020).

Not communicating with someone who isn't expecting to hear from you is not ghosting.

The golden rule of not ghosting is simple: if you've built some kind of connection with someone and clear and direct communication would help them know where they stand with you, then give them that.

Tell them you enjoyed your date and you'd love to see them again.

Or tell them it was fun to hang out but you don't want to take things any further.

Or tell them you've enjoyed getting to know them the past four months but you've given it some thought and the relationship isn't working for you anymore.

Or tell them you're confused and conflicted about how you feel right now, and start a conversation with them about that.

Lots of us aren't sure when or how to start conversations about how we feel or what we want from a relationship. But like with most important but vulnerable conversations, avoiding them normally just delays the inevitable, and often makes having those conversations more difficult or awkward later. So if you have something to say you think that someone you've been dating should know, you don't even need to wait to be asked. It's always OK to ask someone "Hey, can we talk about where we're at?"

(We also have to be prepared to hear things *we* don't want to hear in dating and accept them — because if we don't, that can encourage people to ghost others in the future.)

Communication is important in any relationship — whatever kind of relationship it is. And honesty and openness are basically always better than avoidance. But as queer men, not communicating directly with each other can have even more far-reaching consequences.

Ultimately, ghosting helps to reinforce the idea that other queer men are only valuable — and only deserve our honesty and attention — when we want something from them. It helps to reinforce the idea that we're all just disposable commodities to each other.

On the other hand, direct communication helps create a greater sense of respect and authenticity in our community. It helps make dating a better experience for all of us.

Because anytime we end up ghosting someone — or just avoiding a difficult conversation for the sake of our own comfort — it's easy just to shrug it off as "how dating works."

But if a lack of vulnerability becomes a pattern, if we get too comfortable avoiding risky but necessary conversations in love, in the long run that tends to cost us too.

Baggage Reclaim

We've spent a lot of this book looking at the specific emotional and cultural baggage queer men often carry.

We've looked at how being queer often makes it harder to be authentic and vulnerable. We've looked at how being queer makes us more sensitive to rejection and more likely to accept conditional love from others. We've looked at how homophobia can fuck up the way we think about sex, about love, about our bodies, and even about what it means to be a man.

I've talked about all of that not just because, at some level, I think it's fun to be miserable, but because this baggage has very real consequences. It blocks us, it boxes us in, and it limits our ability to love ourselves and each other. And as tempting as it can be to ignore all that baggage and hope life works itself out on its own, that's usually not a good strategy. To move past our baggage, we usually have to face it, accept it as it is, and find healthy ways to work through it.

Because, yes, being queer is often fun, liberating and exciting. And that's great. It's great that so many of us are determined to live our lives in the ways that bring us the most happiness and fulfillment.

Still, existing as a queer person can also be a heavy, emotionally challenging experience. That means releasing ourselves from our baggage is often a difficult process, but it's one we have to be good at if we want to live — and love — better.

So with that in mind, come join me by carousel four, let's reclaim some of this baggage and see where that can take us.

Life is ups *and* downs — especially when you're queer

It's a cliché, but it's true: life naturally comes with ups and downs. Despite what it can look like online, no one's life is a never-ending stream of fun, positive and perfectly Instagrammable moments. Life fucking sucks sometimes. For everyone.

And sometimes, the problem is not those negative experiences themselves, but the tendency a lot of us have to avoid, deny or just ignore those negative experiences. Often, the measure of our overall happiness and fulfillment isn't determined by how open we are to positive experiences, but how well we can accept negative experiences too.

Part of that is because the things that tend to bring us the most fulfillment in life — long-term goals — always come with challenges and sacrifices. (We'll talk about that properly in the next chapter.)

But a more immediate reason for that is to do with how we process emotions. Because yes, while we can avoid or ignore the negative emotions that come with negative experiences, in short, we can't numb feelings selectively. So while we can detach from our negative emotions so we don't feel them as strongly, that also stops us feeling positive emotions — including love and connection — as strongly. The cost of avoiding feeling bad is that we limit our ability to feel good, and like we belong.[1]

Again, that's why if we just ignore our emotional baggage and hope it goes away, it usually ends up limiting our ability to feel happy and fulfilled, especially in relationships.

And though there are lots of different sources of negative feelings, one we don't talk about enough as queer people is grief, the pain of loss. We talk a lot about the trauma of being queer, but less about the grief that often comes with being queer.

---

[1] Brené Brown, *Daring Greatly: How the Courage to Be Vulnerable Transforms the Way We Live, Love, Parent, and Lead* (Avery, 2012), 137.

"Grief" is a word that's often associated with bereavement, and queer grief is especially associated with the loss of so many queer men to HIV/AIDS at the height of the epidemic in the 1980s and 90s. (The scars of those losses are still with many older queer men today.)

But the truth is, we can experience grief after any loss — a life or otherwise. We can even grieve for things we never even had.

And because of the homophobia that still exists, queer men still lose out in all kinds of ways we shouldn't have to. We lose family and friends who outright reject us. We lose out on closer relationships with family and friends whose prejudices mean we have to keep them at a distance. Basically none of us gets an authentic adolescence of dating and romantic exploration with the people we're actually attracted to like most straight teens do.

We also lose out on time. Because we have to fight harder to find our authentic place in the world, lots of us aren't ready to build stable, fulfilling relationships until later in life. Then, once we do find the emotional maturity it takes to love and be loved, the baggage from the wounding and confusing path we took to get there can stick around, limiting our ability to connect emotionally with other men for a long time.

We lose out on all of those things, not because of anything we've done, but because we exist in a society that normalizes being straight and cisgender and still stigmatizes everything else.

In short, homophobia steals from us.

It steals romantic relationships, friendships, family relationships, and even careers from us. It steals time. It steals authenticity, it steals connection, it steals belonging. And maybe worst of all, it steals love from us. It makes the things we deserve as much as any other human being — and the things we need to feel happy and connected — harder to get than they should be. And we have the right to grieve those losses.

That's also why the fight to eradicate all forms of homophobia is so important. Even subtle homophobia — in straight people or within ourselves — helps to keep us from living the happy and fulfilled lives we deserve to live.

And I know, it isn't all doom and gloom. In many ways, things are better for queer people than they've ever been. But even low-level homophobia — and the baggage it creates for us — are a major factor in why many of us struggle to find the love and fulfillment we want.

And so, because the grief over what we lose out on — and in some cases, never had — can feel especially heavy, we have to learn to process it. We have to mourn the time we spent living inauthentically because we didn't know any other way. We have to mourn the authentic relationships we were too afraid to be in, and the relationships that fell apart because we didn't believe queer love was possible, or just didn't believe it could happen to us.

Because sure, these experiences do help us grow and make us more resilient. And the losses aren't just ours — they also affect the narrow-minded people who lose us, who don't get to see the truest versions of who we are. But this isn't just about saying "What doesn't kill you makes you stronger." It's also about saying "Some struggles are dumb and unjust, and it's OK if they make you mad sometimes." It's about accepting that we're all human, and that there's a limit to how much heaviness we can endure.

And since men in general often find it hard to deal with negative emotions — and being queer can give us more of them to feel — it's especially important we find healthy ways to acknowledge, feel and process the emotions we'd often rather we didn't have.

How to deal with negative emotions more healthily

Negative emotions obviously come in all shapes and sizes. Someone being rude to you on a dating app won't feel the same as a close friend passing away. The end of a two-month relationship won't affect you the way separating after a ten-year marriage would.

But whether the source of the negative emotions is rejection, loss, injustice or anything else, the challenge of dealing with them is usually similar. The goal is to feel and work through those emotions so they don't affect you any more negatively than they have to.

Unfortunately, unprocessed pain or grief can rear its fugly head in all kinds of ways, from mood swings, increased anger and irritability, to long-term emotional detachment or even a dependence on alcohol or drugs to manage those feelings.[2] And inevitably, those knock-on effects from unresolved negative emotions often end up harming our ability to form healthy relationships with others even further.

And what's more, there's often no way around negative emotions, only through. So we have to resist the masculine urge to bury our feelings, or fight or drink or fuck our way around them. Like I've said, we have to be willing to face them if we want to let ourselves be happy.

There are a few important ways to do that.

Start by accepting how you feel

One of the hallmarks of authenticity is being able to accept the world as it is — and yourself as you are. But a lot of people, queer and otherwise, have a tendency to ignore the emotional parts of ourselves. We treat ourselves like emotionless machines because we've got places to be and shit to do. But we're not machines. We're emotional, needy, sometimes horny sacks of meat who need time to rest and, sometimes, just to be human.

And again, as men especially, we're socialized to bury or ignore any of our feelings we don't like. But none of us can heal if we keep pretending we aren't hurt. We can't do anything about our negative emotions if we're not willing to admit we have them.

If it helps, try separating your feelings from who you are as a person. This is the difference between treating feelings as an experience (I'm feeling sad, I'm experiencing sadness) versus

---

[2] See Robert Taibbi, "Six Signs of Incomplete Grief," *Psychology Today* ◆ (June 7, 2017).

something we are (I am sad, I am sadness itself). All feelings are important signals about what's going on in our lives. That's why we evolved to have them. But all feelings are temporary — they visit us, they influence us, but they are not us.

That's why it's not generally a good idea to respond impulsively to every single feeling as it comes. But it is important to notice or acknowledge what you're feeling as you feel it. The goal is not to block those emotional signals about what's going on in our lives, because those signals contain important information. We are responsible for our actions, not our emotions, but it's much harder to choose responsible, healthy actions if we're not aware of what we're feeling.

That means the first step is being honest with yourself about how you feel — and accepting those feelings as valid, whatever they are.

Take better care of yourself

Yes, queer men can be trash to each other. But we really can be trash to ourselves too. We don't always speak about ourselves kindly, or give ourselves grace when we mess up, or prioritize our needs because it's often more convenient to pretend we don't have them.

But strong or persistent negative emotions slow us down. If you're struggling after a breakup or difficult experience, it can affect your body. It can make it harder to think clearly. It can make things you normally do easily more difficult or just more stressful. So just like you'd replan an exercise routine if you broke your arm, it's OK — and probably a good idea — to rearrange your usual routine if you're struggling emotionally right now.

You might want to prioritize spending time with friends, or spending time outside, or exercising more, or resting more. It's also OK to take a break from your usual commitments and responsibilities, if you can, to lower the pressure you might feel under.

Prioritizing your well-being won't always speed up how quickly you process negative emotions, but it will make everything more bearable while you do.

Don't be afraid to ask for help

Lots of us find it difficult to ask for support. Because it takes vulnerability to say, "I'm struggling, can you help?" some people see asking for help as weakness. But it's not.

The simple truth is, difficult experiences and emotions are often easier to deal with when they're shared. Even if sharing a difficult experience doesn't fix the cause of the problem, it usually makes us feel better about it.

Support can come in lots of different forms. It can just mean spending more time with friends. It can mean messaging a friend to say, "Hey, can I call? I'm struggling today." It can mean joining a support group in your area or online. (There are groups dedicated to helping people through specific problems, like bereavement or addiction, as well as more general groups.) Or, if it's an option for you, it can mean starting to work with a therapist or counselor.

Yep, you probably know that joke that every tiny thing that inconveniences a queer person is homophobic. But it literally *is* homophobic that queer people don't always get the emotional support we need to help us navigate living in a homophobic society better. So if you have the means and you've never tried therapy before, it's definitely worth looking for a therapist, locally or online, who's a good fit for you. Despite what some people think, you don't have to be in crisis or going through a divorce or have a full PTSD diagnosis to go to therapy. Working with a trained professional is also a great way to help yourself navigate life's "normal" ups and downs.

Don't lose sight of the positives

One thing that sucks about negative emotions is that we're actually hardwired to experience them more strongly than positive emotions.[3] (Yeah, I know. One more scam about being human.)

---

[3] Kendra Cherry, "What Is the Negativity Bias?," *Verywell Mind* ◆ (September 14, 2022).

It's probably an evolutionary thing. From a survival perspective, it's more important that we experience feeling shit-scared of a lion more strongly than thinking that some squirrel is cute. Evolution is about keeping us alive, and not necessarily happy, after all. But that means today, even if you're not that worried about being eaten by lions, your brain still has a tendency to dwell on negative emotions and lose sight of the bigger picture.

Yes, breakups can suck. But you probably got plenty out of the relationship while it lasted. Or at least, maybe you learned something about yourself or what you're looking for in a partner. And once you're past the pain of the separation, being single has its advantages too.

This isn't about minimizing your negative emotions. It's not about forcing yourself to feel optimistic when you genuinely don't. But it is about saying that during difficult experiences, there are often also positives. You can be grateful for the good things a relationship brought you while being sad or angry that it ended. And you can be grateful for all the exciting things that come with being queer, *while* being angry about the homophobia we still have to deal with.

Still — as we talked about before — breakups are hard because your brain literally gets addicted to the feeling of being in love. That's why breakups hurt. That's why it can be tempting to miss doing all the cute things you did together and forget that you ultimately weren't a good fit for each other. That's why you can miss the toe-curling sex you had together and wonder whether that makes up for the fact he cheated on you with two of your best friends. At once.

Ultimately, the principle of "fuck yes or no" still applies, no matter how you feel about the relationship. It's hard to build a fulfilling relationship with someone you're just not compatible with. And you literally can't build a fulfilling relationship with someone who doesn't want to build one with you, whatever their reasons. You deserve someone who is ready and able to love you as much as you're prepared to love them. So you can remember what was positive about a relationship *while* feeling sad that it ended.

Try to grow around your grief or loss

Finally, there's a common assumption that after a breakup or bereavement or other major loss, the pain eventually goes away and you just carry on with your life. But loss often doesn't work like that.

After a painful or difficult experience, we normally do heal with time. The emotions it creates normally grow weaker over time. But grief is not linear. It can grow and shrink, sometimes in unpredictable cycles. It's also wrong to assume that negative life experiences — like all life experiences — don't stay with us somehow.

In other words, it's not weird if you still miss an ex months or even years later. It's not weird to miss an ex even once you're with someone new. It's not weird to miss an ex even if they messed you around and broke your heart. It's not weird to miss an ex even if you broke up with them and you feel like you should be over them by now.[4]

Again, emotions are often layered. You can love a new partner and still miss some things about an old one. You can be mad about something someone did but still miss who you were when you were with them. You can notice all the different feelings you feel about a situation while accepting them all as valid.

The endgame with negative feelings caused by grief isn't to erase them or even get past them completely. The goal is to move on *with* them. It's to grow around them. It's to accept that all life experiences — good, bad, some combination of the two — stay with us as we go on with our lives, but we keep moving forward anyway. Because often, that's all we can do.

---

[4] Yep, all those theories that we need a certain amount of time to get over a relationship of a certain length — as well as that we experience grief in specific stages — aren't universally true, sorry.

The Long Haul

As queer people, it can be hard to think about the future. As much as we typically gain more acceptance and better rights over time, we're often reminded that we're just one despotic group of politicians away from having some of our hard-won rights and freedom taken from us.

That's definitely part of why many of us focus on "now," and chase instant validation over longer-term fulfillment — it's hard to work toward a satisfying future if you don't believe you'll ever find one.

And yet, longer-term commitment is often the defining factor in finding greater fulfillment not just in our relationships, but in our lives in general. Certain types of fulfillment really only come from a long-term commitment to a goal or to a person.

And while that kind of commitment might not be for everyone all the time — and even some people ever — it's worth talking about. It's worth talking more about what longer-term relationships can bring into our lives, and what, despite the external challenges we face, we have to do to make them work.

Death by a thousand cuts: How long-term
relationships fail

Compatibility is important in relationships. We've talked a lot about that already. But if 100% compatibility doesn't exist, it's inevitable that even very compatible partners will disagree sometimes.

In fact, some relationship conflict is usually a good thing. Highly authentic people will inevitably disagree sometimes, and typically won't shy away from expressing their thoughts and opinions even to other people who don't share them. So we should consider some level of disagreement in relationships not just as normal, but also as healthy.

And yet, some relationships are clearly better at dealing with conflict than others. In some relationships, conflict brings the partners together, while in others it pushes them apart. Why is that?

In 1976, psychologists John Gottman and Robert Levenson teamed up to try to find out why. They spent decades studying over three thousand different couples — straight and, later, queer — and over time they learned how to predict, with around 90% accuracy, which couples would stay together and which would separate.

In short, what became clear was that no, the couples who stayed together didn't necessarily argue less, but they did have the skills to repair the relationship after fighting. They tried to find mutually beneficial solutions instead of just blaming each other, they apologized for hurting each other's feelings, and they knew how to use humor and empathy to defuse tense situations.[1]

In other words, the "master" couples, who stayed together, had learned to "lean in" to conflict. They'd built a relationship where both partners felt comfortable facing conflict and trying to resolve it.

On the other hand, the "disaster" couples, the partnerships that didn't last, typically turned away from conflict. They'd ended up

---

[1] There's a good introduction to Gottman and Levenson's research on relationships at https://www.gottman.com/about/research/couples/. And actually, when Gottman and Levenson studied same-sex couples, they found that factors like our ability to use humor during conflict, and our belief in being equal partners — unlike in straight couples, where the man is often more dominant (oh hello, patriarchy) — made many of us who were in long-term relationships better at it than lots of heterosexuals. How about that? For more, see https://www.gottman.com/about/research/same-sex-couples/.

creating an environment where the partners often felt guarded and suspicious around each other, and especially when conflict arose.[2]

And so, as the conflicts piled up, the partners in the "disaster" couples were pushed further and further apart, even if each individual conflict wasn't that significant. When their relationships eventually reached breaking point, it was a death by a thousand cuts.

Gottman and Levenson identified four behaviors that, if present during conflict, signaled with surprising accuracy that a relationship would deteriorate over time. And with a level of outward drama I can only assume they knew would appeal to queer men, they called these behaviors "The Four Horsemen of the Apocalypse."

The first is **criticism** — personally attacking your partner's character. ("Bitch, you never put other people first!")

The second is **contempt** — insulting or acting superior to your partner. ("Hunty, you're just too dumb to understand that.")

The third is **defensiveness** — denying responsibility and playing the victim. ("Gurl, maybe I'd do the dishes if you were nicer to me!")

And the final horseman is the ultimate high-drama move of **stonewalling** — withdrawing, shutting down emotionally, or even refusing to talk to your partner entirely.

These behaviors not only made conflict resolution more difficult during an argument, but longer-term they also helped each person to conclude that their partner didn't value or appreciate them.

On the other hand, the "master" couples, whose relationships lasted, could disagree without attacking or withdrawing from their partner. They usually responded to conflicts with empathy, kindness, and understanding.

Instead of criticizing each other, they showed appreciation for each other and tried to understand the other's point of view. They took responsibility instead of blaming each other, and apologized when

---

[2] I know, it seems kind of catty to call the couples who couldn't sustain their relationship "disaster couples." I'm just using the terminology from the study.

necessary. And when one partner put out emotional "bids" — made even the tiniest attempt to be heard or acknowledged by their partner — the other responded, almost without fail, with kindness, warmth, and empathy.[3]

It wasn't that the "master" couples always said the "right" thing or never hurt their partner's feelings. They *mostly* avoided saying anything that hurt their partner, and if they did, they apologized. In fact, Gottman and Levenson found that in the relationships that lasted, there were at least *five* times more positive interactions than negative interactions during conflict.

Ultimately, the "master" couples had the skills to repair their relationship after rifts. They knew how to weather conflict, and often found by facing conflict together — as partners versus the conflict, not one partner versus the other — it only strengthened their relationship.

At the same time, those couples had something just as essential — the belief that using those skills would be worth it. Even in the middle of a fight, they could see something bigger than the conflict itself: that the relationship was *worth* repairing.

The value of the long haul

In John Gottman's words, "One of the saddest reasons a marriage dies is that neither spouse recognizes its value until it is too late."[4] And that makes sense. If it takes work to build and maintain a relationship,

---

[3] A bid might be as simple as one partner saying, "It's so nice outside today" or "Did you see how fine Chris Hemsworth looks in this photo he just posted?" and the other responding warmly with "Yes, hun." The exact content of the bid or the response to it isn't usually important. A successful bid is simply when someone tries to get attention or recognition from a person they care about, and that person responds or acknowledges them in a warm way.

[4] John M. Gottman and Nan Silver, *The Seven Principles for Making Marriage Work: A Practical Guide from the Country's Foremost Relationship Expert* (Harmony, 2015), 5.

and then it takes effort and empathy to repair a relationship after conflict, why try unless you believe in that relationship?

Because again, as much as short-term relationships have value, there are a host of specific benefits that you only really get from being with someone longer-term.

Yes, staying with the same partner longer-term can bring a level of stability that lots of us want and need from our relationships. But happy longer-term relationships aren't just about stability. They also offer deeper levels of intimacy, understanding, and connection. Getting to know someone over a longer period of time allows that deeper sense of trust, security and emotional safety to develop. All that shared history, those shared experiences, and shared personal growth help to create depths of trust and intimacy that you just can't get from shorter-term connections.

In the age of internet dating, though, it can be easy to lose sight of that. The apps commodify us. They can make looking for a partner feel like choosing a brand of deodorant off a supermarket shelf. We're encouraged to be and to try to find someone who is *consumably* attractive — who looks great on a profile and is ready to slot perfectly into our lives.

But that's not and has never been how dating works.

Relationships are built, not consumed. Relationships have always been about saying, "Here's a person I'm interested in and want to try building a connection with" and not "I'll take one, please."

None of that is helped by the fact that thriving long-term queer relationships still aren't as visible as they could be. So for us it's often harder to see or imagine where a longer-term commitment can take us. And that can make it harder to believe that the effort and small sacrifices it takes to make a long-term connection work will be worth it.

And so, a lot of us settle into believing that short-term connections — hookups, perpetual first dates, two-week boyfriends — are all queer men are capable of. Or, if we do find a relationship that feels promising, we get scared and break things off the moment it hits its first inevitable conflict. And sometimes, we repeat those cycles over and over, not because deeper connections aren't possible, but because if we don't believe they are, that tends to become a self-fulfilling prophecy.

It's your life and your body, and you get to decide what you do with them. And sometimes, it's great to decide *not* to have a plan — to live open to possibility and chance.

But a lot of queer men struggle because they aren't really deciding. They might be convinced what they want doesn't exist, or they might not be aware of what they want. So they're just going wherever the wind — or Bruno or Krish — might blow them.

And in some ways, that can be a fun life. But over time, it's often a life of diminishing returns. Without some kind of goal or purpose to connect the dots, the individual dots can get boring and unfulfilling. And in relationships, it's often the more challenging dots, the ones that require commitment and even sacrifice that help to unlock the most happiness and fulfillment.

Because the truth about "fuck yes or no" is that it's rarely the "fuck yeses" alone that bring the most fulfillment. It's often the "nos" — the things we turn down so we can focus our time and effort on what we really want — that make all the difference.

Again, one of the worst parts of being queer in a world that isn't built for us is how it can feel like our lives can't ever have deeper meaning. It can feel like we can't build the close relationships we want, or that we can't raise the families we want, or that the deeper fulfillment that can only come from relationships that last years, if not decades, simply isn't accessible to us.

But that's not true.

Love doesn't care about gender, or sexuality, or anything like that. Love is always an option, for all of us.

So if you care about forming more fulfilling romantic relationships and they seem to be eluding you right now, it's worth asking yourself whether you're sure you're open to being in one. Are you prepared to put in the work and sacrifices it takes to build one? Are you avoiding taking a chance on someone because you're afraid it might get hard, not work out, or just that it might not bring perfect happiness, rainbows and blowjobs at every turn?

In our culture of quick wins and instant highs, it is easy to think like that. But like life in general, no relationship will feel great 100% of the time. Even in the healthiest relationships, nobody feels madly, deeply in love all the time. Sometimes love is just quiet warmth and affection with someone you care about.

When you choose a long-term partner, they're not just the person who you'll have cute dinners with, take vacations with, and see naked a lot. They're also the person you'll disagree with sometimes, who unintentionally says the wrong thing sometimes, or who somehow never remembers to wipe down the countertop after they've used it even though you've asked twenty fucking times. They're the person you'll occasionally clash with and have to do the essential work of repairing your relationship with.

Yes, we have to choose our partners well. We have to choose people we like to be around, we have to choose people we're compatible with and we have to choose people we fight well with.

Then once we've chosen well, we have to choose to start building.

Love and connection don't just find us. People we can create it with sometimes do. But then it's up to us to build that love and connection, even if it won't be perfect all the time.

If we want to access the deeper love that only commitment can bring, we have to put in the effort to create, nurture and build it. We have to choose love — and we absolutely can, if we want it.

Looking

In a world of uncertainty, at least there's one important thing queer men can rely on: no matter how a dating app conversation starts, it's only a matter of time before somebody asks, "So what are you looking for?"

And yes, it's a great question. What are we looking for? A blowjob on our lunchbreak? A cashpig to buy us new AirPods? NSA or FWB or TLC or VPL or whatever word or phrase everyone seems to be using by the time you're reading this?

But whatever your answer at any given moment, it *is* good to know what we're looking for. It's a simple truth that we're much more likely to get what we want if we're good at asking for it.

At the same time, one important side effect of working through your baggage as a queer man is that you often become more aware of what you want on a deeper level, and not just on the surface.

And as you peel back those layers, like the fabulous queer onion you are, it often becomes clear that despite the specific things we might want on the surface, our deeper motivations can be surprisingly universal.

*What are you *really* looking for?*

In her book *Daring Greatly*, vulnerability expert Brené Brown writes, "Connection is why we're here. We're hardwired to connect with others, it's what gives purpose and meaning to our lives, and without it there is suffering."[1]

From that perspective, most of the things we chase are either about gaining a sense of connection — the feeling that we belong, that we're seen, accepted, and loved as we are — or about finding ways to soothe or numb our sense of loneliness and disconnection.

For queer men, finding that kind of fulfilling, authentic connection can be especially hard. The invalidation and rejection we face often helps to shut us down emotionally. And so, as you know, we often compensate for that invalidation by chasing quick highs. We chase another hookup because sex can temporarily bring us the feeling of being wanted, which isn't quite feeling loved, but it's close.

Or we're drawn to queer spaces like bars and clubs hoping to find the feeling that we belong, that we're part of a community. But once we're there, we often don't find community. We find rejection and even invalidation, maybe because we're not masculine enough, or muscular enough, or not dressed-like-an-absolute-harlot enough, or because we don't fit some other narrow definition of what a desirable queer man should be. And in turn that helps to reinforce the message that a deeper sense of love and connection isn't easily available to you when you're a queer man. (Even if, again, that's totally untrue.)

But as much as many queer men end up actively avoiding love and connection by telling themselves they don't need it, that they can manage on their own, it's almost never true. Research has shown that for most people with a more avoidant attachment style — people who tend to push love and connection away — it's not that they don't have any desire to connect with other people, it's that they've learned to repress it.[2]

---

[1] Brené Brown, *Daring Greatly: How the Courage to Be Vulnerable Transforms the Way We Live, Love, Parent, and Lead* (Avery, 2012), 8.

[2] Amir Levine and Rachel S. F. Heller, *Attached: The New Science of Adult Attachment and How It Can Help You Find — and Keep — Love* (TarcherPerigee, 2012), 113–14.

The simple truth is that we're hardwired for connection, to feel loved and like we belong. So the next time someone on an app asks you what you're looking for, even if it doesn't feel socially acceptable to reply, "an innately human sense of love and belonging," you can still recognize that, deep down, that may be the true answer.

And since we exist in a culture where deeper connection between queer men can feel rare, it's time we talked about some connection green flags. Let's explore what a deeper romantic connection might look like and, just as importantly, how to spot who is likely to be able to form one with you.

The connection pyramid

Earlier, we talked about Maslow's Hierarchy of Needs — a hierarchy of the biological, physical and emotional things we need to live a healthy, happy and, ideally, fulfilled life.

In this chapter, I'm going to propose a relationship hierarchy of needs that works in a similar way — the personal qualities the people in a relationship should have for the relationship to feel fulfilling on different levels.

I came up with it via a lot of late-night conversation and not a small amount of navel-gazing, and I've called it the **connection pyramid**, partly because it's shaped like a triangle, and partly to honor ancient Egyptians Niankhkhnum and Khnumhotep, history's first recorded same-sex couple.[3]

You can call it "The Holy Dorito of Connection" or "a not-ideally-shaped buttplug" if you like, but in any case, here's what it looks like:

---

[3] Well, probably. Historians disagree on whether the portrait in their tomb shows them kissing or just that they were brothers, even twins. Still, it seems most likely that this was an epic ancient queer love story. And I love that for them. See Harper-Hugo Darling, "Khnumhotep and Niankhkhnum," *Making Queer History* ◆ (March 18, 2017).

**Higher
Purpose
Traits**

Shared causes
Shared ambitions
Shared passions

Higher Connection Traits

Authenticity   Vulnerability
Shared values   Mutual empathy and respect

Higher Personal Traits

Reliability   Independence   Mutual support
Positivity and acceptance

Foundation Traits

Basic lifestyle compatibility   Basic communication skills
A commitment to growth   The ability to receive love

THE CONNECTION PYRAMID

The connection pyramid has four levels, and the upper levels build on the one below it. Let's talk about each level one at a time.

The lowest level is made up of the ***foundation traits*** — the basic personal qualities that any romantic relationship needs to function. They're personal traits that are necessary to make a relationship work — even if they're personal qualities that aren't always easy to take for granted.

Basic lifestyle compatibility

We covered chemistry and compatibility in detail earlier, but basic lifestyle compatibility just means that the way both of you live is conducive to building a life together. A lot of us care about finding someone we can write a cute love story with, but it's usually more important to find someone we can write a great life story with.

That might mean dating someone who either lives nearby or is prepared to deal with the distance. It might mean having weekly schedules that allow you to spend time together. And it definitely means being aligned on how you fit into each other's lives and what you fundamentally want from the relationship.

Like every aspect of compatibility, lifestyle compatibility often isn't that exciting to think about, but without it, it's hard to build a longer-term relationship with someone.

Basic communication skills

A lot of people have this hope that one day they'll find the one perfect person who just "gets" them, and they'll never have to explain anything or ask for anything again. But unfortunately, no real-life relationship ever has worked like that. To make any relationship work, we have to be able to say what's on our minds, gurl. We have to ask for what we need. We have to be able to talk about what we think and feel with our partners.

Without that skill, not only is it difficult to get to know someone authentically, it also becomes a massive pain to make decisions, from what you're going to do on a weekend to what kind of relationship you want to build together. Nobody, not even the people we know best, can read minds. So being in a relationship where communication is possible is essential.

A commitment to growth — individually and within the relationship

Two other common misconceptions about relationships are that they come to you prepackaged and fully formed, and that making any allowances or compromises for the relationship is a sign of incompatibility. But that's not how relationships work either.

Nobody couples up with the perfect person. Again, no partnership has 100% compatibility. And the way you deal with that is by having a willingness to keep learning about yourself, your needs, your partner, your partner's needs, and your relationship itself. That way, it — and both of you — can grow.

Like we talked about, happy relationships have conflict as much as unhappy relationships do. What makes happy relationships work is that everyone in them has the compassion, self-assurance and self-awareness to listen, to reflect on how they might be contributing to a conflict, and to try to do better next time. That's it. Being able to grow and adapt is far more important — and realistic — than getting everything right all the time, which isn't possible.

The ability to receive love

I know. You might be thinking, "Who on Lady Gaga's green earth would not want to feel loved?" But you might be surprised.

In short, people who avoid love often do it because they don't believe they deserve love. And so they tend to reject or dismiss other people's interest in them, and can reject it all the more strongly the more loving it is.

That's because though going through life thinking you don't deserve love is pretty miserable, it's often familiarly, even comfortably, miserable.[4] If you believe you don't deserve to feel loved, it tends to become part of your identity, and unfortunately, adjusting our self-image is difficult and even painful. (Often more painful than staying stuck feeling unlovable, as fucked up as that sounds.)

And because queer men face so much stigma and rejection — because it's easier for us than average to find evidence that we're unlovable or unworthy of love — plenty of us struggle with feelings of unworthiness and tend to push love, and the vulnerability necessary

---

4 Once again, Brené Brown probably says it best: "[In my research] there was only one variable that separated the people who have a strong sense of love and belonging and the people who really struggle for it. And that was, the people who have a strong sense of love and belonging believe they're worthy of love and belonging. That's it. They believe they're worthy." Brené Brown, "The power of vulnerability," *TED* ◆ on YouTube (January 3, 2011), 7:11–29.

to make love work, away.[5] But for a relationship to function, everyone in it has to feel fundamentally worthy of being loved. It's really difficult to build a loving environment with someone who doesn't believe they deserve to be in one.

Ultimately, these traits are the four fundamental relationship green flags. They form the basic foundation of a healthy and fulfilling relationship.

Still, as essential as that foundation is, most of us want more than the basics. So next let's talk about the traits that turn a functioning relationship into a loving one — *the higher personal traits*.

Reliability

Reliability is the foundation of authenticity — and isn't just about turning up at the right place at the right time.[6] More than anything, reliability is about making sure our words and actions align. A reliable person follows through on the things they say. They're able to make even the small day-to-day commitments that make a relationship work, that make their words and promises mean something, and that allow others to trust them and the things they say. A relationship without reliability quickly becomes a guessing game, and that's no fun for anyone.

Independence

Personal independence is important in relationships because, despite the advice you might have learned from internet memes and inspirational wall decals, a relationship is not supposed to "complete" you, and your partner is not your "other half." You're both supposed

---

[5] There's also evidence that other men showing interest in us tends to trigger our internalized homophobia, which makes us see both him and ourselves as less attractive. So that's another reason to keep chipping away at those negative internalized beliefs, hun. See Walt Odets, *Out of the Shadows: The Psychology of Gay Men's Lives* (Penguin, 2019), 23–24.

[6] Though that is important too, eternally late gays.

to come to the relationship as whole, complete, independent people, whose lives enhance each other's. But you're not supposed to depend on each other to feel fundamentally complete or valid.

Connection exists between people, so it can't really exist if two people act like they're one. Yes, in a healthy relationship there are compromises and sacrifices. But there are also boundaries. There are people whose lives are richer because they are together, but those people should also have independent lives within the relationship.

Mutual support

Speaking of which, mutual support, or interdependence, is another key relationship trait. Interdependence is when everyone in a relationship is fundamentally independent, but is also able to rely on and support each other when necessary.

As we touched on in the last chapter, that can be as simple as offering emotional support — saying things like "I hear you" or "I'm here for you." But it could also mean supporting someone through a difficult life transition such as a career change or bereavement. Or it could mean offering support when someone messes up or falls short — supporting their personal growth even when it's a messy or difficult process.

Positivity and acceptance

Someone's ability to be generally positive and accepting goes a long way toward making sure spending time with them is enjoyable. Just like it's difficult to love someone who doesn't believe they deserve to be loved, it's difficult to solve problems and even make decisions with somebody who doesn't believe there are solutions, or who's angry with the way the world is — or they are — all the time.

Positivity often looks like kindness, optimism or good humor. If someone is generally upbeat and confident about their ability to find solutions and/or defuse a tense situation with a well-timed dick joke, that usually makes it easier — and more fun — to be around them.

Acceptance is the ability to be open to the world as it is, to be ready to face new and unexpected situations, or to be open-minded about seeing the world from other people's perspectives. It's the foundation of empathy and understanding.

And without both positivity and acceptance, people tend to think in ways that are unhelpfully fixed and rigid, or that deny the reality of the world as it is, or they feel threatened when other people don't share their exact point of view. And generally, that kind of attitude is not that fun to be around.

Next come the **higher connection traits**, which build on the personal traits by allowing a relationship to go from feeling loving to also being fulfilling. They allow everyone in the relationship to form an especially trusting bond and feel like they belong. Relationships can absolutely exist without any of these traits, but for a real "fuck yes" relationship, you'll want at least some of them to be present.

Authenticity and vulnerability

We've talked about authenticity and vulnerability enough already that there isn't a lot else to add here. But as we've seen, it's hard to connect with someone who doesn't have a genuine sense of who they are. And as we've seen, the key to building trust and intimacy with someone isn't just spending time with them: it's being able to be vulnerable with them.

This means not only working on our own ability to be authentic and vulnerable, but also choosing partners who've done that too.

Shared values

Having plenty of common values with someone — shared beliefs about what's important in life — is usually the foundation of deeper compatibility.

People with shared values are likely to have similar or overlapping answers to questions like "What is worth fighting for in life?" or just "What is a fun way to spend a weekend?"

Part of this is practical: if you want a life that's as adventurous and hedonistic as possible but your partner thinks a good life is quieter and simpler, it's going to be hard to find things you can do together and both enjoy.

But this also runs deeper: the more similarly you both see the world, the easier it is to understand and support each other. If 100% romantic compatibility doesn't exist, part of getting to know someone is learning how to manage that incompatibility and how to love and support each other in the ways you're different. But that process becomes much easier if you start on third base — and already have plenty in common — instead of first.[7]

Mutual empathy and respect

Empathy and respect go beyond mutual support, and are about forming a deeper admiration for each other and the lives you're living — together and apart.

Empathy means understanding and sharing your partner's feelings, not just acknowledging them or sympathizing with them. And respect is about admiring who someone is, what they stand for, and what choices they've made in their life, even if some of those choices might be different from yours.

Both are key to forming deeper connections because they help everyone in a relationship to feel like it's a deep and genuine partnership, and not just a relationship of physical proximity.

And finally, we're at the apex, the glittering drag queen at the top of the tree — the **higher purpose traits**. These are qualities that help to make a relationship not just loving and fulfilling but meaningful — qualities that give a relationship and everyone in it a deeper sense of purpose.

---

[7] Yes, this is just a baseball metaphor, not a "baseball used as a metaphor for sex" metaphor. We're still in the (mostly) wholesome part of the book.

In this case, they're three concepts — ***shared causes***, ***shared ambitions*** and ***shared passions*** — that are basically three flavors of one big idea. In short, if you and your partner have some kind of bigger goal or purpose you can work toward together, your relationship is likely to bring you even more meaning and fulfillment.

To be clear, that goal doesn't have to be "stop war" or "solve world hunger." (Though if you want to try, please, go for it.) Two traditional shared projects a couple might work toward are building a home and raising children. But it could just as equally be doing charity work together, organizing community events together, creating something together or running a small business together.

Whatever the goal is, big or small, it's about having something you both believe in and can work toward together. The point is that having some bigger goal, beyond the relationship itself, can give a relationship a deeper sense of meaning and purpose.

Again, I'm not saying you should start every new app conversation with "Hey gurl, wanna take down the patriarchy together!?" But I am saying that once things start getting serious with someone, if you get the sense that building a home with them would be fun, or that you could be great parents together, or that having some shared projects would be fulfilling, that might just be the biggest green flag of all.

Again, people in healthy relationships should have somewhat independent lives. They won't share every goal, ambition or pastime. But by finding shared goals, by building something meaningful together, the connection and meaning in the relationship are likely to be amplified. Being in a relationship with someone you can or could have something to work toward together is likely to help you feel like you've found not just a great partner, but a soulmate.

So that's the connection pyramid — and those are the key qualities to look out for if you're interested in forming more meaningful, longer-term connections with other men. And to be clear, other than the four foundation traits, the connection pyramid is not about giving you a checklist of qualities you need to spot before starting a relationship with someone. It's about giving you a way of weighing up the potential in a relationship if building a deeper connection is important to you. It's about knowing what to look for beyond an initial spark or attraction if you want something more from a relationship than just a quick hit of validation.

Some are traits about people as individuals, the qualities you want a partner to have and (spoiler alert) that you'll need to develop too. Some are traits about compatibility, the ways two people might be well matched or well suited together. And crucially, none of them are about the way anyone looks, or the body anyone is in.

As much as it can feel like queer men just aren't cut out for commitment or deeper connections, it isn't true. At all. We have the capacity to love and be loved as much as anyone else. We're just not always as great at looking for love and connection as we might be. But by changing what we look for — and even the way we see — we change the things we're likely to find.

PART IV:
MAKING CONNECTIONS

Finding

It was the best of times. It was the worst of times. It was the age of options. It was not the age of choices. It was the age of meeting. It was not the age of connecting. It was the age of the motherfucking internet. And a lot of the time it was *exhausting*.

On one hand, most of us — something like two-thirds of same-sex couples — are meeting online now.[1] And it doesn't look like internet dating is going anywhere soon.

On the other hand, that statistic only represents people who *did* find a long-term relationship online. Plenty of the people who've spent years struggling to find what they want online will tell you a different story.

They'll say they spent a lot of time swiping, matching and chatting without getting very far. Or they'll say that online dating spaces make them feel overlooked and even disposable, or that the constant trying but coming up empty-handed has started to get really depressing.[2]

So what gives?

Why is online dating — clearly — such a struggle for some of us? And what can we do about it?

---

[1] Ella Braidwood, "Nearly two-thirds of same-sex couples meet online, says study," *PinkNews* ◆ (February 12, 2019).

[2] Catherine Pearson, "'A Decade of Fruitless Searching': The Toll of Dating App Burnout," *The New York Times* ◆ (August 31, 2022).

How to make better connections online

The big advantage of internet dating — especially when you're part of a minority community — is that it makes dating more convenient. The big disadvantage of internet dating is that dating isn't supposed to be convenient, exactly.

In one sense, it's great we're so well connected. It's great it's never been easier — or safer — to connect with literally thousands of other queer people, knowing we'll be a good fit for at least some of them.

In another, this ease and convenience is not helping. It can feel like internet dating has turned us more into consumable dating products than real people. It spoils us for choice, and not always in a good way.

We're so overwhelmed with options that it's easy to seize up and never give any of them a chance. If we do give someone a chance, all that choice means that the second a relationship hits its first speed bump, it's easy just to call it quits and start over with someone else. (Often just to repeat that same cycle next time.) And maybe worst of all, the illusion of infinite choice that we get online — that we're surrounded by thousands of great options — isn't helpful. Connecting with well-matched, high-compatibility partners is still rare. Attraction may be common, but true connection definitely isn't.

It's not that dating is supposed to be inconvenient. It's supposed to be fun and exciting. But the convenience of online dating can make it feel like all we have to do is sign up, upload a couple of pictures and our basic stats, and then wait for the perfect partner to come our way. But that's not how any of this works, or has ever worked. As we've seen, relationships take effort. In fact, the effort, intention and consistency it takes to build a relationship are kind of the whole point — they're how you show you're genuinely interested in someone.

Put it this way: IKEA is also about convenience. IKEA is also about doing things in new, fun and modern ways. But crucially, the good folks at IKEA made sure their flatpacks come with instructions. You're never left to assemble your Kukhål or Rumpaklaff just by trial and error. And maybe it's about time we had one of those white pamphlets for online dating too.

Here's what it might include.

We are not our profiles

I don't know how else to explain this, but the internet is *not real.* The duck emoji is the same size as the house emoji. A lot of people in real life look kind of different from how they do in photos. Even with the best intentions, nobody can fully capture who they are in an online profile.

Throw in a bit of a need for validation and a touch of male competitiveness, and suddenly every corner of the internet where you find queer men can feel kind of performative. Our dating profiles become highly curated and partly fictionalized snapshots of who we really are. And maybe that's inevitable, given that internet dating essentially makes us compete for matches with thousands of other people. We're incentivized to show off the best possible version of ourselves, even if those versions are people we can't always measure up to in person.

That also often sets us up for disappointment when we meet new people. It's easy to start with an idealized impression of who someone is, then when the in-person reality of who they actually are hits, it can feel surprisingly discouraging.

What's more, research shows that we're actually really terrible at judging how well we'll get on with someone from an online dating profile.[3] One reason is that a lot of the connection traits we talked about in the last chapter — like how open-minded someone is, or how vulnerable they're prepared to be — are difficult to pick up on just from a dating profile. It's also hard to tell what kind of chemistry you'll have with someone until you meet face to face.

---

[3] Amanda Gardner, "Psychologists highlight pitfalls of online dating," *CNN Health* ♦ (February 6, 2012).

That means it's easy to get excited about the idea of someone online, then end up low-key crushed when you meet in person and there's little real-life connection.

But what's more annoying is that the opposite is also true: you've probably rejected plenty of people online that you'd have really hit it off with in person. (I've definitely met tons of people in real life I've really clicked with that I probably wouldn't have pursued online.)

To be clear, it's not that internet dating as an entire concept is dumb, or that Tinder was sent here by Satan himself to fill us full of false hope. The apps can be great tools for making great connections. We just have to make sure we don't see online dating as some kind of magic wand that does everything for us. Really, it's just a matching service, the online equivalent of a friend saying, "Hey, I know someone you might like. Should I introduce you guys?"

That means that a lot of the time, a great first step in online dating is actually to *lower* our expectations about what it can do. (We'll talk about some of the implications of that later.) While we have to weigh potential matches up via what's on their profile — because that's all the information we have — it's good to remember we're doing that, at best, half-blind. Because at best, our profiles are just snapshots, teasers, the pre-movie trailers, of who we really are.

Take things offline sooner rather than later — unless you're just looking for pen pals

If the world of online profiles is basically a cute but fake fantasyland — like Disney World, only with more shirtless torsos — you'll want to be strategic about the amount of time you spend there.

Specifically, since it's hard to tell from someone's profile how you'll vibe with them in real life, it's a good idea to meet them in person to find that out sooner rather than later. (Unless, of course, you're only looking for conversation.)

Yes, asking to meet someone too soon is definitely a thing. If you ask before they've had chance to get a decent impression of you, they're more likely to say no, and your invitation might even come across as desperate or pressuring. And you obviously want to chat with someone long enough to be sure you trust them and that they're who they say they are.

But if you often find yourself in match purgatory, wondering, "Do any of these hoes even want to meet anyone!?" it can help to be more intentional about asking people to hang out once you've had chance to get to know them a little.

Sure, not everyone you ask is going to say yes. Sure, there is value in finding pen pals if that's what you want. But if your goal is to make real-life connections, then stay focused on that. Once you're ready, shoot your shot. Say something like "It's been really fun chatting. Do you want to continue this conversation over a drink sometime?"

That way, you find out who is interested in taking things further, and who you can stop putting effort into pursuing. Again, you're trying to use online dating as a matching service, and trying to stay focused on moving to the next stage — meeting in person — as soon as possible. That's a major way to reduce dating app frustration.

Focus on quality over quantity

Again, the best but also the worst thing about online dating is that it gives us a *lot* of options. That becomes a trap when it leads to lots of superficial connections when we'd really rather find a few meaningful connections. (Or even just one.)

The danger of too many options is that it can be overwhelming. This is the paradox of choice, the fact that having too many options usually just makes us seize up and avoid taking action. All this choice also seduces us into thinking that maybe the perfect person is out there, if only we keep swiping long enough. So we end up turning down tons of great matches thinking it's worth holding out for something much better — but usually it isn't.

I'm going to avoid putting on an aluminum foil hat and going on about how the dating apps are financially incentivized to keep us swiping. They make money when we use the app, not when they give us what we're looking for, after all.[4] But the bottom line is that if we let them, the apps encourage us to engage in lots of temporary, more shallow connections, instead of focusing on a few more meaningful ones.

The simple truth that underpins "fuck yes or no" is that genuinely great matches are rare. You are not for everyone and everyone is not for you. There are plenty of people you could build a fulfilling relationship with, but there aren't millions of them.

That means that unless you're new to dating or just want to date around to get more experience, it's not a great strategy to match with everyone, or say yes to a real-life date with everyone. The way to use all the choice we have to your advantage is to whittle down your options to the matches you think you're most likely to click with.[5]

The key is to be more intentional about who you connect with. Try to focus on a few, more promising matches and not just scattergunning your way through all the profiles hoping for the best. If it's an app where anyone can just message anyone without matching, don't feel bad about turning down people who aren't a good fit for you. And importantly, resist the urge to keep swiping when you're bored or waiting for someone to reply. Otherwise you risk spreading your energy and attention among so many people it gets hard to follow through with anyone properly.

Yes, if it's difficult to judge three-dimensional people from two-dimensional profiles, we're never going to be able to narrow down our options to a few great matches perfectly. But if you're looking for long-term connections, you want to focus on pursuing a few promising

---

[4] Still, it'd be fascinating to see a dating app that made money only when it got its users actual results. I don't know, $5 for a second date, $25 for a cute weekend away, $100 for a marriage proposal? Maybe someone should get on that...?

[5] And by the way, if the app you're using has a matching algorithm, it may be the people that algorithm digs up for you, or it may not. See Emma Hughes, "It's 2021, why are dating app algorithms so bad?," *Wired* ◆ (June 27, 2021).

matches and to the point where either you both want to become something official, or at least one of you has realized it's not a match.

And this applies once you get offline too, by the way. We've talked about the myth of the "spark" before, how lots of us turn down promising connections if we don't instantly feel every amorous feeling we think we're supposed to on a first date.

So unless a first date is completely underwhelming — unless you come away thinking, "Oh, that really wasn't fun" — make it your policy to ask for a second. Try to take each promising connection to at least three dates before you decide whether you want to keep seeing them. It's really difficult to know that with confidence from one or even two meetups.

Look for "promising," don't filter for "perfect"

Even if it's hard to judge exactly how well you'll click with someone just from their profile, it's still smart to be intentional about how you decide who is worth a shot in real life.

Because we're overwhelmed with so many options online, it's easy to fall into a "no fault" rule for matching — to filter people by rejecting anyone who shows any hint they might not be for us. I'm not talking about major incompatibilities or red flags, I'm talking about "Urgh, not sure about that outfit," or "Oh, he's into [insert hobby or interest here], hard pass."

Being that hyper-selective — that picky — can feel good because it makes us feel in control, like we're effectively cutting down our options to the best matches. But if you make your criteria too specific, or focus on things that ultimately don't matter much, it's usually counterproductive.

OK, maybe in one photo he's wearing a jacket that doesn't really go with his shoes. But maybe basically every other thing about the relationship would be great, and maybe your fashion tips are exactly what he's been waiting for his whole life, sis. And OK, maybe he spends some of his time doing some hobby you don't care for. But maybe you'd still be able to have a great relationship together while occasionally, you know, doing things without each other.

The way you manage this is to shift your decision around matching or showing interest online away from "yay or nay" — or even "hot or not" — and start asking yourself who seems promising, who has potential, who seems worth a shot. Look for people you find physically attractive, sure, but also look for people who have a couple of interests in common with you, or who say they're looking for the same thing as you, or who just look intriguing to you. (We'll talk about what to put in your profile so others can do that with you in the next chapter.)

Because outside of clear deal-breakers — things that make it a definite "no" for you — you can't be sure who's a true "fuck yes" until you meet in person. So online, "fuck yes or no" isn't about deciding who would be a great partner. You don't have enough information for that. It's about deciding who is worth a shot in person, then seeing if they're interested in meeting you too.

It's a subtle shift, but it can make a big difference. It's about seeing first dates or hangouts not just as chances to verify what you've already concluded about someone from their profile, but to see how you actually interact in real life.

In other words, yeah, "suck it and see" really is a great principle to rely on in online dating. And as much as it's smart to be selective about who you decide to hang out with, you'll likely get better results if you look for promise, if you look for potential, rather than just filtering out matches based on a "no fault" rule.

Put yourself in the best environment to get what you want

I know, a lot of queer men think it's basically all the same people on all the dating apps, so the specific apps you use don't matter. But in practice, it often does.

Like, you *could* host your next birthday party in a garbage dump and technically it could be fun. But you probably wouldn't.

The thing about the apps — and dating environments in general — is that, in practice, some usually are better at facilitating some types of connections than others. We've touched on this before. And if an app's primary appeal is that you can filter potential matches by distance, sexual preferences and willingness to receive unsolicited nudes, that's probably going to be an environment that's better at facilitating quick hookups over more meaningful or long-lasting connections.

And even if that wasn't true, as humans we rely a lot on the social cues we pick up from the people already in an environment to decide what is "good" or "acceptable" behavior there. That's why we behave differently at a gay bar versus a church versus a nude beach (at least, most of us do). We tend to act in line with what other people are doing in those spaces.

The same is true in online spaces. Each dating app or environment comes with its own culture and customs, so while most of us might be on multiple apps, we're likely showing different sides of ourselves in different places. (We really do contain multitudes.)

Yes, some people do find love on hookup apps. The world is full of glorious possibility. But generally speaking, the environments that are best at facilitating longer-term connections are the ones that are best at encouraging authenticity and vulnerability. So apps that don't allow anonymous or fake profiles are a great place to start. And apps that encourage people to share more about themselves than just a few hot pictures and their Instagram handle are even better.

Of course, we have to be prepared to share ourselves more authentically on the apps as well. We have to be good at sharing our personalities and interests, communicating what we're looking for, and even showing that we're human and not perfect sometimes. (Again, more on that in the next chapter.) The apps can't do that for us. It's up to us. But we're much more likely to do it in an environment where other people are doing it too.

Be direct and be communicative

What's especially frustrating about using the apps is that people often aren't that communicative. They don't respond, they don't say what they mean, or they leave us guessing. And unfortunately, a lot of this just comes with the territory. Some people don't check the apps regularly. Some people do but don't take them that seriously. Lots of us are speaking to enough people that responding in depth to everyone ever would take more time and energy than we have. (Yes, "They don't respond" is often really "*We* don't respond.")

So, as we've talked about, if someone doesn't reply, it's usually best just to move on. Still, with a bit of effort, we can be better at this.

Make it a habit to invite promising matches to meet in person — and if they aren't interested, get used to responding, "No worries, good luck finding what you want." Get into the habit of telling other people kindly but directly if they want to meet but you don't. If you meet someone you think might be better as a friend — or a workout buddy or fuckbuddy or whatever — get used to telling them that too. It's also OK to be unsure or conflicted about what you want. But it's better to say that than lying or leading someone on.

Yes, being more communicative usually takes more effort, but that's another reason it's good to focus on quality over quantity in dating. It makes it easier for us to be more direct with each other, which gives us all an overall better experience online.

As frustrating as the apps can be sometimes, online dating is still a great way to meet new people. At least, it can be. They key is just being aware of the specific challenges that come with using the apps.

Because, in short, if we're not aware of those challenges, and we're not intentional about using the apps to get what we want, we're less likely to get it.

If we want to make better connections online, we really have to stop saying, "Do what you want with me, daddy," and say, "We're going this way, bitch" instead. If we want to use these online tools to start longer-term relationships, we can. We just have to use them more intentionally.

Offline connections are still a thing too

In some ways, the internet is one of the best things that has ever happened to queer dating and relationships. It's made it possible for all of us to log on to our little devices and connect with tons of other queer people easily and safely, and from absolutely anywhere. And that was a literal game-changer.

Still, as we've seen, the apps can often feel underwhelming. They have a habit of amplifying lots of the not-so-great things about our community — old favorites like our superficiality, our prejudices and internalized homophobia, not to mention our meanness and deep-rooted hang-ups about loving each other. They've even changed in-person queer culture to the point that while queer bars and clubs used to be go-to places to meet other queer people, plenty of us now go to them just to spend time with friends, and don't really see them as places to make new connections.

And sure, I get it. There's an ease and a comfort with the apps. That's the whole point. And if you live in a rural or conservative part of the world where queer in-person spaces don't really exist, they might be your only option.

But the apps have also taken over our lives so much that it's easy to forget there is an entire world beyond our screens — a real world, if you will — where you can also make new connections.

As it turns out, the offline world is an especially great place for making more authentic, more genuine connections. It's a place where it's much easier to focus on getting to know someone one-to-one, rather than splitting our attention between tons of people at once. It's a place where we only tend to meet people because we have something in common — a mutual friend, a hobby or interest, somewhere we like hanging out — which increases the chances you'll meet someone you're highly compatible with. And maybe best of all, it gives us a head start: we get to know a real person, not just a profile.

And even if all of that wasn't true, being open to making new connections offline as well as online will only increase your chances of meeting people you like.

So if you don't mind, I'd love to talk a bit about my favorite twenty-first century dating app. It's called "IRL." It's free to use. You don't even need to download it. It doesn't work all the time, but when it does, it often works great.

There are tons of great real-life spaces to connect with other queer people

When it comes to finding real-life spaces to connect with other queer men, the first places most of us think of are spaces like queer bars and clubs. And they can be decent places for meeting people.

But again, a lot of people in those spaces are more interested in hanging out with their friends than meeting new people. Plus, a loud bar or club centered around alcohol and/or sex often isn't always a great place for forming more substantial connections. And if going to bars or clubs really isn't your thing, then they might not be spaces you'll connect with people who are like you, either.

Still, whether queer bars and clubs are your thing or not, the good news is there are loads of other spaces to meet great people too.

Larger cities usually have queer groups or clubs for lots of different hobbies and interests, like queer sports teams, book clubs, choirs, game nights, dinner clubs and more. Some cities also have singles events for queer people, and there are travel companies that organize trips and retreats specifically for single queer men.

These are all great places, not just to make friends (though that matters too) but also to make potential romantic connections. And because they're environments that are centered around an interest or activity that you have in common — and not just partying — you'll likely have better odds of meeting people you can build a deeper connection with. You'll also have plenty to talk about when you do.

And if there isn't already a group for the thing you love to do, you could always start one. Try to find a group of queer people who share your interest and then get them together. Because again, being part of a group of people who have more in common than just "we all really like dicks!" is a great way to build deeper connections and community.

Personal connections are also great ways to connect with other queer people. Go to parties. Host parties. Invite a ton of your favorite people to dinner sometime so they can meet each other. Introduce queer friends to each other if they might click well. Talk to your friends about your dating preferences and see if they know anyone you should meet.

Maybe that all sounds obvious, but since so much queer dating is online now — and internalized or regular homophobia can encourage us to keep our romantic and friendship lives separate, especially with our straight friends — it's easy not to try to find these kinds of connections. And since we often have high compatibility with friends of friends, that's definitely a missed opportunity.

Whatever you do, the goal is to find or create opportunities to hang out with queer people that aren't online, and that aren't just about sex and/or alcohol. Focus on doing things that you enjoy, where you can be yourself, and see who that brings into your life, gurl.

Also: Speaking to someone you don't know doesn't have to be frightening

Yes, some people find it easier to meet new people than others. Some people have very real social anxiety. Queer people aren't always nice to each other and experiencing even a low-key rejection can hurt.

If social confidence is something you struggle with, there are lots of ways to find more of it.

One important thing to acknowledge — especially in the age of apps — is that if you see another person just existing, you, as another person who just happens to be existing, can just go up to them and say hi. Yes, it's more complicated than that, but at the same time it's not actually much more complicated than that.

The reason most of us get nervous about speaking to people we don't know is that we fear rejection. If you're used to basing your self-worth on what other people think about you, approaching someone you don't know, who may or may not be interested in talking to you, will feel like a big emotional risk.

But as usual, the better you get at not determining your self-worth from other people's opinions of you, the easier it is just to shrug it off if he doesn't want to talk, or if he already has a boyfriend, or if he responds with something weird or rude. And often, the more positive and more confident you are in approaching someone new, the more likely you are to get a positive reaction.

That said, there are also some important practical things to bear in mind to increase your chances of getting a positive reaction.

If in doubt, start with something chilled or low stakes. That way, they're not going to feel put off by you being too forward too soon, and you're not going to feel too disappointed if they don't engage the way you'd hoped.

"Hey, how's it going?" often works great.

"Hey, I'm Max. How do you know Tarek?" is great at a party where you have a friend in common.

At a bar, a warm and genuine "I love your jacket" or "I really like your hair" can work too.

If that feels like too much, you can lower the stakes even further by striking up a conversation over something more boring and transactional. "Are you next?" can work if you're waiting together at a bar. "Hey, is that table free?" might work in a café. Otherwise, a warm smile is a great low-stakes way of showing a basic level of interest in someone.[6]

---

[6] And yes, it sucks that this can still be a big issue, but keeping it low stakes is an especially good idea if you're not sure someone you want to talk to is queer. If it's worth a shot, start with something transactional and non-flirty, then see how he responds. You'll usually get a sense of whether he's interested — or at least that he's not going to flip out if it turns out he's straight.

From there you can gauge his response and act accordingly. If he seems interested — if he engages with your question, smiles back, or generally seems friendly — you can keep talking to him. If he sounds put out by you engaging with him or doesn't respond warmly, then you know and can move on.

And if he engages, that's when you can start to raise the stakes a bit more and say things that would feel too forward or direct to open with. Eventually, if he's shown enough interest, that's the time to go in with "Do you want to connect on Instagram?" or "It was really great to meet you. Do we get to hang out sometime?"

A lot of us worry about coming across as creepy or too forward, but the key to not being creepy or too forward is not so much about *what* you say but about *when*. It's about building a bit of a connection with someone and giving them a chance to trust you before you invite them to invest more time or effort in you.

In practice, this can get complicated by the fact that a lot of us are low-key terrified of connection, wary about love, and even a bit scared of each other. So it's important to remember that if someone responds negatively, it might have absolutely nothing to do with what you did or said, and might be more about him and his emotional baggage.

But staying open to these in-person, real-life connections can radically change the way you connect with other queer men. Lots of queer men in long-standing relationships and friendships met on a night out, on the subway, through a queer sports team, on vacation, at the gym, or just after one of them said hi in the supermarket. Not all of us meet online, and almost anywhere can turn out to be a great place to meet people if we stay open to it.

We Deserve Dating Tips Too

"Write a book about queer dating," they said.

"It'll be fun," they said.

"Just come up with some great tips — 'don't forget to floss!' and 'invite him on an ice-skating date!' — and throw in a couple of dick jokes. It'll be great!!" they said.

But how wrong every one of these imaginary people were.

Because as we've seen, the biggest barriers that stop queer men connecting more deeply have nothing to do with dental hygiene or date suggestions. (Or, I'm sad to say, dick jokes.)

They're about trauma, they're about a prison called *masculinité*, they're about finding authenticity and self-acceptance in a world that still sometimes loses its shit when two people of the same gender fall in love — and other, you know, light topics.

And yet, don't we deserve fun, practical dating tips too? Don't we deserve for dating to be fun too? Don't we get to think about "normal" dating things sometimes too?

Yes, we do.

We absolutely do.

So crack open the Dom Pérignon. Or pick up your fourth iced coffee of the day, if that's more your thing. And join me for a bit of Fun Dating Tips 101.

The secret to great conversation: Be generous

Human connection happens over human conversation. So while a lot of one-word replies and the occasional "yeah, you?" might land you a quick hookup, if you want to connect with someone more deeply, it's usually going to take a bit more effort.

But luckily, the art of great conversation really just comes down to one rule: be generous.

Take a generous interest in someone. Be curious about him. Ask him questions. Want to get to know him.

If he says he's a gaymer, ask him what he plays.

If he says he likes to travel, ask him about his next trip.

If he says he learned guitar as a kid, ask him if he still plays or why he stopped.

If he's shy and isn't sure what to say, ask him about his day, his weekend plans, what he loves to do most, what fills him with dread, what his plans are for the inevitable climate apocalypse, whatever.

Equally, be conversationally generous when you talk about your life. If he asks how your day was, give him more than "fine." Tell him what you've been up to, what was great about your day, what sucked about your day, what fills *you* with dread, how *you're* planning for any future apocalypse, whatever.

Of course, this applies equally online and off. But online, if there's one place it *especially* matters, it's starting a conversation.

So if you want someone's attention, do not, do not, DO NOT just open with "hey" or "hi." If you want someone to reply, definitely do not, do not, DO NOT send just a wave or heart emoji. Ask him about something specific in his profile. Pay him a compliment. Ask him how his day is going. Do literally anything that shows you're interested in him beyond the absolute minimum level of effort.

Yes, "hi" often works great in real life, where people are more likely to engage with you because you're right there in front of them. And I know, lots of us are so jaded with online dating we're afraid of making an effort. But if you're putting in minimal effort and expecting a lot of effort from him in return, then gurl, you probably shouldn't be too surprised if you don't get it.

Whether it's at the start of a conversation or in the middle of one, good conversation is about giving. It's about giving each other cues to bounce off and connect over. Sure, you might not know a lot about what he wants to talk about. Sure, nobody's an expert on everything. So ask him about it. And if you're ready to build a deeper connection with someone, show you care about him enough that if something is interesting to him, you want to know a bit about it too. (If you care about someone, you care about the things they care about too, right?)

Being generous in conversation also means listening more. It's often said you have one mouth and two ears because you should spend twice as much time listening as you do talking. And that's a nice idea, though evolution doesn't quite work like that, Becky.[1]

Still, even if science points were not made, dating points were. One-sided conversations suck. One-sided conversations aren't fun. One of the most important ways you can show you're interested in someone is listening to them. As we've talked about, conversations are often about "bids" — tiny attempts to feel heard and valued by the people we care about — so listening shows someone you care.

How to date more confidently

Dating anxiety is real. It's normal to feel a bit nervous when meeting someone new. It's normal to wonder what they'll think about how we look, how we're dressed, the way we talk or the things we have to say.

So some level of dating anxiety is just part of putting yourself out there and making new connections. But if it's stopping you from

---

[1] You have two ears so you can tell what direction a sound is coming from, just like you have two eyes so you can judge depth and distance. Yes, I am very fun at parties.

242 Boys Who Like Boys

meeting new people, that's often a good time to question whether you're getting too hung up on others' opinions. Because what if a bad or lukewarm response from someone on a date is just a sign that you're probably not a match? And what if "Do I like *them*?" and "Can this person give me what I need from a relationship?" are better questions to ask than just "Will they like me?" when it comes to dating?

Confidence comes from authenticity, and a big part of authenticity is accepting yourself as you are and your needs as they are. That also means accepting that some people just won't like you as you are, or be able to fulfill your needs as they are.

Plus, as we've talked about, more meaningful human connection only happens when we're prepared to share the things about ourselves that aren't perfect or that we're scared might make people reject us. Because the uncomfortable truth is, that kind of authenticity and vulnerability ultimately *will* reveal fundamental incompatibilities and cause some people to misunderstand or dislike us. But it will also help us to connect with the people who are right for us.

And that means the art of dating more confidently is pretty simple: care more about your opinion of yourself than his opinion of you.

Turn up to a date focusing more on figuring out whether he's a good fit for you than obsessing over the possibility you might not be a good fit for him.

Again, being authentic does not mean giving zero fucks about everyone else's opinion to prove a point. But when you can disagree with someone respectfully but confidently, that doesn't just boost your self-esteem because it sends a signal that you value your own perspective and opinions, it's often really attractive to others too.

Because sure, visible abs are hot, but visible confidence is even hotter. (At least, it is to other self-confident men ready to date you seriously.)

So bring all the self-assurance and authenticity you can to a date. Get used to caring more about your view of yourself than anyone else's on a date. Accept that some people you date will disagree with you or even dislike you — and that's fine. Learn to see a bad date as a sign of incompatibility and not a sign that you're an unlovable fuckup who's probably going to die alone. Because the more you do all of those things, the faster and more deeply you'll connect with the people who are meant for you.

The first few dates you have with someone are ultimately just tryouts: a chance to find out whether you like each other, whether you're a good fit for each other, and whether you want to see each other again. And if it isn't all of those things, well, now you know, and you can both try again with someone else some other time.

And speaking of confidence, one classic sign of self-confidence in dating is the ability to take a compliment. So learn to take them — or at least, learn to stop putting yourself down unnecessarily.

If you need to use your phone to calculate a tip, resist the urge to laugh it off by saying "I'm such a dumb bitch!!"

You might have some body image issues (many queer men do), but anytime you take your shirt off, resist the urge to say how out of shape you feel since you haven't been to the gym in at least twenty minutes.

I know. It's a defense mechanism. If you bring up all of your imperfections first, you're in control. He can't use them against you. But defense mechanisms are rarely attractive, because they're usually about avoiding vulnerability.

It's OK to have insecurities. Everybody does. What makes all the difference is the way you handle them. Opening up about your insecurities and imperfections once you've gotten to know someone a little is a great way to show vulnerability and build more meaningful connections. But opening up too soon, before trust has had time to develop, can feel more like a desperate plea for validation than a genuine bid for connection. It often comes across as inauthentic, and therefore creates a barrier to connection, because it suggests you base your self-worth on someone else's opinion of you.

So learn to answer a genuine compliment with a "thank you," and nothing else. Resist the urge to make announcements about the things you've single-handedly decided are wrong with you.[2] Try to focus on the ways you genuinely think you are great, and the great things you would bring to a relationship with someone.

Sow a little chaos by giving him genuine compliments too. Look for things in him that are worth complimenting: maybe his smile or good looks, but especially his kindness, his positive outlook, his confidence, his open-mindedness, his authenticity.

It takes vulnerability to give and receive genuine compliments, but doing a bit of both is a powerful way to build confidence — yours *and* his. So use that power wisely.

How to craft the ideal dating profile for connection

Yes, we are not our profiles. Yes, it's impossible to capture a real three-dimensional person on a two-dimensional profile. But also yes, there is an art to crafting the kind of profile that's most likely to attract what you want.

Probably the most common mistake when it comes to online dating is trying to get the maximum possible matches or connections. But as we've talked about, your ultimate goal is not quantity, it's quality. You want high-compatibility matches, not all the matches you can possibly collect.

This means accepting that it's OK — actually, it's great — to craft a profile that might put some people off. It's more important to say, "I prefer quiet nights in than crazy nights out" if that authentically represents who you are — and therefore who a potential match will be dating — than just focusing on looking as cute and fun as possible.

Yes, lots of us do it. It feels safer to focus on looking cute and fun than to share any part of ourselves that could get us rejected. But

---

[2] Sometimes when we're fearful that someone will use our insecurities or imperfections against us, it's just that — fear. Still, your regular reminder that if someone you're dating starts using your insecurities to try to make you feel bad, he's definitely not for you. (And arguably not for anyone just yet.)

that's another subtle form of manipulation. It stops potential matches from figuring out whether it's a "fuck yes" or "no" for them. And by stopping potential matches from being able to reject us when it's a clear "no" from them because of low compatibility, we end up wasting our time and theirs.

So yes, try to choose photos that share snapshots of different parts of your life — like your hobbies, your social life, your family life, even parts of your work life if what you do is important to you. You don't need professional-quality photos to stand out, but — since it's not obvious to everyone — make sure your photos are well lit, that at least a few show your face, and that you don't have so many group pictures people have to guess which one is you.

But where you really prime potential matches for connection is in the parts of a dating profile that are about who you are — not just how you look. Sometimes that's the "About me" section and sometimes, on apps like Hinge, it's where you answer prompts or questions designed to get potential matches talking to you.

Again, it can feel weird or awkward to share personal things with potentially hundreds of strangers. And again, there are limits. The goal is not to share every detail of your personal trauma on your profile. But when you start to share some specifics about who you are and what you love — "On my fourth half-marathon and counting," "Never one to turn down a game night," "Kind and emotionally available and hope you are too" — you give the people who might like the sound of that the chance to respond positively to it.

You'll come across as more approachable if you express yourself as warmly and positively as you can. "Last-minute trips are my jam" is better than "Staying at home is for losers!!" And if you're not sure what to share, maybe ask a few friends to tell you five things about you that the right partner for you might just love.

And importantly — don't rush this part of the process. Most of us sign up to the apps eager to get swiping and meeting people, but sharing more about yourself than three emojis and your Instagram handle is *essential*. It's always worth taking the time to make sure your profile shows you off in the best light, and is specific enough it gives potential matches some great conversation starters. ("I love spontaneous trips too! Where did you go last?")

Finally, it always helps to say a little bit about what you're open to or looking for — partly as a conversation starter and partly to help filter out anyone who definitely isn't open to the same things as you.

If you want something longer-term, great, say that.

If it's just sex, great, say that.

If you're open to getting to know people and seeing where things lead, great, say that.

If you're not sure what you want right now, great, say that too.

And yep, I'm firmly in the camp of being open about the basics of your sexual preferences right from the start. I understand why some people are hesitant to do that — we want to be seen as more than just a sexual category, or might feel embarrassed about broadcasting that to anyone who swipes by. But if it's a potential deal-breaker for you, I think it's better to figure that out as soon as possible.

If it makes you feel better about it, try to find a fun or personal way of sharing that information. In one profile I had, I included the phrase "Sex is like the seventh most important thing to me in a relationship, but since it is important, I'm mostly [arrow emojis]." (No, I'm not going to clarify which ones specifically in this book.)

It was a fun way of sharing that information — so it could filter out anyone my preferences made me incompatible with — while being a great conversation starter about the things that are more important to me. (Things like connection, respect, kindness and vulnerability, if you're asking. I'm happy to be specific about those here.)

As with any kind of authenticity, learning to share yourself more genuinely online is a process, not a single lightbulb moment. You'll try things out, see what people respond well to, and tweak things they don't. But as you get better at sharing who you are, you'll start to see the matches you attract — and your confidence at starting and holding a conversation with them — drastically improve.

How to look — and feel — great

On one hand, a lot of queer men have a complicated relationship with self-improvement. (We'll talk about this properly in the next chapter.) Whether it's about our bodies, dress sense, confidence, conversation skills, or whatever, we have a habit of never feeling enough. So obsessing over self-improvement forever is definitely not it, sis.

And on the other, there's definitely a lot of truth to the saying, "If you want to attract a high-quality partner, you have to be a high-quality partner." If you want to up your dating game, or just look and feel better when it comes to dating, a little self-improvement can go a long way.

Presenting yourself well is a great way of showing that you value yourself. It's a marker of high self-esteem and high standards of self-care. And as much as we shouldn't judge a book by its cover, in case you hadn't noticed, bitch, most of us do. In a world with more dating options than we could ever have time to explore, presenting a good first impression is important for grabbing people's attention.

So yes, it pays to pays to take your health and fitness seriously — for you and your body first, and for everyone else second. It pays to make regular exercise part of your routine, whether that's working out, swimming, yoga, joining a sports team or gym class, tennis, cycling, running, whatever.

Science says, at a minimum, two things matter with exercise. The first is getting at least thirty minutes of moderate-intensity aerobic activity five times a week. (That includes brisk walking, so walking at the speed most queer men do definitely counts.) The second is getting in some kind of resistance or muscle-strength training at least twice a week, like a gym workout, bodyweight exercises, or yoga. That's enough to improve your energy levels, raise your mood and keep you healthy.[3]

---

[3] See "How much physical activity do adults need?," *cdc.gov* ◆ (June 2, 2022).

If you want to improve your physical fitness level, it's fine — great, even — to get started with small steps. Focus on types of exercise you like, and as you begin to build a routine, that'll make it easier to stick with it.

Your diet matters too, but diet plans are overrated. A lot of people who go on diet plans end up going back to their old habits once the plan is over. It's much better to make small, incremental changes to your diet that are likely to last.

Despite what every expensive diet plan you can buy on the internet might want you to believe, the basics are pretty simple. If you want to lose weight, get used to eating less, and cutting out random snacking on unhealthy foods especially. If you're trying to bulk up, you'll need to combine a weightlifting plan with eating more, while sticking with quality, unprocessed foods. In either case, it's worth finding specific help and support with your particular goals, whether that's with a professional trainer or dietitian, or via all the free information there is online.

But whether you have specific weight goals or not, there is one general rule that makes all the difference in nutrition: the more natural and the less processed a meal is, the better it is for you.[4]

Again, it's about building habits. It doesn't mean you can't eat any processed food ever. It doesn't mean depriving yourself of every food you enjoy. But it does mean that chicken fillets are better for you than frozen chicken nuggets, a tray of oven-roasted vegetables is better for you than a deep-dish pizza, and low-sugar soda and natural juices — or even just water — are better for you than lots of high-sugar soda.

We're obviously just scratching the surface here, but healthy eating and healthy living are two of the most important forms of self-care there are. They'll give you more energy, more motivation, better skin, a healthier glow, and probably make you better at sex too.

---

[4] Jillian Kubala, "Healthy Food vs. Highly Processed Food: What to Know," *Healthline* ◆ (March 8, 2023).

What you wear and personal grooming matter too. How we dress is one way to express ourselves and show other people how we want them to see us. That doesn't mean you have to wear outrageous, attention-grabbing outfits all the time, or spend a fortune on clothes. It just means figuring out the styles, brands, and fits that look best for your body type. It means learning to craft an overall vibe or feel in a look — preppy or edgy or plain or loud or wholesome or slutty or formal or whatever. It means creating the looks that suit you or that you just feel yourself in.

Yes, floss regularly. Use mouthwash. Electric toothbrushes are better than manual ones. Turn up to dates showered and smelling fresh if you can, unless you know you arriving sweaty is his kink. (As I've discovered a couple of times, it's definitely not mine.) Keep your hair well groomed. Yes, in all the different places. Bushy armpit hair is usually not the lewk of the century, and staying trim down there usually shows off your assets better. You can get it waxed or even lasered off, but a decent body hair trimmer also works a treat.

Use moisturizer. Wear SPF anytime you'll be exposed to UV rays. You don't need to spend a fortune on skin products, but getting the basics covered will help keep your skin healthy, especially as you age.

And last but definitely not least — get some sleep. I know you're busy. But quality sleep is not negotiable. Most adults need seven to nine hours a night to function properly.[5] Anything less builds up a "sleep debt" that'll catch up with you eventually. An evening routine to wind down before bed is a good idea. A "no screen time an hour before bed" policy is a great idea.

Again, the goal is not to obsess over self-improvement so much that you never feel ready or worthy of sharing yourself with other people. But presenting yourself well and looking after your body are essential parts of building confidence in dating, and will help encourage other confident people to want to spend time with you too.

---

[5] Eric Suni, "How Much Sleep Do We Really Need?," *Sleep Foundation* ◆ (May 9, 2023).

Dating should be an adventure

Yes, coffee, bar and dinner dates are the workhorses of dating. They're reliable, safe, low-pressure environments to get to know someone. But not all of us were born to ride workhorses. Sometimes it's fun to ride a unicorn. Or whatever.

Making the effort to suggest a more unusual date idea is a great way to show you're definitely interested in someone. Mixing things up by inviting them to do something more adventurous can be a great way to make getting to know someone more fun. Plus, open-minded and adventurous people are attractive, right?

So try a beach date, or a hiking date, or a day trip date, or a dance class date. Suggest a cooking class date, or a comedy club date, or an ice-skating date (there, I said it), or a museum date, or a board game date, or a video game date, or a stargazing date.

Naturally, it's great if you can come up with something you think you'll both enjoy. And you're often right to save the more adventurous ideas for a second or third date. But once you've gotten to know each other beyond a basic level, a less obvious type of date is a great way to give yourselves something different or exciting to bond over.

Some of my most fun and memorable dates were more like mini-adventures: a drink and a walk on the beach, a trip to see his favorite spot in the city, dinner and a comedy show.

Yes, it can feel like a risk to invite someone to do something a little different. But fortune favors the brave, bestie. And that cute guy you like might just favor it too.

So try to enjoy the ride

Yes, queer dating sucks sometimes. Men are trash sometimes. Love is weird and messy and irrational most of the time — whether you're queer or not.

But damn, what a privilege to be able to play. What a thrill it is to live in a time when safe, public queer dating *is* more possible than ever. How lucky we are to have access to that arena — and each other.

You've heard of sports, right? Yes, that thing lots of straight people enjoy?[6] That thing people turn up to, not knowing whether their team is going to win or lose, sink or swim? That thing where people turn up anyway because the thrill is in turning up, in trying, in finding out, game after game after game.

Well, what if the same is true of dating?

What if you worry less about whether each date will turn out to be "the one" — because that isn't a thing — and just focus on enjoying getting to know new people?

What if you worry less about that dinner date that just went badly and focus on being glad you took a chance on a connection that looked promising, or that you learned something new about what you do and don't want in a partner?

What if you choose to see the funny side when you realize you have two exes in common, or you hooked up years ago but forgot about it, or you've already seen his butthole on Twitter?

What if the beauty of dating is that it can be messy and human and surprising?

Actually, what if the beauty of *life* is that it can be messy and human and surprising?

And what if the best way to navigate this beautiful, chaotic and sometimes excruciating life we get as boys who like boys is to try things out, avoid forcing anything, and see what naturally flows?

Sure, that doesn't suddenly make queer dating easy, or negate all the ways queer dating sucks and really shouldn't. That doesn't mean queer dating won't feel frustrating or hopeless sometimes.

But it does give you permission to enjoy queer dating for what it is, hate it for what it is, or just take it for what it is.

---

[6] Yes, once again *I* am being trash. Plenty of queer people love sports and if you are one of them, I love that for you.

Plus, it does make you a more fun, more human person to date. And that's something too.

Enough

A friend of mine once joked, "Maybe I'm pansexual because I keep dating lost boys who refuse to grow up." And, well, maybe you've been there too.

Lots of queer men do experience "Peter Pan syndrome." Plenty of us do seem to be stuck in eternal adolescence, or just seem to mature emotionally later in life compared to many straight men.[1]

There are likely a few different reasons for this. The big one is that yes, most of us can't openly start exploring (or even talking about) authentic romantic attraction and relationships as teenagers, like most straight kids do. As a result, important parts of us don't even begin to mature until we're older, once we're comfortable enough in who we are to pursue the kinds of relationships we truly want.[2]

But it's not just that. It's not helped by the way our emotional baggage tends to make our relationships more complicated and less stable, so coming out often feels like it's out of the frying pan into the fire. Then add the fact that almost none of us has easy access to healthy and bigotry-free support in building happy queer lives and

---

[1] I was surprised I couldn't find any research on this, especially since it's a regular theme throughout *The Velvet Rage*. For one gay man's take, see Lee Suckling, "Why do gay men act like teenagers?," *NZ Herald* ◆ (December 10, 2014).

[2] See, for example, Gabrielle Kassel, "Teenage Dream or Teenage Scream? Why LGBTQIA+ People Experience 2 Kinds of Adolescence," *Healthline* ◆ (September 7, 2021).

relationships — something that even very supportive straight parents usually can't give us — and, in a phrase, it's a hot mess, gurl.

As a result, it's not surprising that lots of us aren't ready to start building healthy and more meaningful relationships until we're well into our thirties, forties, or even beyond.

And before we continue, let me be fully clear about one thing: emotional maturity isn't about reaching "straight" milestones. There is nothing smart or mature about deciding maturity can only mean settling down in a committed relationship, having career goals and/or buying a home. Equally, there is nothing immature about being happy single, wearing string vests and high tops well into your forties, or — of great relief to me personally — delighting in the art of genital-based humor.

True emotional maturity is about two things. First, it's about taking care of ourselves, physically and emotionally, short-term and long-term. It's about understanding our needs and making choices that help us get them fulfilled. Second, it's about taking care of other people. It's about communicating with other people well, and being aware of the impact our actions have on others.

In short, emotionally mature people are good at building strong relationships because they're good at taking care of themselves *and* others, and balancing both sides when they conflict.

Emotionally immature people often struggle in relationships because they're either too good at behaving in ways that get them what they want but harm others, or so good at putting other people first that they harm themselves. And often, they can't recognize those patterns so they end up stuck repeating them.

Because that's basically the thing here: recognizing the ways we're harming ourselves and our relationships is often painful. It's often frightening, even threatening. And as we'll talk about, it involves the discomfort of facing up to who we really are — warts and all.

And since so many of us struggle to muster the authenticity and vulnerability to do that, our dating pool is full of men who have the emotional maturity you'd expect from a teenager. They might be very mature in some ways — they might have successful careers, their own home, excellent dental hygiene and plenty of friends — but when it comes to relationships, the space where their emotional maturity should be is just an empty void with a sign that says "Coming soon!"

Because, sure, let's go there. When our immaturity greatest hits surface, they often *are* behaviors you might expect from a teenager still trying to find their place in the world.

We sometimes care way too much about what other people think of us because we have such a poorly formed opinion of ourselves. Or we struggle to regulate our emotions and end up responding to them in ways that damage our relationships — by being gossipy, flaky or hot-tempered, by cutting people off when we don't get our way, or by never taking responsibility for our side in a disagreement.

We have a habit of using lies or manipulation to get what we want because we haven't learned any healthier ways of getting our needs met. Or we learn to value ourselves conditionally based on how we look, who we know, which brands we wear, or how we'd never even speak to anyone who isn't as cool as us because, fuck, that'd make us so uncool by association.

But as we've seen throughout this book, when we do those things it rarely leads to a fulfilling life — or a life of strong and fulfilling relationships. But it's usually the life we end up trapped in when we're unable or unwilling to grow up.

And unless our fear of never growing up becomes greater than our fear of the growing pains that come with growing up, we stay stuck. Without being ready to face that discomfort, it's hard to live more purposefully and become more than impulsive validation chasers.

To do that, we have to confront a paradox of personal growth that seems especially relevant to what it means to grow up as a queer man. Like most paradoxes, it's beautifully — if mind-fuckingly — simple.

Personal growth means recognizing where we want to be but aren't yet. It's hard to grow purposefully without knowing what your goal or destination is.

And yet, as contradictory as it seems, personal growth also means accepting, unconditionally, where we are and who we imperfectly are, so we can make an effective plan for moving closer to our goals.

That's because to recognize what we're not, we have to be able to accept what we're not. And it's because without that acceptance, there's a risk we'll never feel enough. We'll stare at the ceiling we want to reach, but because personal growth has no ceiling, when we get there we realize there's even further to go. So if we can't accept ourselves unconditionally, we end up only painfully aware of what we're not.

But that's the paradox.

Personal growth means recognizing that, yes, we could be more. But it also means recognizing that, on a fundamental level, we're also enough already — we're still valid as we imperfectly are.

It means holding both of those balls — yes, the metaphorical kind — in one hand at the same time. It means cupping both balls tenderly and lovingly, even if they seem to openly contradict each other, and one hangs slightly lower than the other. (Again, metaphorically.)

Because as queer men especially, we have a habit of focusing more on who we want to be, often as a way of compensating for the parts of ourselves we think are bad or inadequate. We get huge in the gym but think we need to be even buffer to feel happy. We become brilliant in our chosen careers but still feel like frauds or impostors. We even build great relationships — romantic and otherwise — and still can't escape the fear that there might be someone or something better out there if we keep looking.

As usual, part of this is living in a society where some people will never accept us as we are. But it's not just about being queer. Part of it is also the general culture of "never enough" we live in, where we're constantly absorbing the highlight reels of literally hundreds of people on social media and asking ourselves why we're not permanently on vacation while simultaneously nailing it at work, while living a perfect-looking life with our perfect-looking partner.

So that means it is a radical act — a radical choice — to say, "I'm enough." It's radical right now to decide, "Actually, I'm OK making do with less. Actually, I don't always need more."

And if we want to be happier, if we want to become more than lost boys who refuse to grow up, we have to be happier making do with less. A change of outlook isn't just helpful, it's mandatory.

I wish you could see that you are enough

This might sound weird, but come with me on a little thought experiment — some philosophical role play, if you're into that.

Imagine, for a second, a parallel world where homophobia just isn't a thing. Imagine we lived on an entire planet of people who were smart enough to be like "Ohh, homophobia is totally a social construct that harms a substantial proportion of the population! Maybe we should just not do that!!"

As a result, whether you're romantically or sexually straight or gay or queer or whatever, nobody really cares. Nobody has to deal with "coming out," people just pursue who they like and nobody bats an eyelid. Being not-straight doesn't mean you're treated differently, or told you're confused or unnatural or "deviant." Being cisgender-and-heterosexual or any kind of *not* cisgender-and-heterosexual are all seen as equally beautiful branches on the tree called "things human beings can naturally be."

It's a world where queer people experience life pretty much the same as not-queer people. We all live our lives authentically, without having to compromise on who we fundamentally are. We don't feel extra anxiety about rejection because we're not constantly scanning our surroundings for potential rejection or threats. We can approach someone we like but know nothing about without wondering whether they'll respond with a barrage of homophobic abuse.

Plus, because we don't fear constant rejection and invalidation from the societies we live in, we don't feel any need to compensate for that by having the hottest body, or the cutest friends, or the most followers online. In fact, rejection doesn't really even cross anyone's mind. We're content to do the things that matter to us, and be the people we want to be, without really thinking about it.

We can feel comfortable in our own skin — even when we're having a bad day, or we look like a bit of a mess. We can ride the wave of life knowing its ups and downs are just part of being human.

It's not that hard to image what that world looks like. But in that world — a world where being any kind of queer never gets more of a reaction than a shrug — what would it *feel* like?

Liberating? Peaceful? Scary? All of the above?

Think about it for a second.

Now zoom out and imagine observing yourself in that world, as someone who isn't you. What would you say that guy deserves? I'm not talking about fancy cars, expensive vacations or a rockin' body. How does that guy deserve to feel, just for being human?

Does he deserve to be happy — even if he's not perfect? Does he deserve to feel loved — even if he can't see every one of his abs? Does he deserve to feel like he's basically fine, and even worthy, exactly as he is?

Because as much as you might feel like I just dropped you in a New Age "Choose Love" seminar, this thought experiment with a hint of spiritual out-of-body experience is a genuinely valuable thing to try.

It's not that difficult to recognize how the straight-centric, cis-centric reality we live in suppresses and stifles us. But even if we understand that intellectually, it can be hard to see beyond this reality because it's all we've ever known. Like a fish that doesn't know it's in water, as long as a culture is invisible, it feels inevitable. It can take a mental quantum leap — like a fish jumping above the water's surface for the first time — to recognize that our reality is not inevitable. It's just one of the billions of cultural realities we could have ended up in.

But anyway, back to this parallel you in this parallel universe. How do we feel about this guy?

I'm going to push the boat out and say, yes, he does deserve to be happy — even if he makes mistakes sometimes.

I'm going to go out on a limb and say, yes, he does deserve to feel loved — whatever he physically looks like.

I'm going to resist the queer male urge to be sassy, snarky or subversive and say, genuinely, yes, he is fundamentally enough, exactly as he is. He deserves to exist in a way that brings him happiness and fulfillment, whoever he is, whatever he looks like, and whatever he has achieved in his life.

The simple truth at the heart of being human — queer or otherwise — is that we all deserve to feel fundamentally worthy by birth: worthy of existing, worthy of connection, and worthy of love. And as we've seen, literally the only factor that tends to determine whether we find love and connection or not is whether we think we're worthy of it.[3]

The baggage-free world I described probably isn't going to become our reality anytime soon. At least, probably not in my lifetime. But real or not, that is the world we deserve to get our self-esteem and self-acceptance from. It's the fictional world we deserve that reminds us of what we really deserve in this one.

Because we do deserve happiness.

We do deserve to feel loved.

We do deserve to feel like we belong.

We deserve not only *not* to be vilified for who we love and fuck, but to be celebrated for it.

We deserve to be celebrated for our diversity, resilience, creativity and independence.

---

[3] Let me quote Brené Brown one more time, because her summary is worth repeating: "The people who have a strong sense of love and belonging believe they're worthy of love and belonging. That's it. They believe they're worthy." Brené Brown, "The power of vulnerability," *TED* ◆ on YouTube (January 3, 2011), 7:11–29.

We deserve to be celebrated for our queerness, not shunned or feared because of it.

We deserve to see our queerness — and everything it makes us — as a superpower.

Periodt.

And we deserve all those things without conditions — whoever we are, whatever we look like, whatever mistakes we've made, and whatever exact brand of queer we are.

So despite what it can feel like, none of us needs to be or live a certain way to be valid either as human or as *any* kind of queer. We do not need to like drag shows. We do not need to be gym rats. We don't even need to stan Beyoncé. We do not need to live in a big city. We do not need to live in a "gay" neighborhood in a big city. We do not need to be having lots of sex. We don't even need to particularly like sex.

We can love baseball. We can be into heavy metal. We can call our close friends "buddy" and not "babe." We can be in any type of body. We can match literally all, literally none, or just some of the stereotypes — that both straight and queer people perpetuate — about what it means to be gay, queer or any kind of LGBTQ+.

Because again, one way our collective struggle with authenticity shows itself is the list of outrageously narrow expectations we decide to attach to "being gay" or "being queer." We then judge ourselves and others for falling short of those expectations, for being "too gay" or "too queer," or not being gay or queer enough, at least in the ways we were expecting. It's a prison of our own making.

And in turn, that perpetuates the trap of always wanting more, and specifically wondering whether, to feel loved, we're supposed to adapt ourselves to meet other people's expectations.

But until we step off the toxic, infinite carousel of just needing this or that to feel fundamentally valid, we never will. It's OK to want more, yes, but until we're good at accepting ourselves as we are — and all of the versions of ourselves we are and were — we'll struggle to feel fundamentally enough.

Because again, the only route to feeling enough in a world that's constantly telling us we need to be more is agonizingly simple: it's learning to be more comfortable with what we're not, and what we lack.

Feeling enough means recognizing what we don't have, who we aren't and maybe never will be, and thinking, "Bitch, that's fine" — and meaning it. Feeling enough is about finding more unconditional love for ourselves. It's learning to appreciate and accept ourselves as we are, whether we'd choose to be exactly like that or not.

That's harder than it should be when you're constantly bombarded with messaging that says we aren't enough, that we need to be more. But here's the simple, difficult truth: feeling enough is a choice.

Ultimately, we decide to feel enough.

We either choose to have values that help us and support or self-esteem, or we choose values that undermine it. We either look for evidence of our unworthiness — that we're not muscular enough, not fun enough, not outrageously queer enough, not extroverted enough, not-fucking-whatever enough — or we choose to accept we're worthy as we are.

And if it's our decision, we should choose what's good for us.

But I'm angry we can't all treat each other like we're enough

So that's it, right? The way to feel more comfortable in our own skin is basically unconditional love? It's working through society's stigma and shame and we'll come out the other side feeling much better?

Actually, not quite.

See, in 2020 some psychologists did a study to try to account for the increased mental health issues queer men experience. For a long time, the prevailing theory of why queer men suffer from higher rates of mental health issues like anxiety, depression and substance abuse

— and yes, self-harm and suicide — was, to put it one way, "straight people think being homo bad, so that make homo people miserable."[4] This is called minority stress theory. It's the idea that when a wider population treats a minority group as inferior or invalid based on some arbitrary, made-up prejudice, that unsurprisingly has a negative psychological effect on the people in that minority group. And as a theory, it goes a long way to account for the extra ways people in all kinds of minority communities, not just queer people, often struggle psychologically.

And yet, for queer people, minority stress didn't account for the whole picture. It was a factor, sure, but when the researchers did what researchers do — isolate and test different variables to see how they affect things — they realized that minority stress explained some but not all of the increased mental health issues queer men experience.

What the psychologists discovered was that queer men don't just struggle because of the way straight people treat us. We also struggle *because of the way we treat each other.*

As well as minority stress, we suffer from *intra*-minority stress. The call is coming from inside the house. The researchers proved that we can be our own worst enemies.

And that makes sense, because as important as self-acceptance and self-validation are, there are limits to what we can do alone. We *do* need some external validation, something to measure ourselves against, to reinforce our own positive self-image. That's part of being

---

[4] The original study is pretty dense, but there's a good summary in Naveen Kumar, "The Gay Community's Obsession With Status and Looks Has Huge Mental Health Costs," *them.* ♦ (April 7, 2020).

If you're feeling hardcore, the full study is John E. Pachankis, Kirsty A. Clark, Charles L. Burton, Jaclyn M. White Hughto, Richard Bränström and Danya E. Keene, "Sex, Status, Competition, and Exclusion: Intraminority Stress from Within the Gay Community and Gay and Bisexual Men's Mental Health," *Journal of Personality and Social Psychology* 119/3 ♦ (September 2020), 713–40.

social animals, of being wired for connection.[5] And as tempting as it can be to spend our entire lives as celibate hermits, if we want to form some kind of relationship with other people, we *do* need their basic acceptance and approval.

If we want someone to date, we need them to accept us. If we want someone to have sex with, we need them to accept us. (At least, if the sex isn't going to be super transactional.) If we want to feel part of a community of people who are like us, or just find like-minded friends, we need those people to accept us.

The idea that having high authenticity and self-acceptance means becoming some kind of rebel lone wolf who could not give two shits about anyone else or how his actions affect other people is not how it works. It's not how it works for other animals either. We tend to think of "survival of the fittest" as survival of the strongest and most ruthless, but even Charles Darwin was like, "Umm, that's not what I meant."[6] All over the animal kingdom, cooperation within a species is often far more important than competition in determining whether that species thrives.

And sure, for us, thriving is less about "not being eaten by lions" and more about "living grounded and fulfilled lives." But as a stigmatized minority, queer men need each other *especially* to help all of us reinforce our authenticity — and even validity — as we are.

What's unusual about homophobia and transphobia as forms of discrimination is that they're uniquely loaded with invalidation. As if

---

[5] See Hyeonjin Jeon and Seung-Hwan Lee, "From Neurons to Social Beings: Short Review of the Mirror Neuron System Research and Its Socio-Psychological and Psychiatric Implications," *Clinical Psychopharmacology and Neuroscience* 16/1 ◆ (February 2018), 18–31.

[6] The phrase "survival of the fittest" was coined by someone called Herbert Spencer, for starters. Daddy Darwin literally wrote, "Those communities which included the greatest number of the most sympathetic [i.e. community-minded] members would flourish best and rear the greatest number of offspring." See Christopher Kukk, "Survival of the Fittest Has Evolved: Try Survival of the Kindest," *BETTER by Today* ◆ (March 8, 2017).

creating a made-up reason to make us feel less than wasn't enough, homophobia and transphobia often also come with the implication that we're not really who we say we are, that we choose to be queer, or that it's "just a phase." (Racism, for example, is also obviously bad. But racism doesn't usually come with the implication that anyone's race is "a choice.")

So for us, feeling part of a community of other queer people is especially important in helping all of us live authentically and recognize our intrinsic value and worthiness, exactly as we are. We need other queer people to help us accept ourselves — including our queerness — and not feel like we have to change or hide who we fundamentally are.

And yet, collectively, we can be really mean to each other. We're prone to saying mean things to each other. We're prone to doing mean things to each other. We're prone to using other queer men for sex or companionship and not thinking twice about coldly dropping them when we've decided to move on. We have a bad habit of seizing on other queer men's imperfections or insecurities to make us feel better about our own.

That's how we helped build an environment where intraminority stress is common — where we feel invalidated by society as a whole and then pass that invalidation on to each other.

But as a community that constantly faces external discrimination, you'd think we'd have more compassion for each other. You'd think we'd have more understanding that other queer people's struggles are just like ours, and you'd think that understanding would encourage us to treat each other with more solidarity and respect since we're on the same (fabulous) team.

And yet, a lot of us don't. We call ourselves a community, but we often struggle to act like one.

And so, if we all want to get closer to feeling enough as we are, it's not just about saying affirmations to ourselves ten times in the mirror each morning. Because as important as all that inner work to find more authenticity and self-acceptance is in itself, the work only gets harder anytime the community we depend on for companionship, love and sex, not to mention solidarity and support, actively undermines it.[7]

You can't self-love your way out of a community where conditional acceptance is the norm. It's hard to see your own value if you're around people who won't give you the time of day if you're not at least a seven out of ten, whatever that means.[8] It's hard to self-validate when you face regular invalidation not just from straight people who don't know better (but should), but also from other queer people who really, *really* should.

That's the heartbreaking reality of why some of us are so wary around each other. It's a big part of why some of us end up thinking things like "I'm attracted to men, but I don't like men," and yes, "Men are trash." And it's a big part of why so many of us end up feeling lonely and distanced from other queer men.

Yes, the stakes really are that high. Every time our learned trashiness shows itself, we make our whole community suffer. We give each other more reasons to mistrust each other and keep other queer men at a distance. We give each other more reasons to be aloof and detached around each other instead of warm and open.

And I know, it's devastating to learn that we can't blame straight people for *all* of our problems. But we have to take responsibility for our part in this too.

---

[7] It's also interesting that a lot of our "go to" or most "sacred" spaces — including big queer events but also the app beginning with G whose name I told myself I wouldn't print in full in this book — seem to be places that bring out the worst in us. They're spaces we flock to hoping to find connection and community, but they can be spaces that bring out our worst competitiveness, cliquey-ness and meanness, and trigger our insecurities the most. For more on this, see Michael Hobbes, "Together Alone: The Epidemic of Gay Loneliness," *The Huffington Post* ◆ (March 2, 2017).

[8] I mean, regularly rating other men on a scale out of ten totally sounds like something a two would do. If you subscribe to that scale, obviously.

We have to be kinder to each other. We have to let ourselves — and each other — off the hook for being human and less than perfect. We have to see more value in being a better community, and supporting and celebrating each other, as we are.

If we don't, we just make it harder for any of us to feel enough.

The secret to feeling enough: Find your community

So there's the not exactly heartwarming news that one of the biggest barriers to queer men finding more happiness and fulfillment is — *checks notes* — ourselves.

But before you run off to a monastery or decide being a celibate hermit really is underrated, just hear me out. All is not lost.

Because, as easy as it is to conclude that all men are trash, it's just not true. There are plenty of kind and well-balanced queer men out there. There are plenty of queer men who do have a good handle on their baggage, who are supportive and understanding, and who are open to making new connections.

And as much as it can feel like most gay or queer men just aren't like you — for whatever reason — that's not true either. There are plenty of queer men you'll have plenty in common with, and who'll support you just as much in the ways you're different. There are plenty of queer men who will treat you like you matter, like their lives are better because you're in it — and whose lives will be enriched by you treating them in the same way.

As much as it can be hard to find great connections, it doesn't mean they aren't out there.

Part of the problem is that the internet age just is a disconnected era. We all exist in a moment in time when not only has the internet made positive in-person interactions rarer than they used to be, but people are also working longer hours for lower real wages, have less faith in our political systems, or are just committed to riding the wave of the super individualistic, "everyone for themselves" culture we somehow found ourselves in.[9]

That's true for everyone, queer or otherwise. But for us, of course, all the rejection and invalidation we experience, whether it's from straight people or each other, only tends to amplify that feeling of loneliness and disconnection.

Ultimately, the most effective fix not just for that sense of isolation and disconnection, but also our fears that we aren't enough, is finding community. The best antidote to the loneliness we feel and the best route to better self-acceptance is to value community more. It's to surround ourselves with people who see, understand and validate us as we are — and it's to be someone who does that for others too.

Lots of us look to build romantic relationships because we think having a great partner will help us feel less lonely and disconnected, and give us the authentic validation we need. (For our queerness, and otherwise.)

And yes, a healthy romantic relationship will give you all of those things.

But equally, it's worth remembering that healthy friendships — or just a healthy sense of community — can give us those things too. As the Authenticity Fairy might say, "Healthy validation is healthy validation, bitch! Get it where you cannn!!"

And no, don't panic. The rousing conclusion of this book about queer dating isn't "Love is a lie, gurl! Just make some new friends!!" But part of it is that if you want to feel happier and more fulfilled — especially anytime dating leaves you feeling drained or frustrated — it's easy to forget how well supportive friendships can meet our needs for love and belonging.

In short, it's east to think that finding a boyfriend is the game-changer we need, but finding like-minded people to spend time with,

---

[9] Will Tanner and James O'Shaughnessy, "An age of alienation: why we must end the dangerous decline in community life," *The New Statesman* ◆ (July 9, 2021).

who share a few of our interests, or just who treat us like we're valued, is important for our sense of fulfillment and belonging too.[10]

It's one of the most reliable ways to get the healthy validation we need, and improve our relationship not just with ourselves, but often with our queerness in general.

And that's why, even if there's lots of value in turning to women or straight men — also, dogs — for support and companionship, there are unique benefits to having other queer men as close friends. There's a lot to be gained from feeling connected to other queer men who understand the specific challenges that come with being a queer man so you can support each other when that's needed. As queer men, there's a lot of value in chosen family — even if you have a great relationship with your biological one.

What's more, having even a couple of strong queer friendships also gives you a great foundation for pursuing romantic connections. It means you'll have someone to turn to anytime a relationship breaks down. It means you'll have support and perspective from people who get what queer dating is like anytime a relationship leaves you feeling lost and confused. And if you're unlucky enough to experience a queer man being trash, you'll have friends who are living reminders that plenty of queer men aren't.

And I know, making queer friends in the era of disconnection often isn't easy. Not everyone lives in a large town or city where there are lots of queer people. Some of us do live in places with large queer communities, but everyone somehow seems to be so fucking busy all the time.

But like with any kind of relationship, great friendships rarely come about without effort and intention. Building better friendships begins with the intention to try.[11]

---

[10] Rob Ledonne, "I Thought I Didn't Need Gay Friends; I Was Wrong," *GQ* ◆ (June 27, 2019).

[11] Richard Reeves, "The friendship recession," *Big Think* ◆ on YouTube (March 31, 2023).

That can mean saying, "Hey, do you want to be friends?" after a date where you're not feeling a romantic connection, and seeing that as a win too. And if you're feeling lonely and isolated, it can mean focusing on building and maintaining strong friendships to ease your loneliness instead of just trying to fix a new hookup or first date.

In short, meaningful queer friendships are the underrated secret not just to dating better, but to fighting the loneliness and isolation many of us feel.

And for every queer man who fits the "mean gay" stereotype — or who is just a bit too obsessed with looks, money, or status — there are plenty of queer men who aren't like that. There are plenty of queer men with the most enviable quality of all: they're ready to help the people they're close to feel accepted and enough, as they are.

This is the kind of queer man we should aspire to be, and the kind we should want to have in our lives.

We can find community in lots of different ways. It can come from being part of a dating pool. It can even come from having a handful of fuckbuddies you can hit up. But if you want to feel loved, if you want to feel like you belong, and if you want to fight our culture of never enough, great queer friendships are often what matter most.

It Starts with Us

I wish I had easy answers. I wish there were easy answers. I wish it didn't feel like we've all been thrown, *Jumanji*-style, into a game we didn't consent to, where the difficulty is set too high, where it's one wrong move and *bam!* you're outrunning another horde of horny bears. (Though sure, you might be into that.)

The reason it's easy to feel hopeless about queer dating is that there's so much about it we can't control. We can't delete homophobia overnight. The worst parts of internet dating aren't going to go away soon. Trashy men have existed since the dawn of time — Judas, gurl, therapy would have helped — so that's probably not going to change either.

And yet, there is still reason to be hopeful.

Because what can make us hopeful, what does give us power, are the things we can control — namely, us.

We don't get to choose the cards we're dealt, but we do decide how to play them. We don't decide what's done to us, but we do decide how to respond. We can't and shouldn't have to take responsibility for the homophobia and stigma we face, but we can — and must — take responsibility for overcoming it and pursuing what matters to us.

In short, it starts with us.

Despite everything, it starts with us.

And despite everything, we often underestimate our power to make meaningful change within our communities.

As we've seen, we're all connected, and not just in some spiritual, conceptual sense. We are connected in a literal, "we rely on each other for relationships, sex and connection" sense. That means, as we've seen throughout this book, our day-to-day choices matter. The way we treat each other matters. Every choice we make has a ripple effect throughout our communities.

If I'm feeling so jaded with dating that I'm mean or flaky online, or if we meet and I spend the whole time acting tetchy and aloof, you're more likely to end up thinking, "Men really are trash" or just "Queer men don't really do dating." And that might make you feel justified in acting mean or flaky or tetchy and aloof next time, and so the great cycle continues.

If I'm feeling so jaded with dating that the only way I can get my needs met or connect with other queer men is through lots of transactional and emotionally detached sex, then I'm helping to reinforce the false belief that our sole value to each other is as sex objects.

One way or another, we have a habit of passing our emotional scars on to other queer men, like some kind of shitty circle of queer life that goes around and around forever.[1]

But again, that is a choice. Consciously or unconsciously, we choose how we act around other queer people. Consciously or unconsciously, we either choose to keep the shitty cycle cycling, or we choose to break it. Whether we realize it or not, we're always choosing to send out either a kind and compassionate ripple into our communities, or a mean and disconnecting one.

That is our power. Those are the choices we get to make.

---

[1] This isn't just a theory, by the way. Adult relationship experiences really can alter the fundamental beliefs we have about love and relationships — for better and worse. See Amir Levine and Rachel S. F. Heller, *Attached: The New Science of Adult Attachment and How It Can Help You Find — and Keep — Love* (TarcherPerigee, 2012), 140.

And if we want to become better at connecting with each other — and if we want to help create a better community — here are some ways we as individuals can do that.

Be kind

You've probably heard the saying, "Be kind! You never know what someone is going through." And wow, yes, points were made.

Except, if we're talking about other queer men, you do have a pretty good idea about what he's going through. You know he's facing some combination of a constant fear of stigma and rejection, an uphill battle to find his place in the world, a family that probably doesn't fully understand him, a cloud of semipermanent grief for everything homophobia has stolen from his life, plus a struggle to rely on even his own community to give him the basic social acceptance we all need. And yet you still might be thinking about treating him like shit. Fascinating!

But seriously: this is the key piece of the puzzle that lots of us seem to miss.

To over-repeat a point, being queer is hard. It's hard emotionally, psychologically, and practically. Most of us carry around a mental catalog of many of the shitty things queer men have said and done to us. We keep those emotional receipts. And yes, those experiences can make it harder for us to be kind and compassionate to each other. But they're also the reason we have to fight extra hard to be kinder and more compassionate with other queer people. We have a responsibility to heal our pain and insecurities so we don't pass them on to each other.

We have to learn to show a basic level of kindness and inclusion to all queer people, regardless of how much they're queer in exactly the same way we are, how attractive we think they are, and how much we might want to fuck them. We have to remember that there's a real, connection-seeking human on the other side of the app — even if we haven't met them face-to-face yet. We have to be unconditionally kind

— kind because it's good to be kind, not because of what it might get us in return — especially to other queer people.

It would be great if we could take for granted that we'd all at least treat each other with basic empathy and kindness. It would be great if we could all be warm and welcoming to each other just for having our queerness, our shared struggle, in common. Because that would be a game-changer.

Lean into vulnerability

One of the biggest reasons many queer men become emotionally cold and aloof is that we get hurt — by straight people and by other queer people — and respond by raising our guard. We stop taking emotional risks and build up this protective armor to stop us getting hurt again. And in some ways, that makes sense. But armor is heavy.

Emotional armor might protect us from pain, but it also stops us from connecting with other people. It stops us from expressing and sometimes even recognizing how we feel. It encourages us to be more judgmental, take fewer emotional risks, and even push great people away. Limiting ourselves emotionally might protect us from bad relationships, yes, but it also closes us off to good ones. It's also often part of the way we pass our pain and insecurities on to others.

The better option is to lean into vulnerability. The better option is to recognize that yes, protecting yourself emotionally is sometimes important and necessary, but if we work too hard to avoid all negative emotions or experiences it also limits our ability to experience joy, connection, and fulfillment.

In lots of ways, learning to be more vulnerable with the people we trust is the harder path. But it's the more emotionally rewarding one.

Relationships — queer and otherwise — hurt sometimes. They wound sometimes. So get used to practicing emotional first aid. Get used to taking time off, from dating, from life, from whatever, when you need it to heal. Get used to relying on friends or your wider circle to talk things through. Work with a therapist or counselor if that's an option for you. Get used to recognizing and processing how you feel so your difficult feelings don't keep causing emotional collateral damage to the other people in your life.

I understand the masculine urge to punch, fuck or just deny your way through your difficult emotions. I feel that urge too. But leaning into your difficult emotions with vulnerability takes a lot more strength. And it's much better for you.

Practice clear and direct communication

If I got a dollar for every queer connection that never really ended but just fizzled out in a hot sizzling cloud of "meh," I could be like twenty people's sugar daddy by now.

A lot of us aren't great about saying how we feel or what we want, and that's not entirely our fault. But it still hurts us.

If we want to form better relationships, we need to normalize pursuing the people we're interested in directly, without tricks or games. We need to normalize getting comfortable being rejected and rejecting others. We need to normalize being open and honest about where we're at with someone, and exactly what we do or don't want from a relationship. We need to normalize having important but difficult or risky conversations when they're necessary.

Relationships — any kind of relationships — don't work without clear communication. And considering we have more channels of communication than we've literally ever had in human history, we can be really bad at being communicative with each other.

We have the power to let him know how we feel.

We have the power to release each other from the pain of second-guessing or not knowing.

We have the power to tell each other what we want and need from our relationships.

And, perhaps most of all, we have the power to ask for clarity from someone when we need it.

But we have to see the value in clear and direct communication to use that power. (And since communication is something many of us struggle with in dating, I put together some clear communication templates that cover what to say in lots of common situations — like showing interest, turning down someone gracefully, asking someone for clarity — in an appendix at the back of the book.)

Shoot your shot

Yes, queer dating is hard. Yes, the odds aren't always great. Yes, you'll face plenty of rejection. But if you sit at home waiting for your ideal partner to slide into your DMs or knock on your front door, you're going to be waiting a long time, gurl. As the cliché goes, you miss 100% of the shots you don't take.

So send that risky text. Go out on a limb and tell him he's cute. Ask for that first date. If you enjoy it, ask for a second. Learn to see rejections as a good thing — as a sign you're trying, you're putting yourself out there.

When we become too afraid of rejection, we limit ourselves and our relationships. We tell ourselves it'll be a no before we actually find out for sure. Instead of letting other people reject us, we reject ourselves by never even trying.

A lot of queer men struggle with being assertive and proactive. Our rejection sensitivity discourages us from taking chances. The hopelessness most of us feel with dating from time to time encourages us to play it safe.

But it's hot when someone is proactive. It's hot when someone chases the things — and the relationships — they want. It's hot when someone is comfortable hearing no.

And sure, to the people who aren't interested in you, being proactive and direct won't mean much. But damn, when you find that person who is interested, he might just be blown away by your directness, your intentionality, your commitment to chasing what you want from life. He might just feel reassured you're chasing him because you like him, not just because he's there.

Then, when everything slots into place and it's that rare "fuck yes" from everyone, you'll be glad you learned to pursue the relationships you want with zero hesitation and zero shame.

Oh, and also: be sure it definitely is a rejection before you take it as one. Again, our rejection sensitivity can make us feel snubbed or pushed away even when that wasn't someone's intention.

Yes, lots of queer men struggle to speak their minds, and lots of us are wary and mistrusting around other queer people. But if someone tells you they don't want a relationship but they'd like to be friends, and you're open to that too, take what they say at face value. Ask them for clarity if you need it. But try to trust what they say, and don't interpret a no about one thing right now as that person rejecting you over everything forever.

Prioritize longer-term relationships too

Whether they're romantic relationships, friendships or something else, many of the relationships we have will be short-lived. People pass into and out of our lives all the time, and that's just a fact of life.

But as we've seen, our lives are usually richer when they include some longer-term relationships too. There are benefits we can only get from longer-term relationships: things like deeper connection, deeper understanding, deeper trust. If we never commit to anyone because we're afraid something better might come along, we lose out on the great things we get from getting to know someone well.

And as we've also seen, these kinds of relationships rarely happen by accident. It takes conscious effort and intention to build longer-term relationships.

That means, if you want to build longer-term relationships, you have to *keep* shooting your shot. You have to focus on getting to know a smaller number of people, instead of chasing every shiny, new person who comes along.

If you want to feel more connected and more fulfilled, you have to fight your need for instant validation, and fight the way the internet encourages us to prioritize quantity over quality. You have to resist the urge to make decisions based only on what might get you laid, and make more decisions based on what's most likely to help you feel connected and fulfilled in the long run.

That might mean cutting down on social media and hookup apps. It might mean cutting down on posting content if you're mostly doing it to get attention and validation from strangers.

It might mean focusing on finding acceptance and community from a smaller number of real-life people instead of lots of internet people you hardly know.[2]

It might mean pushing past a promising but not perfect first date so you can see how you feel by the third date, instead of just jumping back on the apps immediately and chasing someone else.[3]

There is a level of fulfillment we can only get from longer-term relationships. But we can't rely on longer-term relationships to happen on their own. We have to be intentional about pursuing them. We have to stick with them even when time exposes the ways they're not 100% perfect, because no relationship is.

If we want to be truly happy, we have to focus on what we want most, not just what we want now. If we want the benefits of stability and consistency, we have to *choose* stability and consistency.

Chase what's real, not what's perfect

The reassuring news is that relationships aren't perfect for anyone. Even for straight people. Even for people who put an ungodly amount of effort into making it look like their relationships are perfect on social media. Perfection, as we've seen, doesn't exist.

That said, we have to face the reality that queer relationships often do present unique challenges.

We might have to accept that some of us aren't ready for serious, long-term relationships until we're older than we might like to be. We might have to give a partner — and ourselves — extra grace while we

---

[2] Research shows we have to spend about 200 hours with someone to become close friends, and we only need *three to five* close friends to feel fulfilled. See Allie Volpe, "The case for fewer friends," *Vox* ♦ (June 6, 2022).

[3] Plus, because vulnerability and direct communication take effort, it's usually easier to build better relationships when you're focusing on a few meaningful connections instead of chasing lots of different people at once.

work through an emotionally triggering conflict or disagreement. We might have to ask for forgiveness from someone we've hurt, or give someone else a second chance if they've hurt us. We might have to tell our families we met our partner at a house party, not a threesome. (Which technically could be a type of house party, I guess.)

Part of the reason lots of us spend forever chasing new partners is because we succumb to the fantasy that the perfect, easy relationship — or perfectly sexy hookup — is out there, if we only swipe long and hard enough or send a "hey what's up?" to enough people.

And I get it. Facing the reality that queer life is shitty sometimes isn't fun. It's more fun — and really comforting — to imagine living in a fantasy world where things are easier for us.

But by chasing what seems perfect even though perfect doesn't exist, we actively reduce our chances of happiness. We chase people we idolize as perfect but who aren't interested in us. We get emotionally invested in relationships that look promising but can't realistically work. We waste time in a seductive fantasy instead of letting the world we actually live in offer us what it can.

We might go about it in different ways, but we're all basically trying to get a similar cocktail of very human needs met. And yet, again, a lot of us judge each other harshly for that. We think of other queer men as too hedonistic or slutty, or resent that someone is either too shamelessly queer or not shamelessly queer enough. We fall into the old trap of thinking, "This person is not queer in the exact same way that I am queer, and I am suspicious!" when, as long it's not hurting other people, there is no one right or wrong way to be queer.

It'd be great to live in a world where homophobia doesn't exist, where we all get to enjoy trouble-free lives surrounded by incredible people, and where everyone's asshole always smells like a tulip. But that is not the world we live in.

The world we live in is imperfect, not least for us. But it's better to choose being imperfectly happy than be perpetually unhappy because we can't accept our imperfect world as it imperfectly is. It's better to chase what's real if imperfectly fulfilling than what our minds — or social media feeds — make seem perfect but can't ever fulfill us because it doesn't exist.

Don't take the rough experiences personally

We've talked a lot about how we can treat each other better, and how we can avoid hurting each other unnecessarily. But the reality of all relationships is that they hurt sometimes. Yes, when it comes to relationships it's better to be in the arena than just watching on the sidelines, but if you're in the arena you're going to get knocked around and bruised sometimes.

And yes, plenty of queer men have put and keep putting in the work to overcome their emotional baggage, but inevitably some are further down that path than others. So for every "men are trash" moment you experience, you really shouldn't take it personally.

The simple truth is, a lot of queer men are so overwhelmed by the trauma that comes with being queer, while simultaneously being so anxious to find connection and community, that they're not fully aware of what they're thinking or doing, or the impact their actions have on other people. In fact, this emotional detachment causes some queer men to behave in ways that only reinforce their sense of loneliness and disconnection, and even in ways that actively push away the people they deeply long to connect with.[4]

An early relationship of mine ended after my ex asked for an open relationship but then got upset and shut down with me emotionally when he found out I'd met someone for a coffee. A few weeks later, I found out he'd been having sex with someone else at that time.

---

[4] "Emotional detachment of this kind is pervasive, Pachankis [the researcher whose work came up in the previous chapter] says, and many of the men he works with go years without recognizing that the things they're striving for — having a perfect body, doing more and better work than their colleagues, curating the ideal weeknight G____r hookup — are reinforcing their own fear of rejection." Michael Hobbes, "Together Alone: The Epidemic of Gay Loneliness," *The Huffington Post* ◆ (March 2, 2017).

When I confronted him about that ridiculous double standard, he was surprised and confused that he'd hurt me, told me how important I was to him and panicked about potentially losing me from his life. But he couldn't even confirm how long his relationships with me and the other guy had overlapped, which made me trust him even less.

Obviously, the double standard hurt. But what cut deepest was how confusing and contradictory his behavior was. The breach of trust — and the disconnection it created — left a significant scar.

At the time, I took it personally. I chose to see it as a sign that something I did meant I deserved to be treated like that. It took me a long time to accept that we are only responsible for our own behavior, not other people's. And when we're treated badly, it has nothing to do with our inherent worthiness.

With queer men, it's not as simple as just "men are trash." Queer men are wounded, and that makes us act like trash. It makes a lot of our relationships volatile, confusing, and outright wounding. To build and sustain a healthy relationship everyone in it needs a handle on their emotional baggage, and unfortunately the odds of that happening in queer relationships can be depressingly small.

To be clear, saying "It's not personal" does not excuse any bad or hurtful behavior. It doesn't force us to keep people who hurt us in our lives. But when other people treat us badly or disrespectfully, it's almost never about us. We have to learn to release ourselves from taking responsibility for anyone else's behavior — good and bad — and fight to make sure it affects our self-esteem and inner peace as little as possible. For our own sakes, more than anything.

Keep growing

We talk a lot about physical glow-ups — body transformations — on social media, but emotional glow-ups are definitely a thing too.

Reacting calmly to a situation that would have triggered you six months ago is a glow-up.

Realizing that you've started rejecting hot but incompatible or emotionally immature guys before things get messy or complicated is a glow-up.

Realizing that being attractive as a queer man is about way more than the bodies any of us are in is a glow-up.

Again, we don't choose the emotional baggage we inherit, but we do choose how we respond to it. We can detrashify ourselves if we want to. We can't control every impulse or desire we have, but we can break old habits that don't serve us and replace them with new ones.

We can lean more into authenticity and vulnerability. We can take a hatchet to our internalized homophobia. We can let ourselves screw up but try to be better next time. We can be patient with anyone who isn't as far along the path of personal growth as we are. We can focus on what we truly value over what only gives us momentary validation. We can support each other better. And we can all be gay, bi and/or queer in all the ways that are authentic to us, whether they fit the stereotypes of what a queer man is "supposed" to be like, or not.

To build more meaningful relationships, we have to accept that culturally, queer men often aren't automatically set up for emotional success. We have to accept that, then do the work to overcome that. That's how we become better at relationships. That's how we grow beyond our baggage and attract other men who have done the same.

Because the truth is, there *are* plenty of great men out there, both for friendships and romantic relationships. There are plenty of queer men who are kind, mature and emotionally available, and queer men who are attractive physically as well as in all the other, even more important ways.

A lot of us think we just need to find the perfect partner — or become the perfect partner — to get the fulfilling relationships we want, but that's usually not what's stopping us. Most of the time we just need to do the work to process our baggage, undo everything that messed us up emotionally, and become genuinely ready to find and accept the love and connection we want.

There's this legendary story from 2006 when a paparazzo found George Michael cruising on Hampstead Heath in London. The British tabloid press had spent years hounding George over his personal life, because, um, that's what they do, and he'd had enough. He allegedly just kept on doing whatever he was doing while he yelled at the photographer, "Are you gay!? No? Then fuck off! This is my culture!"[5]

And you know what? He was right. This *is* our culture. And gay culture and queer culture in general are not straight people's culture. Our lives don't have to look like straight people's lives — or any other group of people's lives.

But crucially, our culture isn't just one thing. "Queer culture" or just "gay culture" isn't only cruising and buff bodies and drag queens and no-strings sex.

"Queer culture" isn't just saying you'll dress sluttier than ever when you go out on Halloween and then dressing just as slutty as you do every other weekend.

Our culture is made up of tons of subcultures — individual cultures we can decide to be part of, or not. Again, we contain multitudes.

So if cruising queer subculture or buff bodies queer subculture or no-strings sex queer subculture genuinely serve you, that's great.

But there's also a "dates over hookups" queer subculture.

There's a "supporting each other in our shared struggle" queer subculture.

There's a "clear communication is important in relationships" queer subculture.

There's a "being hot is about more than being muscular and super masculine" queer subculture.

There's a "sex is great but, damn, so is emotional connection" queer subculture.

All of these queer subcultures already exist — and we can all be a part of as many of those subcultures as we want to be.

---

[5] Andy Towle, "Tab: George Michael Sex Cruise on Hampstead Heath," *Towleroad* ◆ (July 24, 2006).

And importantly, culture isn't just something that happens to us. Bitch, we *are* culture. We create it, them, all of them.

Because as inevitable as the wider straight-dominant culture that often stigmatizes us can feel, it isn't. And our homegrown cultures aren't either. A lot of us have a fixed idea of what "mainstream" queer culture is — whether that's a love of wild parties, skimpy underwear, lots of sex, or whatever. But there are definitely more queer people who don't fit all of those stereotypes than those who do.

Again, there's no right or wrong way to be queer. We are not just one thing. And again, we can underestimate our power to shape and create the cultures we want to be part of. We have the power to look at our lives and look at our choices to create the subcultures that honor who we most want to be.

If we want queer dating to be different, or if we want a different queer subculture to exist, we just have to be part of creating it. If we want something different, we have to start breaking habits and patterns that don't serve us. If we want something different, we have to start saying no to the things that aren't giving us what we truly want.

And what's more, you don't need to be on TV or be a brand deal-certified influencer to leave your mark on a culture. Gurl, we are all influencers. Part of the reason queer men feel so much status anxiety is because we're all so busy watching each other to figure out what we have to do to be fundamentally accepted by each other. And so, ultimately we decide whether being acceptable to each other is based purely on how we look, or how "masculine" and aloof we are. Or we can decide that being an attractive man means being supportive and kind, and mindful of our trashiness, and good at communication, and warm and empathetic, and not afraid of being vulnerable.

Our day-to-day actions decide that. Our day-to-day choices create culture. Not the other way around.

* * *

"Hi Max, how are you this week?"

"I'm good, Claire. How about you?"

"Yes, great, thanks," Claire replied. "So where do you want to start today?"

"Well, um, I've met someone," I said. I sort of screwed up my face in disbelief. "I've met someone I really like."

"Oh, that's great news," Claire said.

It had been a fun year. I'd spent most of it as a digital nomad, traveling around the world and, among other things, writing this book. In Spanish there is this outstanding word *putivuelta*, which literally means "hoe circuit," to describe when you get to a club or party and do a lap of the room just to see who's there. (English speakers do this too, obviously, only we're too strait-laced to have a word for it.) So I'd been calling the year *mi putivuelta mundial*, my *putivuelta* world tour — a chance to do a big lap of the world, just to see what, and maybe who, was out there.

It was a fun year, but it was a weird year for dating. It was annoying to keep meeting great people, only to have to move on a few days to a couple of weeks later. And it was especially weird to be writing about love and connection — and specifically about how queer men can unfuck themselves enough to be ready to love and connect with other men longer-term — while my life circumstances meant it was hard for me personally to do that. So when the opportunity came up to spend three months in London — like, in one, actual place for more than two weeks — I took it.

"Yeah, we matched just before Christmas," I told Claire, "and decided to meet in this cute Jamaican rum bar near his apartment. It's not that there was this intense spark, but we both found spending time together fun and agreed to do it again. We managed to squeeze another two dates in before we both left for the holidays, and I've already seen him twice in the week since we got back."

"That all sounds great," Claire said.

"Nico is from the Philippines," I went on. "So obviously my hyper-international ass took the opportunity to show off I knew a couple of different words for 'handsome' in Tagalog. We already call each other 'pogi,' which is as sickening and cute as it sounds."

(One thing a *putivuelta* world tour will teach you is how to be cute in a lot of different languages.)

"He has this fancy job in finance, which, based on past experience, made me wonder whether we'd be a good fit, but we are. I was glad to be surprised about that. I was glad one line on his profile didn't put me off. He's fascinated by what I write and has his own creative ambitions too.

"But most of all, it's just easy. We laugh a lot. I don't feel like I have to hide or filter myself around him. We can stay up 'til 3 am talking, fucking or talk-fucking, depending on how we're feeling. We come from very different worlds, but it feels so easy to be together. Sure, it's not perfect. He sometimes writes 'dins' as shorthand for 'dinner' on WhatsApp and I don't know how I feel about that. But if that's the worst thing about this, I think I can cope...?"

"I'd hope so," Claire laughed.

Still, given the journey I took to get here, there was one important plot twist.

"Oh, and also," I said, "it turns out we chatted nine months earlier on a different app, and, um, I left him on read after about four messages."

Nico had shown me the receipts. He thought it was funny.

"We agreed four messages probably doesn't count as ghosting. And I explained I was just in town for the weekend at the time, so he doesn't hate me for it," I continued. "I guess this was exactly what Shakespeare had in mind when he said, 'The course of true love never did run smooth,' the prescient bitchhh."

Maybe. But it was a good reminder that so much in dating and relationships is about being in the right time and place.

"I don't know how long this will last — or even if I'll be staying in London longer-term. But I feel confident about dealing with that, talking with Nico about it, and in the meantime, enjoying this for what it is. Because whether this is just for a couple of months or for longer, it's what I really needed."

"I'm really happy for you, Max," Claire said. "But just to be clear," she joked, "do you still think men are trash?"

"Claire, I met someone I like. I wasn't kicked by a horse."

She laughed.

"No, but seriously: I definitely have a lot more compassion for what we struggle with. I recognize our collective trashiness, but honestly, I worry about it less. And maybe best of all, I've noticed how I feel a thousand times more confident about navigating all of this — including my own emotional baggage — than I used to be."

I smiled at Claire with a rare sense of self-satisfaction. It felt like everything had slotted into place. It felt like everything that went into this book had done what I hoped it would — at least, it did for me.

A few weeks later, it had become time for me to leave London. The night before my train, Nico and I sat with a bottle of Merlot on his building's rooftop overlooking the Thames. Through the February mist, the lights of the Tate marked out its blocky silhouette across the water.

"You know," Nico said, "I was just thinking about how rare it is to find someone it just feels so easy to be with. Every queer man should have this. Why is this the exception and not what's normal?"

That was another thought that deserved to reverberate around the universe.

And it was true. Whatever luck had led to us crossing paths, twice, we couldn't have controlled. But it dawned on me that the fact we'd made it work when the time was right was definitely on us. It was how we'd approached this connection. It was how we'd shown up for each other — and ourselves.

We'd both had some soul-crushing relationships that had left us wary and limited in the relationships that came after. But those rough experiences didn't seem to matter anymore.

We'd come to realize the difficult truth that, as queer men, it *is* a huge achievement just to be ready and open to love. It is a huge achievement to get past our individual and collective baggage enough that we're ready and able to love and connect with each other freely and wholeheartedly.

But as queer men, that is our challenge — to learn to love. To be ready to connect. To be open to what the world offers, and resist the temptation to push the love we're offered away.

Growth is a strange thing. There's a pain in giving up who you used to be. There's a pain in realizing that you might have gotten what you wanted sooner if you'd raised your standards sooner, or you'd been better at saying no to the connections that weren't serving you in the way you wanted. But there's also beauty in trying to see every experience in our lives — mostly good, mostly bad, a bit of both — as an opportunity to learn something that helps us get a little closer to where we want to be.

Nico leaned into my shoulder. "I'm going to miss you, pogi," he said.

"I'm going to miss you too," I replied, "whatever happens next. But I'm so grateful our paths crossed when they did. Spending time with you has changed my mind about everything."

I meant it. Spending time with Nico had changed my mind about dating, about queer men, about what we're capable of. But that wasn't just luck. Before that, the ideas that wound up in this book had set all that in motion. I'd begun to feel much more confident about dating and relationships — and much better equipped to face the challenges they bring. I was less afraid. I was less guarded. Whenever the right connection came along, I'd become ready for it.

Without exaggeration, writing this book had set me free.

It taught me that even if there are no easy fixes, even if there are no perfect solutions, there is a path forward. It taught me that by accepting that the work starts with us — and by accepting that we have everything we need inside of us already — we can start connecting more deeply and more genuinely with each other.

Even if healthy and fulfilling queer relationships can feel like the exception, not the norm, they do exist. We can lift the barriers to love and connection we face. We can build the meaningful relationships many of us want and deserve. Many of us already have.

So whatever makes your heart — and not just your dick — happy, and whatever makes you feel like you belong, I hope you find it.

Whatever you need to feel happy and fulfilled, I hope you chase it.

And whatever you're looking for, I hope you find it.

Enjoyed this book? Want to make our community an even better place to date?

Why not...

Lend your copy to a friend!
Talk about it with the people you date!
Bitterly recommend it to an ex!
Refuse to fuck anyone who hasn't read it!

And if you can...

Please leave an online review somewhere...?
(That really helps, thank you.)

Appendix: Clear Communication Templates

The only rule when it comes to communicating clearly in dating is to be direct and authentic about how you feel, while also being as kind as you can.

Still, if you're not sure where to start, I've written out some specific phrases you can use in a few common dating situations. Obviously, you'll want to tailor the details to your specific circumstances and what feels authentic to you.

I've written these as imaginary text messages or app DMs, but you can obviously use the phrases when you're speaking to someone on the phone or via video call — or even face to face.

When you want to start a conversation on a dating app

> [Hey / Hey handsome / Hey cutie], how are you?

> Hi [*name*]! It's nice to match with you. How's your week going?

> Hey [*name*], you're a [basketball player / keen traveler / gaymer] too, huh? How's it going?

Hey, I love that you've been to [*place / festival / event*]! It's really [cool / fun / fascinating], right?

When you want to start a conversation with someone on a social network that's not a dating app (e.g. Instagram, Facebook, Snapchat)

Hey, you know [*mutual friend*]? We [are friends from school / met on a night out once / used to play kickball together].

(Direct messaging in reply to a photo) Wow, this is cool! Where is this place?

When you want to ask someone to meet in person

This all sounds great and I'd love to keep talking in person. Do you want to get a coffee or a drink sometime?

You sound like a nice [guy / person]. Do you want to meet sometime?

Are you free this weekend? Do you want to hang out?

Phrases like "We should meet" or "I want to meet you" don't always land that well, because they can feel pushy or one-sided. If you want to hang out with someone, it's usually better to extend them an invitation — and not just frame it through what you want.

When you want to decline someone's offer to meet

> It's been fun chatting but I'm not sure this is a romantic match for me and I don't want to waste your time. Good luck finding what you're looking for :)

> Thanks, but everything's a bit crazy at the moment. If you're still interested in few weeks' time, you're welcome to try me again then.

> Hey, thanks for the offer. I've actually met someone [I've really clicked with / I'm dating seriously] so I'm not meeting anyone new right now. Good luck though :)

When you enjoyed a first date and want another

> Hey, it was great to meet you [earlier / last night]! I had a really fun time. I'd love to keep getting to know you if you're up for it too. Maybe next week?

> Hey, I had a nice time with you [last night / yesterday]. You're a really sweet guy. Can we do it again soon? Maybe [dinner / a movie date / a walk in the park] sometime?

When you didn't click on a first date and want to be clear you're not interested in a romantic connection

> Hey, it was fun hanging out with you [earlier / last night]! I hope you don't mind me being direct but this isn't really what I'm looking for in a relationship at the moment. Hope you find what you're looking for :)

It was great to meet you tonight! I'm glad we finally got to hang out. [This wasn't really a romantic match for me / You're not really my dating type], but if you're interested in hanging out as friends sometime I'd definitely be up for that.

It's important to play this by ear. You don't want to be the asshole who ends every unexciting date by loudly announcing that it wasn't a match for you — especially if you get the vibe that they weren't into you either. But if it feels like someone is trying to gauge your interest in a romantic connection, it's respectful to be upfront even if the answer is no.

When you're genuinely busy but want to keep someone's interest until you can see them

Yes — I'd love to hang out [sometime / again sometime]! [Work / Life / Everything] is pretty busy at the moment but I really want to make time for you once I'm past that. Can we pencil something in [next week / in a couple of weeks]?

When you want to postpone or cancel a date

Hey, I'm sorry for the change of plan but I can't make [this weekend / next Thursday] anymore. [Something came up at work. / I've got a family situation to deal with. / This week turned out really crazy and I hate rushing around.] I'd still love to see you though — can we reschedule?

Hey, I'm sorry but I want to cancel our date this weekend. It's been nice getting to know you but I had a think the past couple of days and I'm not sure this is what I'm looking for right now. Thanks for understanding and maybe see you around :)

Everyone has different expectations about how much notice it's respectful or reasonable to give when there's a change of plans. But once you know you need to cancel or rearrange, you should let him know ASAP — and ideally with at least twenty-four hours' notice.

When someone has previously shown interest but is quiet now and you want to check what's going on

> Hey, hope you're doing OK. Just thought I'd check in and see whether you're still down to hang out next week. I'm still game if you are, so let me know :)

> Hey, how's it going? I know you've been busy recently but I feel like I was getting mixed messages from you so I just wanted to check and see where you're at. If you're not feeling it, it's cool, but I'd appreciate you letting me know.

Of course, asking someone directly to let you know where they're at doesn't mean they will. But if they're unable or unwilling to give you the clarity you want after you've been clear about asking for that, that is a signal or response too.

When you think someone you've been sleeping with is catching feelings and you don't want to progress to a romantic relationship

> Hey, it's been great spending time with you. I wasn't sure exactly where you're at but I just wanted to be upfront that I'm not looking for a [romantic / committed] relationship right now.
>
> I'm happy to keep seeing you if that works for you but I don't want either of us to get hurt. So if you're looking for something more romantic, we can definitely wind this down.

When you want to see if a (so far) sex-only relationship has romantic potential

> Hey [baby / handsome], it's been fun hanging out recently ;) I've been thinking, and I'd definitely be interested in taking this relationship in a more romantic direction. I'm not sure where you're at with that, so maybe we can chat about it next time I see you?

When someone who's been acting hot and cold or sending you mixed messages wants to hang out

> Hey, thanks for your offer. Honestly, I feel like I'm getting mixed messages from you and I only like to make time for dates when both of us are definitely interested. Good luck finding what you're looking for :)

> Hey, it's nice to hear from you but I'm not interested in pursuing this anymore. See you around :)

When someone won't take no for an answer or wants clarity you can't or don't want to give them

> Sure, I appreciate your openness but this isn't what I'm looking for right now. Good luck finding the right person for you.

> Hey, there's not a lot else I want to say. You're a great person and I'm sure you'll be a great match for someone else. It's just not what I'm looking for at the moment.

***When someone has acted in a way that made you
uncomfortable or their behavior crossed enough of a line
that you feel you need to say something***

> Hi, yes, it was nice to meet you last week. I want to be honest
> with you though, when you said you [cheated on your last
> boyfriend / thought I was really cute for an Asian guy / sleep
> with forty-seven firearms under your bed] it made me feel
> uncomfortable so this definitely isn't a match for me. Good luck
> finding what you're looking for.

> Hi, I've been upfront with you that [this isn't / you're not] what
> I'm looking for right now. I'm not interested in taking this any
> further so please stop [texting me / asking if we can hang out
> again / sending me dick pics].

Further Reading

These are nine books and one article that especially influenced the ideas in this book, or are just worth reading if you want to improve your relationships as a queer man.

- Brené Brown, *Daring Greatly: How the Courage to Be Vulnerable Transforms the Way We Live, Love, Parent, and Lead* (Avery, 2012)

- Leo Buscaglia, *Love: What Life Is All About* (Ballantine, 1996)

- Alan Downs, *The Velvet Rage: Overcoming the Pain of Growing Up Gay in a Straight Man's World* (Hachette, 2012)

- Janet W. Hardy and Dossie Easton, *The Ethical Slut: A Practical Guide to Polyamory, Open Relationships, and Other Freedoms in Sex and Love* (Ten Speed Press, 2017)

- Michael Hobbes, "Together Alone: The Epidemic of Gay Loneliness," *The Huffington Post* (March 2, 2017) https://highline.huffingtonpost.com/articles/en/gay-loneliness/

- Amir Levine and Rachel S. F. Heller, *Attached: The New Science of Adult Attachment and How It Can Help You Find — and Keep — Love* (TarcherPerigee, 2012)

- Mark Manson, *The Subtle Art of Not Giving a F*ck: A Counter-intuitive Approach to Living a Good Life* (Harper, 2016)

- Walt Odets, *Out of the Shadows: The Psychology of Gay Men's Lives* (Penguin, 2019)

- Yung Pueblo, *Inward* (Andrews McMeel Publishing, 2018)

- Matthew Todd, *Straightjacket: How to Be Gay and Happy* (Bantam, 2018)

Internet Reference Links

Because internet links tend to look kind of chaotic in footnotes (and have a habit of breaking or changing) I've put them here instead, listed by chapter and footnote number. I've also marked these references with links with a "◆" symbol in the relevant footnotes.

To be honest though, unless typing long and convoluted URLs into your browser's address bar is something you especially enjoy, you could just find these sources by putting the article's title and author names into a search engine.

I Hate to Say It… But Men Kind of *Are* Trash

3   *https://hbr.org/2019/11/research-how-men-and-women-view-competition-differently*

4   *https://www.bbc.com/future/article/20190313-why-more-men-kill-themselves-than-women*

6   *https://pubmed.ncbi.nlm.nih.gov/19696380/*

9   *https://www.themarginalian.org/2014/06/30/leo-buscaglia-love-2/*

Authenticity

2   *https://www.imperial.ac.uk/Stories/overturning-darwins-paradox/*

5   *https://highline.huffingtonpost.com/articles/en/gay-loneliness/*

7   *https://www.vice.com/en/article/evj47w/the-exhausting-work-of-lgbtq-code-switching*

Vulnerability

1   *https://www.refinery29.com/en-gb/problem-with-coming-out-inviting-in*

4   *https://psychcentral.com/lib/signs-of-emotional-unavailability*

Rejection

5   https://www.ncbi.nlm.nih.gov/pmc/articles/PMC7084542/
6   https://nautil.us/love-is-like-cocaine-235787/

Chemistry and Compatibility

1   https://www.thesunmagazine.org/issues/489/the-radical-idea-of-marrying-for-love

Sex Is Great

1   https://www.verywellmind.com/sex-as-a-stress-management-technique-3144601
2   https://pubmed.ncbi.nlm.nih.gov/17610060/
6   https://www.ted.com/talks/terri_conley_we_need_to_rethink_casual_sex

...And Consent Is Sexy

3   https://www.ncbi.nlm.nih.gov/pmc/articles/PMC4799731/

DTF? Or DTL?

3   https://onlinelibrary.wiley.com/doi/abs/10.1111/pere.12307

Abs

1   https://www.attitude.co.uk/news/world/more-than-half-of-gay-men-say-they-are-unhappy-with-their-body-exclusive-291498/
2   https://www.thepinknews.com/2023/01/31/lgbtq-youth-dissatisfied-with-their-body-study/
3   https://www.bbc.com/news/uk-51270317
5   https://neurosciencenews.com/dating-apps-superficial-psychology-17980/
6   https://www.insider.com/guides/health/mental-health/how-social-media-affects-body-image
7   https://elemental.medium.com/six-pack-abs-are-mostly-genetic-ba07dd929b0a
8   https://www.insider.com/fitness-influencers-steroids-secret-dangerous-body-dysmorphia

Stability, Variety and Open Relationships

3 https://time.com/5434949/divorce-rate-children-marriage-benefits/

4 https://www.huffpost.com/entry/gay-open-relationships_b_1217880

6 https://www.them.us/story/30-percent-gay-men-open-relationships-new-study

"It's Just a Preference"

2 https://sitn.hms.harvard.edu/flash/2017/science-genetics-reshaping-race-debate-21st-century/

3 https://digitalcommons.denison.edu/episteme/vol30/iss1/2/

5 https://www.indy100.com/news/lgbt-racism-bame-stonewall-ethnic-minorities-8421526

6 https://www.theguardian.com/commentisfree/2016/nov/24/no-asians-no-blacks-gay-people-racism

7 https://www.washingtonpost.com/news/capital-weather-gang/wp/2017/11/27/our-personalities-are-shaped-by-the-climate-we-grew-up-in-new-study-says/

11 https://www.nytimes.com/2021/04/30/opinion/john-mcwhorter-n-word-unsayable.html

13 https://www.psychologytoday.com/gb/blog/science-choice/201612/what-is-narrative-bias

Straight Acting

1 https://www.theguardian.com/books/2018/mar/17/the-crisis-in-modern-masculinity

2 https://medium.com/matter/masc4masc-b72369ba0d10

3 https://www.ncbi.nlm.nih.gov/pmc/articles/PMC2902177/

4 https://www.them.us/story/gay-men-masculinity-mental-health

6 https://www.sciencedirect.com/science/article/abs/pii/S074756321630259X

7 https://qz.com/1190996/scientific-research-shows-gender-is-not-just-a-social-construct

Ghosting

2   *https://www.vox.com/23130613/fewer-friends-how-many*

3   *https://medium.com/@hingeapp/ghosting-d3248b07bc5f*

Baggage Reclaim

2   *https://www.psychologytoday.com/gb/blog/fixing-families/201706/six-signs-incomplete-grief*

3   *https://www.verywellmind.com/negative-bias-4589618*

Looking

3   *https://www.makingqueerhistory.com/articles/2016/12/20/khnumhotep-and-niankhkhnum-and-occams-razor*

4   *https://www.youtube.com/watch?v=iCvmsMzlF70*

Finding

1   *https://www.pinknews.co.uk/2019/02/12/lgbt-online-dating-study/*

2   *https://www.nytimes.com/2022/08/31/well/mind/burnout-online-dating-apps.html*

3   *https://edition.cnn.com/2012/02/06/health/online-dating-pitfalls/index.html*

5   *https://www.wired.co.uk/article/dating-app-algorithms*

We Deserve Dating Tips Too

3   *https://www.cdc.gov/physicalactivity/basics/adults/index.htm*

4   *https://www.healthline.com/nutrition/junk-food-vs-healthy-food*

5   *https://www.sleepfoundation.org/how-sleep-works/how-much-sleep-do-we-really-need*

Enough

1   *https://www.nzherald.co.nz/lifestyle/lee-suckling-why-do-gay-men-act-like-teenagers/6MV7Y4WL3WRLWTTNJBBMCJS6NU/*

2   *https://www.healthline.com/health/healthy-sex/second-queer-adolescence*

3   *https://www.youtube.com/watch?v=iCvmsMzlF70*

306

4   https://www.them.us/story/gay-bi-racism-looks-grindr-anxiety-depression

    https://www.ncbi.nlm.nih.gov/pmc/articles/PMC7354883/

5   https://www.ncbi.nlm.nih.gov/pmc/articles/PMC5810456/

6   https://www.nbcnews.com/better/relationships/survival-fittest-has-evolved-try-survival-kindest-n730196

7   https://highline.huffingtonpost.com/articles/en/gay-loneliness/

9   https://www.newstatesman.com/politics/2021/07/age-alienation-why-we-must-end-dangerous-decline-community-life

10 https://www.gq.com/story/i-thought-i-didnt-need-gay-friends-i-was-wrong

11 https://www.youtube.com/watch?v=VpOanohqdNA

It Starts with Us

2   https://www.vox.com/23130613/fewer-friends-how-many

4   https://highline.huffingtonpost.com/articles/en/gay-loneliness/

5   https://www.towleroad.com/2006/07/tab_george_mich/

About the Author

Max Thomas is the pen name of author, musician, and occasional flâneur Ed Bell when he's writing about queer culture. *Boys Who Like Boys* is Max's first book. He hopes you enjoyed it.

maxthomas.net
@maxthomasnet

Acknowledgments

Most of all, I'm grateful to all the queer men who shared their authentic experiences, hopes, and disappointments in dating with me as I wrote this book. I wish I could tell you I've personally experienced every single thing that went into each chapter, but I haven't. With so many different perspectives and experiences, this book is much richer than it would have been otherwise.

And yes, I really wrote this book on a *putivuelta mundial*, writing in short-stay apartments, in cafés and on trains, and trying to avoid the aisle seat so the whole plane wouldn't see me reading *The Ethical Slut*. I'm grateful to all of the places — Barcelona, London, New York, Costa Rica, Cyprus, Athens, Vienna, Ljubljana, Dubrovnik, Mexico City, Gran Canaria and more — that opened my eyes to different aspects of queer culture and helped remind me that wherever we are, our experiences (and our baggage) always have a lot in common.

I'm grateful to the small army of editors and relationship experts whose thoughts and feedback helped shape every idea in this book.

And lastly, I'm grateful to you, our community, for showing up and doing the work to make our communities better places to date and love — and just be. I'm proud of who we are and who we're becoming.

Printed in Great Britain
by Amazon

27219793R00182